OPPENHEIM
TOY PORTFOLIO

2007 Edition

The Best Toys, Books, & DVDs
For Kids

Joanne Oppenheim
and Stephanie Oppenheim

Illustrations by **Joan Auclair**

With thanks to our family and the many other families who helped us test for the best.

—*Joanne & Stephanie*

OPPENHEIM TOY PORTFOLIO 2007 EDITION: THE BEST TOYS, BOOKS, & DVDS FOR KIDS. Copyright © 2006 by Oppenheim Toy Portfolio, Inc. All rights reserved. Printed in the United States of America. No part of this book may be used or reproduced in any manner whatsoever without written permission except in the case of brief quotations embodied in critical articles and reviews. For information contact: Oppenheim Toy Portfolio, Inc., 40 East 9th St., Suite 14M, New York NY 10003 or call (212) 598-0502.

This book may be purchased for educational, business, or sales promotional use. For information contact: Stephanie Oppenheim, Publisher, Oppenheim Toy Portfolio, Inc., 40 East 9th St., Suite 14M, New York NY 10003 or call (212) 598-0502 or e-mail stephanie@toyportfolio.com.

Designed by Joan Auclair

ISBN: 0-9721050-6-9

Rating System

Our rating system for quick reference!

- ooooo An outstanding product, not to be missed.
- oooo A very good worth-the-money product.
- ooo Good, not fantastic. Will have limited appeal, but not for everyone.
- oo Good idea, poorly executed; or great execution, terrible idea.
- o Thumbs down, or "What were they thinking?"

What They Win

ooooo **Oppenheim Toy Portfolio Platinum Award.** These represent the most innovative, engaging new products of the year. See the 2007 Platinum Award List.

oooo **Oppenheim Toy Portfolio Gold Award.** Given to outstanding new products that enhance the lives of children.

ooo–o Nothing.

Other Notable Awards

 Oppenheim Toy Portfolio Blue Chip Classic Award—Reserved for classic products that should not be missed just because they weren't invented yesterday. Products must be in the marketplace for five years to be considered for this award.

Oppenheim Toy Portfolio SNAP Award—Given to products that can be used by or easily adapted for children with special needs.

Applauding Manufacturers. We applaud the manufacturers that submitted products to our review knowing that we write about the good, bad, and otherwise. Unlike many other toy testers, we don't charge fees to submit products. We don't take ad dollars. We don't sell any products. Our editorial independence means we can say what works and what doesn't. No manufacturer refused to send us products for review. (We will keep you posted if that changes!)

Praise for
OPPENHEIM TOY PORTFOLIO

As seen on NBC's TODAY Show, Oprah, and CNN

If thoughts of holiday shopping have you fretting about what to buy for the little ones, help is on the way... the Oppenheim Toy Portfolio is just out... recognizing the year's best new toys.

—USA Today

...cuts through the confusion and offers the consumer sound information about what's good—and not so good.

—Associated Press

Sane comprehensive survey... absolutely worth the price.

—Miami Herald

Put away the aspirin, because there's a new book... that should make your toy-buying decisions smart and easy.

—Houston Post

Definite parental appeal.

—Booklist

The authors of the Oppenheim Toy Portfolio have yet again answered the call of parents who are tired of guessing which are the best toys and products for children—they've published a book.

—New York Family

The Oppenheim Toy Portfolio tells parents which are the best and dumbest toys.

—Business Week

Contents

Introduction   **vix**

I • TOYS

1 • Infants: Birth to One Year   1
The Horizontal Infant • Crib Toys • Equipment for Playtime • First Lap & Floor Toys • The Vertical Infant • Rattles & Teethers • Floor Toys • First Toys for Crawlers • Tub Time • First Huggables • Best Travel Toys for Infants • Best New Baby/Shower Gifts • Toddlers-in-Training Toys • Looking Ahead: Best First Birthday Gifts for Every Budget • Best Books for Babies

2 • Toddlers: One to Two Years   33
Active Physical Play • Strictly Outdoors • Sit-Down Play • First Construction Toys • First Stacking, Nesting, and Shape-Sorter Toys • Pretend Play • Art and Music • Bath Toys • Basic Furniture • Best Travel Toys for Toddlers • Best Second Birthday Gifts for Every Budget • Books for Toddlers

3 • Preschool: Three to Four Years   75
Pretend Play • First Trains and Track Toys • Construction Toys • Early Games • Puzzles • Science Toys and Activities • Active Physical Play • Art Supplies • Music and Movement • Preschool Furniture Basics • Best Travel Toys • Best Third and Fourth Birthday Gifts for Every Budget • Books for Preschoolers

4 • Early School Years: Five to Ten Years   127
Pretend Play • Dolls • Track Sets • Remote Control Cars & Other Vehicles • Construction Toys • Games • Puzzles • Activity Kits & Art Supplies • Musical Instruments • Active Play • Science Toys & Equipment • Best Travel Toys & Games • Best Birthday Gifts for Every Budget • Books for Early and Later School Years

II • Oppenheim Toy Portfolio Platinum Book Awards — **177**
Babies and Toddlers • Preschool • Pop-Up Books • Early School

III • Oppenheim Toy Portfolio Platinum DVD Awards — **193**

IV • DVD Plug Ins & Game Platforms — **197**
High Tech for Preschool and Early School Years • High Tech for Older School Years and Teens

V • Using Ordinary Toys for Kids with Special Needs — **207**

Contact Companies	211
Safety Guidelines	215
Index	220

Introduction

Our Fourteenth Edition

We're pretty cranky. Last year we gave the toy industry a big fancy "A" for innovation and quality. Our book was overflowing with glowing reviews of new and classic products. This year we regret to report that the mark has gone down considerably, to a B- (and that's being generous). When asked by reporters what the industry needs to keep kids in toyland, our answer is simple. Make toys that work. Make toys that indicate that you've met a child. Make game directions clearer. Make instructions for constructions understandable to someone without an engineering degree. Make toys less ugly, less garish. Make toys you can get out of the package without a wire cutter and box cutter. You get our point.

Not to fear, with all of our whining we still found a great list of products (thankfully, they brought up the curve). What you will notice, however, is that we've left in many past winners because they're still worth knowing about and bringing home to the children in your life (in fact many classics remain a better bet than some of the newer choices). Whether you are a new parent or grandparent, or an uncle, aunt, or family friend, you will find reviews in these pages that can help you bring home memorable and engaging products that will entertain and fit your child's developing needs. That is what we do for you. This year in particular, in a year of limited good choices, we are confident that we provide a really valuable service.

Our mission remains the same—to take the guesswork out of choosing products that are not a waste of your money or

INTRODUCTION

your child's time. We've taken all the toys, books, DVDs, and music out of their packaging and put them to test.

We've done things a little differently this year. To give you a more portable guide, we've slimmed things down a bit. All of the books, videos, and music we've reviewed in the past are on our website, www.toyportfolio.com. We add to those lists throughout the year. Our Gold award winners for books, videos, and music are posted online. In this edition you'll find only our top Platinum picks for this year in these categories.

Quick Rating at a Glance. In addition to awarding products a Platinum, Gold, or Blue Chip rating, we have also marked products with "play balls" right after the price to give you a quicker read on what worked and what didn't. You'll find our lists of this year's award-winning and top-rated products in the opening pages of this book. In addition to our PLATINUM AWARD Winners list, you'll find lists of outstanding products for group play, parent-child interactions, and office quiet time; top-rated science, educational, special needs, and gender-free products; our top picks for Under $10, $15, and $20; as well as Break-the-Bank (grandparent!) gifts.

You'll find full descriptions of these as well as other excellent new products, along with shopping information, in each of the age-appropriate chapters of the book. As always, we've included our BLUE CHIP classics, since we believe it would be a shame for kids to miss such products just because they weren't invented yesterday.

Children's products have a short shelf life. In fact, over 60 percent of this year's book is entirely new content—a response to the thousands of new choices introduced this year (6,000 new toys alone).

What Are the Trends for 2007?

Notable Trends

Asthma-Friendly Toys. A new line of toys from Kids Preferred, designed to reduce the allergens associated with triggering asthma attacks. A great concept—(if it works) and also well executed in terms of design.

Gender-Free Kitchens. We are pleased to report that the two major plastic toy kitchen makers (Little Tikes and Step 2)

INTRODUCTION

have embraced the idea that boys need to role play at being capable cooks! Both companies should be applauded for taking the pink out of the kitchen.

Great Games. There continue to be great choices in family games for all ages. Our award list is chock-full of games that got high marks from our testers. (That said, we all request that companies vet their directions better.)

Generational Markers. Want to feel old? Magic 8 Ball is 60 years old. The Ant Farm is 50 years old, as is Play-Doh. Twister is 40 years old. UNO is 35. So, what's old is new again, except, of course, those of us who played with these toys as kids!

High Tech Gadgets for the Preschool Set. Picking up on the tech frenzy for older kids, toy makers are making versions of many of our favorite gadgets for 3s & up, some with more success than others. The League for the Hard of Hearing warns that constant noise in your child's ears can have life-long implications. Don't assume that toys have been regulated for a "safe" volume level.

The Real Thing Doesn't Cut It. A bunch of new toys that may inspire you to ask "why"? For example, there's a new toy called "Thumb Warriors" (Radica)—when your own thumb won't do for a thumb wrestle. The company says "arm your thumb" . . . with a plastic reptilian creature. Also, how about the card game, "Rock, Paper, Scissors"?

Play With Me! Over the years we have spent a lot of time urging parents to get down on the floor and play with their kids. So we were delighted when we heard this again and again as part of the new marketing mantra at several major toy companies. Toys come with handy activity suggestions as well. The toys are not always great, but the concept is first rate.

Sign of the Times. Who would have imagined a game where the game play is to avoid a nuclear core melt down? That's exactly what players are asked to do in the new Simpsons Don't Panic Game—"The Game of manic multi-tasking mayhem!"

Crocheting Isn't Just for Grandma. Last year we saw an explosion of knitting kits. This year crocheting is the thing. Can you believe that Granny Squares are trendy?

Manners. Move over, Emily Post, Whoopi Goldberg and others have addressed the topic of manners. We find most of these "behave yourself" titles a bit too prescriptive, but the sentiment is correct, thank you very much.

Potty Dolls and Potty Books. Still really a hot topic in toyland with dolls that pee and poop (with varying degrees of success). New this year, a book about how boys and girls pee differently and then perform their peeing prowess at a circus (no joke).

Trolls. They're back, again.

Up, Up, and Away! Toy planes were understandably nowhere to be found in the years after 9/11. This year they're back—and are really among some of the best toys we reviewed this year. No matter what the age group, there's a plane for you.

On the Upside

Crafts for Boys. Usually the domain of "girls," we were delighted this year to find several kits that will appeal to boys as well as girls. Using a paintbrush to develop fine motor skills and learning how to follow step-by-step instructions are equally important for boys.

Fewer Stupid "Smart" Toys. Toys that claim to teach babies school skills before they can talk are thankfully on the decline. There are still notable exceptions. For example, a toy labeled for six-month-olds, who are not yet talking, asks the baby to find the shape or color object and fit it in place.

Pretend Power. There's a miniature play setting for every interest: castles, airports, a pirate ship, a zoo, an amazing crane, and a tree house are just some of the great props for pretend that made our top list.

Game Time. Classic games, as well as a new crop of innovative games, are among the best choices in toyland. Most kids will jump at a chance to play any truly "interactive" game with their folks. Games are also a no-tears way of developing math, language, geography, and reading skills, and gamesmanship, too. They give families an opportunity to share some important values (being a good sport, for example) and also time to talk while the game's being played.

Volume Controls Are In! Perhaps to bolster parental sanity,

INTRODUCTION

toy makers have added volume controls to their electronic wonders (and even the revolutionary option of playing with the sound off). We usually find that less noise means more play value in the long run.

Who's the Boss? Thank goodness there seem to be fewer intrusive toys that dictate how kids must play. Indeed, play is one of the areas where kids can and should be empowered to use their own creative powers.

On the Downside

Age Labels. We received many new products this year where the toy fit in the choke tube completely, but merely stuck out just enough to pass the test. Our question to manufacturers is, why take a risk? There are also many new lacing games with strings marked "18 months and up." These pose an unnecessary strangulation hazard. Watch out for pull toys with strings more than 12" long (with no safety release), as these too are potentially dangerous. We received craft kits marked "2 & up" with feathers in them. More plastic bags (very attractive on the shelf), but too many come with no airholes. These bags pose a suffocation danger. Our recommendation is to ditch the bags at once.

Blind Meanness. The new American Idol Game (Screenlife) subjects players to the meanness of the judges without any weight given to your child's actual performance. It's one thing for Simon to be cruel if you can't sing, but what's the point of being ridiculed based on nothing?

Dirty Diapers As Toys. For several years toy makers had left the "gross" out of the playing field. No more. One game, "Monster Under My Bed" (Fundex), includes a plastic dirty diaper as one of the playing pieces (yuck!).

False Praise. In the past we have written negative reviews for electronic games that are mean if you give the wrong answer. No one needs to say "you're too slow." But now there's a new crop of electronics that suffers from a common parenting pitfall: false praise. One writing toy (VTech's Write & Learn Letter Pad), tells your child that he did a great job no matter what. We're all for positive reinforcement, but this goes too far.

Great Idea, Poorly Executed. We had more toys this year

that just didn't do what they said they would. For example, a toy truck that was supposed to sense the chalk on the sidewalk and trace it. Just didn't work. A remote-controlled flying Superman toy from Mattel (where the man of steel seemed to have been exposed to kryptonite). He wasn't a great flyer.

Just a bad idea. Cause and effect is an important developmental milestone for babies and toddlers. Unfortunately, under the mistaken belief that "more" is better, we had more toys this year where, if your baby touched a button, she was met with a frenetic explosion of lights and sounds. Way too much and, by the way, misses the point of these toys entirely.

Fine Print Warnings. We got arts and crafts kits that had way too many warnings about staining fabrics, furniture, and, even more alarming, what to do if your child "ingested" any of the toy. Why package such potential problems?

Smelly Toys. A disturbing number of plastic toys came in with very strong odors. This was also true of foam products. Whether it's a baby toy (that will be tasted) or a puzzle for your five year old, we find the smells unacceptable.

Rococo Plastic. We have never seen so many truly ugly toys that we know will sit in some landfill for centuries. While there's nothing technically wrong with many of the toys in this category, what happened to aesthetically pleasing objects that feed the expectations and tastes of our children?

Puzzles for Babies? We were sent several puzzles with oversized pieces marked for 12- and 18-month-olds. It doesn't matter how big the pieces are, babies do not have the visual discrimination to understand part vs. whole images or to understand the logic of putting them together. Nor do they have the dexterity to turn and fit pieces of a jigsaw puzzle together. It's like reading *War and Peace* to your preschooler. We wonder if any of these puzzle makers have ever played with a 12–18-month-old baby?

Your child's not stupid. Age labels are off kilter . . . not just for babies and toddlers, but for older kids as well. We had bead kits and construction sets that are misleadingly labeled for much younger ages than would be possible. While we are all for parental assistance, we think a lot of frustration could be saved if toys were more honestly labeled to fit.

Barbie goes OC. We have to admit that we found the Barbie Hot Tub Party Bus with light-up hot tub and pull-out bed a bit too much like a setting from the OC for the five-and-up crowd for our taste (but our testers really liked it). In fact, fold-out beds were available for several other dolls this season.

PhD required. While some games had ambiguous directions, others had direction overkill. One card game designed for 8-year-olds was tested by a family with numerous post-graduate degrees, and even with all that brain power, no one could keep track of all the permutations.

Misleading Boxes. Our testers were particularly up in arms about boxes that did not warn that additional purchases were required, or boxes where it looked like you were getting more than you actually were (e.g., race sets with only one car!).

No More Steering. In what we assume is a cost-saving move, most ride-on and ride-in toys for the youngest riders no longer have real steering—forcing kids to lift up the whole toy when they want to change direction.

Hurry Up, Baby! The marketing message to new parents is clear: "Smart toys" will help your baby learn faster and achieve more. They don't mention that developmentally, babies learn best through real-life experiences and that too many lights and sounds can stimulate babies to distraction. Babies and toddlers are not ready for symbolic learning. The fact that a toddler can recite the alphabet is nothing more than a great parlor trick—ask the same toddler what "l-m-n-o-p" means and see what happens. There is no one magic toy that will guarantee an Ivy League acceptance (or even a spot in your city's competitive preschools)!

The Ultimate Downside. All of this rushing gives kids the unfortunate message that learning is hard and that maybe they're not very good learners. The most important thing parents can do is provide an environment that helps develop their children's confidence and a positive sense of themselves as learners. Many of the academic skills they need will be learned with much less difficulty later on, when children are more developmentally ready.

Trust your instincts and relax; the misguided "sooner is better" mentality is not a view shared by the majority of child development experts. Your toddler does not need to know how to spell *cat* or five words that rhyme with *star*. For children at every stage of development, toys that match their emerging abilities can best foster learning.

Talk, read, play with, and enjoy your child. Children learn language when people talk and listen to them. Literacy grows from the pleasures discovered in sharing books with meaningful stories and memorable illustrations. It is not served by rushing babies and toddlers with letter and sound drills. During early childhood the everyday discoveries of life have more educational value than any quiz machine you can bring home. Interactive people are far more important to learning than interactive machines!

Just Toys—What Difference Do They Make?

So what's the harm? After all, this is the 21st century. This is the age of technology, and even the Consumer Product Safety Commission is considering adjusting its age guidelines.

But pushing kids to do things that are developmentally inappropriate delivers a powerfully negative message that colors how kids think about themselves as competent, able doers. Parents, bombarded with the "smart toy, smart child" message, may also wonder if there's something wrong with their toddler who's incapable of rhyming in three languages or spelling *unicorn* by age three!

We used to "invest" in our toys. A favorite doll would be our companion in good times and bad (real and pretend), and our toys grew with us. Preprogrammed toys do not have the same lasting play value, however. For the most part, they are the toyland equivalent of a one-trick pony.

Pretend No More. Pretend play is not merely something cute that children do while they are waiting to grow up. It's through pretending that children begin to think symbolically, letting one thing stand for another. The ability to make their own symbols, by turning a mud pie with sticks into a birthday cake with candles, provides the underpinnings for more abstract symbolic systems that they'll understand when they're older.

Changing Expectations. Play is also one of those wonderful states where kids can step into roles of control—even if it is pretend. So playhouses with sound effects that tell kids it's raining—"shut the window"—or small trucks with drivers who run the show with voice commands, steal words from the mouths of babes. As more and more tech toys invade toyland, the expectations of what a toy does seem to be changing in the minds of children as well as adults. As toys become more literal, children also become more passive observers; the true value of play is turned upside down, with children reduced to pushing buttons and reacting to what the toy does instead of being active players. Kids end up moving around the play schemes dreamed up by adults—and being robbed of the power of play.

We're all for technology, but not when it is used to strip away the value and fun of play from children.

Expanded Coverage

We have included reviews of the best products we tested this year as well as highlighting some notable losers. Unfortunately, there isn't space for all the products we review—so be sure to visit our website, www.toyportfolio.com, where our database of reviews is available. We'd like to thank all the families who contributed to this book. As always, we welcome you, our readers, to give us your feedback on the selections. For new readers, you'll find our review process and criteria for our award program below.

Happy playing!

Joanne   Stephanie

How We Select the Best

We shop for children year 'round—only we get to do what most parents wish they could do before they buy. We open the toys, run the DVDs, read the books, and play the music. We get to compare all the toys that may look remarkably similar but often turn out to be quite different from each other. For example, we put the toy trains together and find out which ones actually stay on the tracks.

How We're Different

We don't sell products. We don't take fees for looking at products. The **Oppenheim Toy Portfolio** was introduced in 1989 as the only independent consumer review of children's media. Unlike most other groups that rate products, we do not charge entry fees or accept ads from manufacturers. When you see our award seals on products, you can be assured that they are "award-winning" because they were selected by noted experts in child development, children's literature, and education, and then rated by the most objective panel of judges—kids.

The Real Experts Speak: Kids and Their Families

To get a meaningful sampling, we deal with families from all walks of life. We have testers in the city and in the country, in diapers and in blue jeans, in school clothes and in tutus. They have parents who are teachers, secretaries, lawyers, doctors, writers, engineers, doormen, software programmers, editors, psychologists, librarians, engineers, business people, architects, family therapists, musicians, artists, nurses, and early childhood educators. In some instances, we have tested products in preschool and after-school settings where we can get feedback from groups of children. Since all new products tend to have novelty appeal, we ask our testers to live with a product for a while before assessing it. Among other things, we always ask, Would you recommend it to others?

Criteria We Use for Choosing Quality Products

- What is this product designed to do and how well does it do it?

- What can the child do with the product? Does it invite active doing and thinking or simply passive watching?

- Is it safe and well designed, and can it withstand the unexpected?

- Does it "fit" the developmental needs, interests, and typical skills of the children for whom it was designed?

- What message does it convey? Toys as well as books and videos can say a great deal about values that parents are trying to convey. For example, does the product reflect old sexual stereotypes that limit children's views of themselves and others?

- What will a child learn from this product? Is it a "smart" product that will engage the child's mind, or simply a novelty with limited play value?

- Is it entertaining? No product makes our list if kids find it boring, no matter how "good" or "educational" it claims to be.

- Is the age label correct? Is the product so easy that it will be boring, or so challenging that it will be frustrating?

Rating System

Outstanding products selected by our testers are awarded one of four honors:

 Oppenheim Toy Portfolio Platinum Award—These represent the most innovative, engaging new products of the year. See the 2007 Platinum Award List.

 Oppenheim Toy Portfolio Gold Seal Award—Given to outstanding new products that enhance the lives of children. Products listed with four play balls have received a Gold Seal Award.

 Oppenheim Toy Portfolio Blue Chip Classic Award—Reserved for classic products that should not be missed just because they weren't invented yesterday. Products must be in the marketplace for five years to be considered for this award.

 Oppenheim Toy Portfolio SNAP Award—Our Special Needs Adaptable Product Award is given to products that can be used by or easily adapted for children with special needs. The SNAP Award winners are listed in the book; past award winners are shown on our website.

Using This Book

Each section begins with a play profile that tells you what to expect during each developmental stage and what "basic gear" will enhance learning and play. We also give suggestions for best gifts for your budget and, perhaps most importantly, a stage-by-stage list of toys to avoid.

Because we know how busy people are these days, our reviews are purposely short and provide information on how to get your hands on the product.

A word about prices: Our award-winning products are not all high-ticket items. We have selected the very best products in toy supermarkets, as well as those that you will find in specialty stores, on line, in museum shops, and in quality catalogs. We have listed the suggested retail prices, but they will vary tremendously depending on where you shop.

Telephone numbers and websites: Where available, we have given a customer service number in case you have difficulty locating the product in your area. Phone numbers and websites are also provided on page TK. For some educational products, you'll find a catalog number for ordering.

Child's Play—More Than Fun!

For children, playing is more than a fun way to fill the day. It's through play that children learn and develop all sorts of important physical, intellectual, and social skills. Like musicians, children use well-chosen toys, books, and music to orchestrate their play. As they grow and develop, so does their need for more complex playthings that challenge and enhance their learning. Toys and stories with the right developmental fit help create a marvelous harmony for learning and fun. The **Oppenheim Toy Portfolio** is a resource book you can use to make that kind of mix.

OPPENHEIM TOY PORTFOLIO PLATINUM TOY AWARDS 2007

INFANTS

Cuddle Pups Puppets (Manhattan Toy), p. 6
ActiviTot Developmental Gym (Tiny Love), pp. 9, 30
NooBoo Symphonic Stacker (Manhattan Toy), p. 20
Lamaze Clap with Me Monkey*/Giggle Bug* (RC2/Learning Curve), p. 21
Amazing Baby Sound Balls* (Kids Preferred)/ **Toss the Taggie*** (Taggies), p.25
Amazing Baby Developmental Blanket Teether (Kids Preferred), p. 28

TODDLERS

Triple Track Tower (Playskool), p. 49
Kiddy Connects and **EduBlocks** (Edushape), pp. 49, 51
Lego Duplo Zoo (Lego Systems), p. 50
Latitude Enfant Grannimals Collection (Pint Size Productions), p. 57
Smushy Elephant (North American Bear Co.), p. 57
iPlay Zoom Around Garage (International Playthings), p. 59
Little People Lil' Movers Airplane (Fisher-Price), p. 60

PRESCHOOLERS

Dolls & Props
Bebe Do with Moses Basket (Corolle), p. 81
Trixieville (Manhattan Toy), p. 82
Lucky the Incredible Wonder Pup (Zizzle), p. 85
Penelope Peapod (Penelope Peapod), p. 123

*indicates a tie in the category

OPPENHEIM TOY PORTFOLIO PLATINUM TOY AWARDS 2007

PRESCHOOLERS *(cont.)*
Hokey Pokey Musical Skirt (Acting Out), *p. 119*
Jumbo Jungle Animals (Learning Resources), *p. 73*

Vehicles
Airport Action (Lego Systems), *p. 96*
Thomas & Friends Echo Tunnel*/Sodor Fire Station*/Recycling Center* (RC2/Learning Curve), *p. 92*

Games & Puzzles
Magneatos Intermediate (Guidecraft), *p. 97*
Caterpillar Race (Edushape/PlaySound), *p. 99*
Animal Bingo (eeBoo), *p. 99*
The Very Books Block Puzzle (Mudpuppy), *p. 103*
My Creativity Center (Alex), *p. 121*

Electronics
Air-powered Action Stadium (Hasbro), *p. 98*
100 Hoops (LeapFrog), *p. 110*
Kid-Touch FP3 Player (Fisher-Price), *p. 120*

Active Play
Ride & Rescue Coupe (Little Tikes), *p. 112, 123*
Dive, Dodge 'n Slide Bouncer (Little Tikes), *p. 114*

EARLY SCHOOL YEARS
Dolls
American Girl Emily (American Girl), *p. 133*
Only Hearts Club Sleepover Collection (OHC Group), *p. 134*
Tiptoes Touche Mediterranean Madge (Manhattan Toy), *p. 134*

Building
Airport (Lego Systems), *p. 139*
Mag XL Magformers (Rainbow Products), *p. 141*

*indicates a tie in the category

OPPENHEIM TOY PORTFOLIO PLATINUM TOY AWARDS 2007

EARLY SCHOOL YEARS (cont.)

Games

Combo King (Gamewright), p. 150
Doodle Tales (Cranium), p. 145
Highrise (Fundex), p. 150
Ringgz (Blue Orange Games), p. 146
Sudoku (Briarpatch), p. 152
Tea Party Game (eeBoo), p.
Ugly Doll Game (Gamewright), p. 100
Uno Spin (Mattel), p. 151
Wallamoppi (Out of the Box), p. 146

Puzzles

Egyptology Puzzle (Mudpuppy), p. 157
Lego City 60 pieces Puzzle (Ravensburger), p. 157

Crafts

Cast & Paint: Krazy Kars* (Skullduggery)/**Monster Trucks Custom Shop*** (Creativity for Kids), p. 159
Decoupage Diva Jewelry Keeper (Creativity for Kids), p. 160
The Foam Airplane Book (Klutz), p. 172
Leg Warminators*/Hug This Shrug Kit* (Fashion Angels Enterprises), p. 164
Super Embroidery Kit (Alex), p. 164

Electronics

Word Whammer Fridge Phonics (LeapFrog), p. 154
Cosmic Catch (Hasbro), p. 143
Mindstorm NXT (Lego Systems), p. 137
Kid Tough Digital Camera (Fisher-Price), p. 174

*indicates a tie in the category

OPPENHEIM TOY PORTFOLIO PLATINUM BOOK AWARDS 2007

INFANTS AND TODDLERS

Amazing Baby Soft Book (Kids Preferred), p. 177
Baby Love/My Blanket (Magsaman, Little Brown), p. 178
Nursery Rhyme Books (Sassy), p. 178
You and Me, Baby (Reiser/Gentieu, Knopf), p. 179
Maisy's Book Tower (Cousins, Candlewick), p. 178
Baby Animals (Nguyen, Chronicle), p. 177
Yes (Alborough, Candlewick), p. 178
"I'm not cute!" (Allen, Hyperion), p. 179

PRESCHOOLERS

Boo and Baa Have Company (Landstrom, Farrar Straus), p. 179
Dooby Dooby Moo (Cronin/Lewin, Atheneum), p. 179
Elusive Moose (Gannij/Beaton, Barefoot). p. 180
Fast Food (Freymann/Elffers, Scholastic), p. 180
The Gingerbread Girl (Ernst, Dutton), p. 180
Move Over Rover (Beaumont/Dyer, Harcourt), p. 180
Library Lion (Knudsen/Hawkes, Candlewick), p. 181
Oscar: The Big Adventure of a Little Sock Monkey (Schwartz/Marcus, HarperCollins), p. 181
A Particular Cow (Fox/Denton, Harcourt), p. 181
Silly Billy (Browne, Candlewick), p. 181

POP-UP BOOKS

My Little Yellow Taxi (Johnson, Harcourt), p. 182
Ruff! Ruff! Where's Scruff? (Carter, Harcourt), p. 182
Sharks and Other Sea Monsters (Sabuda/Reinhart, Candlewick), p. 182
MOMMY? (Sendak/Yorinks/Reinhart, Scholastic), p. 182
Sabuda and Reinhart Present: Castle (Olman/Sabin, Scholastic), p. 183

EARLY SCHOOL YEARS

Alphabet Explosion! Search and Count from Alien to Zebra (Nickle, Random House), p. 183

Adèle & Simon (McClintock, Farrar, Straus), p. 183

Happy Birthday, Jamela! (Daly, Farrar, Straus), p. 184

Olivia Forms a Band (Falconer, Atheneum), p. 184

Owen & Mzee (Hatkoff et al., Scholastic), p. 184

Pancakes for Supper! (Isaacs/Teague, Scholastic), p. 184

Edwina, the Dinosaur Who Didn't Know She Was Extinct (Willems, Hyperion), p. 185

Flotsam (Wiesner, Clarion), p. 185

Mama, I'll Give You the World (Schotter/Gallagher, Random House), p. 185

Museum Trip (Lehman, Houghton Mifflin), p. 185

Pandora's Box (Marzollo, Little, Brown), p. 185

Snow Globe Family (O'Connor/Schindler, Putnam), p. 186

Take Care, Good Knight (Thomas/Meisel, Dutton), p. 186

Yoon and the Christmas Mitten (Recorvits/Swiatkowska, Farrar, Straus), p. 186

Historical Fiction

Brothers (Yin/Soentpiet, Philomel), p. 187

Night Boat to Freedom (Raven/Lewis, Farrar, Straus), p. 187

Satchel Paige, Don't Look Back (Adler/Widener, Harcourt), p. 187

Nonfiction

First Picture Spanish (Brooks/Mackinnon, et al., Usborne), p. 188

John, Paul, George & Ben (Smith, Hyperion), p. 188

Rainforest (Marent, DK), p. 188

The Usborne Book of Art (Dickins, Usborne), p. 188

Why Are the Ice Caps Melting?/Who Lives in an Alligator Hole? (Rockwell, HarperCollins), p. 189

OPPENHEIM TOY PORTFOLIO PLATINUM BOOK AWARDS 2007

EARLY SCHOOL YEARS (cont.)

Chapter Books

The Looking Glass Wars (Beddor, Dial), p. 189

The Miraculous Journey of Edward Tulane (DiCamillo/Ibatoulline, Candlewick) p. 189

Peter and the Shadow Thieves (Barry/Pearson, Hyperion), p. 189

Sherlock Holmes and the Baker Street Irregulars, The Fall of the Amazing ZalIndas (Mack/Citrin, Orchard Books) p. 189

Toys Go Out (Jenkins/Zelinsky, Random House), p. 189

Water Street (Giff, Random House), p. 190

Weedflower (Kadohata, Simon & Schuster), p. 190

Editor's Note: Two books that are must-reads

The Prince's Bedtime (Oppenheim/Latimer, Barefoot Books), p. 190

Dear Miss Breed: True Stories of the Japanese American Incarceration During World War II (Oppenheim/Scholastic), p. 191

OPPENHEIM TOY PORTFOLIO PLATINUM DVD AWARDS 2007

Bear Snores On (Scholastic Video Collection), p. 194

Caillou, The Everyday Hero (PBS), p. 194

Cars (Pixar), p. 195

The Greatest Game Ever Played (Disney), p. 195

Growing Up with Winnie the Pooh: Love & Friendship (Disney), p. 195

Popular Mechanics for Kids: Lightning and Other Forces of Nature (Koch Vision), p. 195

Wallace & Gromit: The Curse of the Were-Rabbit (Dreamworks), p. 195

OPPENHEIM TOY PORTFOLIO SPECIAL NEEDS ADAPTABLE PRODUCT AWARDS 2007

ActiviTot Developmental Mat (Tiny Love), p. 207
Lamaze Clap With Me Monkey (RC2/Learning Curve), p. 207
Toss the Taggie (Taggies), p. 207
Peek-a-Blocks Bucket of Builders (Fisher-Price), p. 208
My First Quatro Set (Lego Systems), p. 208
iPlay Zoom Around Garage (International Playthings), p. 208
Little People Lil' School Bus (Fisher-Price), p. 208
Lucky the Incredible Wonder Pup (Zizzle), p. 208
Jumbo Jungle Animals (Learning Resources), p. 209
Funky Artist (Alex), p. 209
Thomas & Friends Echo Tunnel (RC2/Learning Curve), p. 209
Magneatos Intermediate (Guidecraft), p. 209
Caterpillar Race (Edushape/PlaySound), p. 209
Tea Party Game (eeBoo), p. 210
Word Whammer Fridge Phonics (LeapFrog), p. 210
Alphabet Puzzle Boards (Lauri), p. 210

TOP-RATED GROUP TOYS 2007

Kids are by nature social beings and enjoy few things more than being with other kids. Still, learning to share and play together can be rough going. We kept an eye out this year for toys that work especially well with groups of kids. For kids who are still at the "it's mine" stage, the key is to find toys with enough pieces to go around. We also looked for products that lend themselves to cooperative play—board games or activity kits that two or more children can enjoy together—or simply play with side by side. We often talk these days about interactive toys, but here are some wonderful products for interactive kids.

Candy Land DVD Game (Hasbro), p. 199
Colossal Barrel of Crafts (Chenille Krafts), p. 116, 124
Cranium Hullabaloo DVD Game (Cranium), p. 197
Egg and Spoon Race (International Playthings), p. 98
The Family Fun Game (Cranium), p. 144
Finger Painting Party (Alex), p. 116
My Playhouse (Alex), p. 114
Naturally Playful Clubhouse Climber (Step 2), p. 43
Wooden Trains/Unit Wooden Blocks
 (various makers), pp. 51, 52, 91, 93

GREAT LEARNING TOYS FOR THE 3 RS 2007

Whether your kids are getting top grades or the other kind, there are playful ways you can help. Here are some of our highlighted favorites that give school skills a boost without your having to break out the flash-cards.

Reading, Storytelling, Listening, & Language Skills
Create Your Own Books (Creativity for Kids), p. 160
4-Way Spelldown (Cadaco), p. 147
Leapster L-Max (LeapFrog), p. 123, 171, 174, 175

Prewriting/Fine-Motor Skills
Lacing Games (various makers), pp. 105
Leap Pad Plus Writing System (LeapFrog), pp. 154

Math, Logic, & Visual Perception
Combo King (Gamewright), p. 150, 175
Math Dash (Learning Resources), p. 150
I Never Forget A Face Memory Game (eeBoo), p. 100
Sudoku (Briarpatch), p. 152
Tangoes Jr. (Rex Games), p. 151

Staying Power & Problem Solving
Bead Kits (various makers), pp. 117, 159, 163
Construction Toys (various makers), pp. 49, 93, 138
Magnetic Building sets (various makers), pp. 97, 141, 209
Puzzles (various makers), pp. 46, 103, 155

TOP-RATED OFFICE TOYS 2007

Whether your office is in a complex or in a corner of your home, when kids come to visit, having a few quiet toys can make the time more enjoyable for everyone. Besides a pack of crayons and paper, here are some top choices:

TODDLERS AND PRESCHOOLERS

Crayola Color Wonder Paper & Markers (Binney & Smith), *pp. 65, 73, 116, 124*
Fairy Collection Woodkins (Pamela Drake), *pp. 123*
My First Quatro Bucket (Lego Systems), *pp. 50, 73, 208*
Kid K'nex Wild Ones (K'nex), *p. 96*
Play Scenes (Mudpuppy), *p. 172*

EARLY SCHOOL YEARS

Bead Kits (various makers), *pp. 117, 159, 163*
It's All About Me (Klutz), *p. 172*
Magz-x (Progressive Trading), *p. 141*
Paper Stained Glass (Klutz), *p. 172*
Pixter Multi-Media (Fisher-Price), *p. 123, 171, 174–175*
Leapster L-Max (LeapFrog), *p. 123, 171, 174, 175*
Gameboy DS (Nintendo), *p. 171, 174*
Lacing Puppets (Lauri), *p. 136*

PARENT & CHILD TOYS 2007

While it's important for kids to know how to play independently, games and cooperative projects provide the raw materials for interactions that can be rewarding for adult and child. Without taking over, adults can help kids get started and be there as "consultants," giving kids strategies for working in an orderly fashion. Making time to do such things together gives you a chance to play and experiment together—a chance to solve problems, think creatively, and even have fun learning together.

Here are some of our favorites:

INFANTS & TODDLERS

ActiviTot Developmental Gym (Tiny Love), *pp. 9, 30*
NooBoo Symphonic Stacker (Manhattan Toy), *p. 20*
Lamaze Clap with Me Monkey*/Giggle Bug* (RC2/Learning Curve), *p. 21*
Amazing Baby Sound Balls* (Kids Preferred)/ **Toss the Taggie*** (Taggies), *p. 25*

PRESCHOOLERS

Airport Action (Lego Systems), *p. 96*
Puppets & Puppet Stage (various makers), *pp. 6, 27, 86, 135, 136*
Tea Party Game (eeBoo), *p. 100, 124, 210*
The Very Books Block Puzzle (Mudpuppy), *pp. 103, 124*
Wooden Trains (various makers), *pp. 51, 91*

EARLY SCHOOL YEARS

Airport (Lego Systems), *p. 139*
Bird House (TWC of America), *p. 170*
Cast & Paint: Krazy Kars (Skullduggery), *p. 159*
Castle (Playmobil), *pp. 129, 175*
Combo King (Gamewright), *p. 150*
Egyptology (Mudpuppy), *p. 157*
Mindstorm NXT (Lego Systems), *p. 137, 175*
Zooreka (Cranium), *p. 143*

TOP-RATED GENDER-FREE PRODUCTS 2007

Many of the toys, books, and videos you bring home may have a built-in Gender Agenda™—products that reinforce stereotypes and shape your child's self-image. It often begins innocently in the nursery with pastel color coding, but quickly moves on to a glut of products with themes of hair-play for girls and gunplay for boys. The gender issue is not just one that is important to girls. The overly aggressive and violent-themed toys and video games directed at boys are even more alarming to us than the dating games or lavender blocks that come with blueprints for a shopping mall.

Can you avoid all gender-specific toys? Probably not. These are often the products kids want the most, not only because they are heavily promoted on TV, but also because children tend to sort the world out in the simple and absolute terms of right or wrong, hard or easy, boy or girl. There are, however, positive choices you can make—where a gender-free product will work for both boys and girls . . . and products that break gender stereotypes.

ActiviTot Developmental Mat (Tiny Love), *pp. 9, 30*
Amazing Baby Sound Balls (Kids Preferred), *p. 25*
Cosmic Catch (Hasbro), *p. 143, 175*
Deluxe Tumble Treehouse (Maxim Enterprises), *p. 89*
Kitchen Appliances (various makers), *pp. 63, 77*
Lamaze Clap with Me Monkey (RC2/Learning Curve), *p. 21*
Lego Duplo Zoo (Lego Systems), *p. 50*
Lucky the Incredible Wonder Pup (Zizzle), *p.85*
Retro Rocket (Radio Flyer), *pp. 39, 72*
Ringgz (Blue Orange Games), *p. 146*
Sudoku (Briarpatch), *p. 152*
Trikke 5 (Trikke Tech), *p. 168, 175*
Word Whammer Fridge Phonics (LeapFrog), *pp. 102, 154, 210*
Zooreka (Cranium), *p. 143*

MAKE A GIFT LIST 2007

Teaching kids to give, not just get, can be fun with any one of these craft kits. These are just a few of our favorite kits that make a finished product kids can give with pride to family, friends, or teachers.

Beeswax Candles (Creativity for Kids), *p. 162*
Decoupage Diva Jewelry Kit (Creativity for Kids), *p. 160*
Hug This Shrug Kit (Fashion Angels Enterprises), *p. 164*
Funky Bead Chest (Bead Bazaar), *p. 163*
Star Box Kit (Balitono), *p. 161*
Paint-a-Doggie Diner (Alex), *p. 160*
Potholders & Other Loopy Projects (Klutz), *p. 165*
Super Embroidery Kit (Alex), *p. 164*
Wake Up! Alarm Clock (Creativity for Kids), *p. 132*

TOP-RATED SCIENCE PRODUCTS 2007

One of the best ways to excite kids about science is to make it a hands-on experience. Here are our favorite picks of this year's top science toys. Many require some adult involvement—providing a chance to make discoveries together.

Backyard Safari (Summit Toys), p. 169
Birdhouse Kit (Balitono), p. 170
Box of Rocks (GeoCentral), p. 169
Dinosaur Excavation Kit (Usborne), p. 169
Discovery Kids SL-70 Telescope (Discovery Kids), p. 169
Hook Fortune Finder (Wild Panet), p. 169
Marshall Brodien Magic Wand Set (Cadaco), p. 170
Magnetic Building Sets (various makers), pp. 97, 141, 209
Mattel Hot Wheels ESS Radar Gun (Mattel), p. 167
Perryscope (Kid Galaxy), p. 170

TOP-RATED PRODUCTS UNDER $10 — 2007

20Q (Radica), p. 174
Amazing Baby Teether Mirror Rattle (Kids Preferred), p. 14
Bendy Beeper Rattle (Sassy), p. 12
Crank 'N Glow Flashlight (Playskool), p. 77
Crayola Color Wonder Paper & Markers (Binney & Smith), pp. 65, 73, 116, 124
Gertie Balls (Small World Toys), pp. 110, 124
Imaginetics (International Playthings), p. 172
K'nex Kids Wild Ones (K'nex), p. 96
My First Quatro Bucket (Lego Systems), pp. 50, 73, 208
Puzzles (Lauri/Ravensburger), pp. 46, 103, 155
Rugged Riggz Trucks (Little Tikes), p. 90, 124
Scratch Art Light Catcher Fun Kits (Scratch Art), pp. 161, 176
Top Speed (Gamewright), p. 173

TOP-RATED PRODUCTS UNDER $15 — 2007

Backyard Flyer (Kid Galaxy), p. 166
Cast & Paint: Krazy Kars (Skullduggery), p. 159
Center Stage Puppets (Mary Meyer), p. 86
Ceramic Allowance Bank (Creativity for Kids), p. 132
Color Dominoes (eeBoo), p. 101
Dishes (various makers), pp. 62, 78
Groovy Girl (Manhattan Toy), pp. 83, 88
Triple Track Tower (Playskool), pp. 49, 73
The Very Book Block Puzzle (Mudpuppy), p. 103, 124

TOP-RATED PRODUCTS UNDER $25 — 2007

Lamaze Whirl & Twirl Jungle (RC2/Learning Curve), pp. 22, 31
Little People Lil' Movers Airplane (Fisher-Price), pp. 60, 73
Monster Truck Custom Shop (Creativity for Kids), p. 159
Musical Stack & Play (Tiny Love), pp. 31, 47
Peek-A-Blocks Bucket o' Builders (Fisher-Price), pp. 50, 208
Works of Ahhh Star Box (Balitono), p. 161
Wrist Pix (Fashion Angels Enterprises), p. 163

TOP-RATED BIG TICKET LIST — 2007

ActiviTot Developmental Gym (Tiny Love), pp. 9, 30
Airport (Lego Systems), p. 139
American Girl Emily (American Girl), p. 133
Bebe Do with Moses Basket (Corolle), p. 81
Dive, Dodge 'n Slide Bouncer (Little Tikes), p. 114
EduBlocks (EduShape), p. 51
Great Big Creamy Bear (Mary Meyer), p. 84
Hot Wheels Flashfire (Mattel), p. 137
Kid-Touch FP3 Player (Fisher-Price), p. 120
Leapster L-Max (LeapFrog), p. 123, 171, 174, 175
Learn-Around Playground (LeapFrog), p. 47
Mindstorm NXT (Lego Systems), pp. 137, 175
My Creativity Center (Alex), p. 121
Pixter Multi-Media (Fisher-Price), p. 123, 171, 174–175
Pushing Car (Haba), p. 38
Retro Rocket (Radio Flyer), po. 39, 72
Wooden Blocks/Trains (various makers), pp. 51, 52, 91, 93

I • Toys

1 • Infants
Birth to One Year

The Horizontal Infant

What to Expect Developmentally

Your Role in Play. To your newborn, no toy in the world is more interesting than you! Babies are more interested in people than things. Your smiling face, your gentle touch, the sound of your voice, even your familiar scent make you the most perfect plaything. Don't worry about spoiling your newborn with attention. Responding to your baby's needs now will make him less needy later. Playing with your baby is not just fun—it's one of the most important ways babies learn about themselves and the world of people and things!

Learning Through the Senses. Right from the start, babies begin learning by looking, listening, touching, smelling, and tasting. It's through their senses that they learn about the world. In this first remarkable year, babies progress from gazing to grasping, from touching to tossing, from watching to doing. By selecting a rich variety of playthings, parents can match their baby's sensory learning style.

Reaching Out. Initially, you will be the one to activate the mobile, shake the rattle, squeeze the squeaker. But before long, baby will be reaching out and taking hold of things and engaging you in a game of peekaboo.

Toys and Development. As babies develop, so does their need for playthings that fit their growing abilities. Like clothes, good toys need to fit. Some of the toys for newborns will have short-term use and then get packed away or passed along to a new cousin or friend. Others will be used in new ways as your child grows. During this first year, babies need toys to gaze at, listen to, grasp, chomp on, shake, pass from one hand to another, bang together, toss, chase, and hug.

Basic Gear Checklist for the Horizontal Infant

- ✓ Mobile
- ✓ Crib mirror
- ✓ Musical toys
- ✓ Activity mat
- ✓ Soft fabric toys with differing sounds and textures
- ✓ Fabric dolls or animals with easy-to-grab limbs

Toys to Avoid

These toys pose choking and/or suffocation hazards:
- ✓ Antique rattles
- ✓ Foam toys
- ✓ Toys with elastic
- ✓ Toys with buttons, bells, or ribbons
- ✓ Old wooden toys that may contain lead paint
- ✓ Furry plush dolls that shed
- ✓ Any toys with small parts

Crib Toys: Musical Toys, Mobiles, and Mirrors

Musicals

Few toys are as soothing to newborns as a music box with its quiet sounds. Today, most musical toys for infants don't come as boxes but as plush toys. We prefer some of the newer pull-down musical toys to dolls with hard metal windup keys that older babies may chew on or get poked with by accident.

INFANTS • Birth to One Year

■ Amazing Baby Developmental Light Up Musical 2007

(Kids Preferred $20 ●●●●½) Hang this in the crib or take it along for overnights at Grandma's. A star-shaped musical in bold colorful patterns, it has a pull-down action that triggers an old-fashioned music box sound. A baby face lift-up flap covers a small Mylar mirror for peek-a-boo sightings. Small lights twinkle under the fabric and the music plays long enough to soothe a baby to sleep. Has a very contemporary look. (866) 763-8869.

■ Woodles Pull-String Musicals 2007

(Gund $25 ●●●●) A new charming collection of pull-down woodland creatures that play music when you pull on the wooden handle. We especially like the giraffe and the cow. Still top rated, **Cuddly Pals Pokey & Spunky** (Gund $20 each ●●●●●). Wind up either Pokey (a bear) or Spunky (a pup), and they will play you a lullaby as they move their heads slowly. Pokey plays "Beautiful Dreamer" while honey-toned-with-white-patches Spunky plays Brahms' "Lullaby." Both have stitched features and a big plastic key. PLATINUM AWARDS '06. BLUE CHIP winner **Peter Rabbit Musical** ($25) also moves his head very slowly as he plays Brahms' "Lullaby." (800) 448-4863.

■ Sleepyhead Bunny

(North American Bear Co. $29 ●●●●●) Pull the long blue-and-white sleeping cap on this floppy pastel bunny, and it plays "Beautiful Dreamer" with an old-fashioned musical sound. Also comes in pink. PLATINUM AWARD '05. (800) 682-3427.

Mobiles

A musical mobile attached to crib rail or changing table provides baby with fascinating sights and sounds. During the first 3 months, infants can focus only on objects that are relatively close. Toys should be between 8" and 14" from their eyes. Mobiles with bright colors and high contrast are easier for baby to see than pastels. Before you buy any mobile, look at it from the baby's perspective. What can you see? Many attractive mobiles are purely for decoration and do not have images that face the baby in the crib. **Editors' Note:** Unfortunately most mobiles we continue to receive both are pastel and have images not directed at baby!

Here are our favorites (all gender-free):

■ Changing Table Flutter Bug Musical Mobile

(Infantino $23 ●●●●) Cleverly designed, this "bug" has four patterned wings with colorful ribbons that flutter as they turn to the music. It's a windup music box with old-fashioned sound, rather than the usual electronic type. This attaches to the changing table for three minutes' worth of diversion. The **Wall Mounted Mobile & Mirror** ($24.99 ●●●●) is reintroduced with new colors and is a good choice for hanging above the changing table. Baby can see her own reflection as well as those of the dangling animals. (800) 840-4916.

■ Lamaze Shine On Me Musical Mobile

(RC2/Learning Curve $50 ●●●●●) A cheerful mobile with a bright smiley sun face tilted down for baby to see. A bird, a butterfly, and some friendly bugs spin as the mobile rotates. Plays jazz, classical, and Latin music that can be activated with a remote control. PLATINUM AWARD '04. (800) 704-8697.

■ Symphony Light & Motion Mobile *2007*

(Tiny Love $49.95 ●●●●½) A monkey, a lion, and a kangaroo are all positioned properly so that baby can focus in on their bright faces. Plays 15 minutes of classical music and nature sounds. This is the newest in our favorite line of mobiles. We still prefer the original **Symphony in Motion Deluxe** ($49.95 ●●●●●), which is brightly colored with small shapes that slide on the arms of the mobile, making a pleasing clicking sound as the mobile turns. Comes with a handy remote control. In our opinion this is the best in the category, followed by the Calderesque **Symphony-in-Motion Shapes** ($39.99 ●●●●●), the most attractive, but with no remote control. PLATINUM AWARD '02. (800) 843-6292.

■ Wimmer-Ferguson Infant Stim-Mobile BLUE CHIP

(Manhattan Toy $20 ●●●●●) Newborns will be fascinated with the

INFANTS • Birth to One Year

black-and-white, high-contrast patterns of the ten vinyl 3" discs and squares that dance and dangle on this nonmusical mobile. Not as cute looking as other mobiles, but babies do react to the visual stimulation of this crib toy. (800) 541-1345.

> ☞ **SAFETY TIP:** Mobiles should be removed by the time baby is 5 months old, or whenever baby can reach out and touch them, to avoid the danger of strangulations or choking on small parts.

> **SMART BABY TRICK: Monkey See, Monkey Do.** Here's the first really neat trick your baby will be able to do. Almost from the start your baby will be able to imitate your expressions. Try sticking your tongue out and see what happens! Who says you need words to "talk"?

> **SMART PARENT TRICK:** Babies stop looking at things that are always there, just as you stop looking at a vase that's always in the same place. Changing things to gaze at will interest babies more. Also, it's hard to focus on too many objects at once. So less may be more.

Crib Mirrors

Even before your baby can reach out and touch, a crib mirror provides her with ever-changing images. It will be a while before baby knows whose face and hands she sees. In time, she'll be babbling to that face and studying the reflection of her hands.

■ Earlyears Crib Mirror

(International Playthings $16.99 ❹❹❹❹) Best choice for newborns, this 14½" x 11" black-and-white, high-contrast graphic will attract baby's attention. Reverse it and you have an infant-safe, distortion-free mirror with colorful trim. (800) 445-8347.

TOYS

■ Me in the Mirror
(Sassy $14.95 ❍❍❍❍) This large (9½") mirror has interesting toys attached for gazing at, and even a place for adding your own photo. Great for tummy time on the floor, or you can attach it to the side of the crib. (800) 323-6336.

> **SAFETY TIP:** Many catalogs and picture books show baby cribs overflowing with quilts, pillows, and toys. These are pretty to look at, but totally unsafe!

BABY TRACKING GAMES
Following a moving object is no small feat for the new baby. Use a boldly patterned soft toy with quiet rattle or squeaky sound to get baby's attention. Give it a shake and move it slowly from side to side in baby's line of vision. In time baby will reach out to touch, but for now, looking and listening is the name of the game. Remember, newborns can't focus on objects more than 8–14 inches from their eyes.

■ Cuddle Pups Puppets *2007* PLATINUM AWARDS
(Manhattan Toy $11.99 each ❍❍❍❍❍) You'll love the feel of these extremely soft velour puppets that are ideal for playing tracking games with your baby. Bring home either the pink **Butterfly,** blue **Monkey,** or green **Frog.** (800) 541-1345.

■ Let's Play Puppets *2007*
(Gund $12.99 ❍❍❍❍½) Choose a blue elephant, **Tootie,** lavender hippo, **Tibs,** or mint green frog, **Pippy,** for early tracking games and heart-to-heart talks. These soft hand puppets come with a baby puppet for parent and child to use together later. For now, these are fun to share with an older sibling as you play with baby together. Also a good take-along toy for distractions on small trips. (800) 448-4863.

INFANTS • Birth to One Year

Everything That Goes Up: Here's a little baby science lesson. Hold your hand up in the air in baby's sight line, saying:
"Everything that goes up comes down, down, down!"
(Gradually spiral your hand down, down, down 'til you gently tickle baby under the chin or on the tummy.) Before long baby will anticipate the tickles, and giggle before your fingers touch!

Equipment for Playtime

Babies are such social beings that they are often happiest when they are in the midst of the action. Many of the following products have serious safety issues that you should be aware of before you buy:

SAFETY TIP: Swings, baby seats, playpens, and saucers are often recalled because they can tip or collapse with frightening consequences. Be sure to check the Consumer Product Safety Commission website if you have inherited a product or find one at a yard sale.

SAFETY TIP: Never place any type of baby carrier on a table, bed, or counter. Even though the baby has never done it before, there's no way of predicting when he will make a move that can tip the carrier.

SAFETY TIP: Many parents find the back-and-forth action of a swing a soothing diversion for a restless infant. We find it difficult to recommend any infant swings, however, because they can entrap limbs and necks, or even collapse. If you choose to use one, we urge you not to leave the room. Use it only with constant supervision.

SAFETY TIP: While stationary entertainment units are safer than the walkers most of us had as kids, you should know that they do not build muscles for walking, and time in these seats should be limited and supervised. Babies do need to crawl before they walk!

SMART PARENT TRICKS

You Don't Say! Some new parents feel awkward about speaking to a baby who can't talk yet. What can you talk about? Anything. Talk about what you are doing, even if you are changing a diaper. Imitate baby's coos, gurgles, and squeals. In the beginning you'll do most of the talking ... but before long baby will be answering. Pause, so baby can take turns! Before long you'll be having real "chats." Research indicates that babies who are frequently talked to have almost 300 more words by age 2 than tots who are rarely spoken to.

Puff 'n' Pop. Puff your cheeks. Then use your hands to pop them to make a funny noise. Soon, baby will reach out to pop your cheeks for you.

Playmats/Activity Gyms

WHAT TO AVOID: As a general rule, avoid playmats and blankets that have lots of doodads, which pose a choking hazard. Also avoid mats with activities all over and no really com-

INFANTS • Birth to One Year

fortable place for baby to lie down on. In addition, we do not recommend plastic activity gyms that now come with a cacophony of frenetic lights and sounds. These gyms have too much heavy plastic over your child's head (it takes only a baby's kick or a big sibling knocking into one of these things to send them over). Most offer the convertibility factor for older babies, but instead, we'd recommend buying a toy for a sitting-up baby when he's ready. See Vertical Infants, Toys for Making Things Happen, p. 20.

Best in Category

■ ActiviTot Developmental Gym
2007 PLATINUM AWARD

(Tiny Love $83 ●●●●●) We've seen a lot of so-called tummy-time products for infants. This one is a gem. An oversized, pear-shaped mat that pops open, has bright graphics, and is fitted out with disks that toys and arches clamp into. There are toys to hang on the arches for baby to bat at, and a mat that inflates for baby to lie on, tummy-side down. A mirror with music box can also be placed for baby to enjoy her own smiling face. Bigger than anything this company has done before, and our parent testers loved it. Not as portable as the original but still got high marks. Select either Tropic Isle or Sun Garden motif. (800) 843-6292.

■ Gymini Duet 2007

(Tiny Love $67 ●●●●½) A clever twist on the original Gymini design with a mat that flips from simple patterns for newborn to gaze at, to an activity mat with sounds and lights to activate on the flip side. Like the original, this has crossing fabric arches that hold dangly toys and a mirror for tummy time. One parent preferred the less expensive versions "without the lights." We'd pass on the new **Gymini Melody Maker** ($67 ●●●)—we found the music uncharacteristically loud and jarring. Still top rated, **Gymini Total Playground Kick & Play** ($69 ●●●●●) PLATINUM AWARD '06. (800) 843-6292.

■ Peek 'n' Play Discovery Dome 2007

(Hasbro $49.99 ●●●) Fifteen different activities for baby and parent to explore together, including a peek-a-boo curtain, a shape-sorting mailbox, and a ball drop chute. Crawling babies often like the fun of going in and out of a space, but this toy just isn't stable enough for older babies who try to pull up on it. We'd also pass on the new **Tummy-Time Together Gym** ($24.99 ●●●). Tummy time is important for this generation of babies who are not put on their stomachs for safety reasons. In the over-the-head activity gym mode, our testers felt that the toy was not stable enough. In the tummy-time mode, there is an angled mirror (which we wish were much bigger), and there is some music (with volume control, a plus), but the toys to explore are limited. We'd pass on this one. (888) 836-7025.

■ **Taf Toys 2 in 1 Smart Gym** *2007*

(Edushape $69.95 ●●●●½) Like last year's **Smart Mat,** this is an oversized playmat with a gym in the middle! 39 x 59, with many textures, colors, and patterns, this has arches that connect securely to hold dangly toys that jitter, ring, and play music. Ideal for gazing at, batting, and kicking, and for multiple discoveries. The huge mat itself has built-in mirror, squeakers, and rattling rings. In contrast to the **ActiviTot,** these arches are not easy to set up, but they work well once you've done it. Our family with triples still raves about the original mat (sans arches) that is ten dollars less. (800) 404-4744.

■ **Lamaze 2-in-1 Gym**

(RC2/Learning Curve $60 ●●●●) A reversible playmat with high-contrast red, black, and white on one side, and bright colors on flip side. Closes up easily with a Velcro closure. Comes with three hanging toys for early gazing. (800) 704-8697.

> **SAFETY TIP: With any gym you use, total supervision is required. Gyms are also not for babies who are beginning to pull themselves up. We prefer fabric playmats to most plastic gyms, which can be accidentally kicked over. Yes, we are repeating ourselves . . . but it's worth repeating.**

INFANTS • Birth to One Year 11

First Lap and Floor Toys: Rattles, Sound Toys, and More

Infant toys can help adults engage and interact with newborns. A bright rattle that baby tracks visually, a quiet music box that soothes, or an interesting doll to gaze or swipe at, are ideal for getting-acquainted games. These toys can be used on the changing table or for lap games during playful moments after a feeding, before a bath, or whenever. **Editors' Note:** Since babies are no longer put to sleep on their tummies, giving them supervised tummy time is very important for developing neck and upper body strength. Some of these toys can be put in front of them.

■ Lamaze First Mirror BLUE CHIP

(RC2/Learning Curve $19.99 ❍❍❍❍❍) A fabric-covered wedge with red piping and a mirror is covered in eye-grabbing, bold black-and-white patterns. The distortion-free mirror is now padded and, like the original, can be removed and hung in the crib. PLATINUM AWARD '98. (800) 704-8697. You can also use the **Me in the Mirror** from Sassy (see p. 6) on the floor.

> **Smart Baby Trick.** Since babies are no longer put to sleep on their tummies, many of our testing families are telling us that their babies are not learning to crawl in the traditional way. To build those little muscles, it's a good idea to build some brief tummy time into their playtime. Most toys designed for this sound better than they are. Many are just too gimmicky. Nothing replaces your getting down there and playing. Putting interesting toys in their reach will encourage babies to use the arm, leg, and neck muscles they'll need to get about as crawlers.

Rattles

Many rattles are too noisy, hard, or heavy for newborns. While most will be used by adults to get baby's attention, the best choice for newborns is a rattle with a soft sound that

TOYS

won't startle and a soft finish that won't hurt. During the first months, an infant's arm and hand movements are not yet refined. Here are some of the best rattles for early playtimes:

■ Bendy Beeper 2007
(Sassy $4.99 ○○○○) Baby will soon be able to grasp the bendy pieces, but even before then, this is a good choice for tracking. Small ball at one end twirls with an easy touch and a quiet squeaker will attract baby's attention. Still top rated, **Circle Rattle** ($3.99 ○○○○½). Also good for early tracking games, this colorful ring has a spotted ball, interesting textures, and smaller rings that clack. So there's a lot to look at, feel, and last but not least, chew on. A classic shape reintroduced in new colors. (800) 323-6336.

■ Mini Pro Grabbies
(Gund $5 ○○○○) These are the lightest rattles we've found, which are perfect for a first rattle and for preemies. Done in velour with a little space for small hands to grasp. Sports themed. (800) 448-4863. Very similar in design but with a different motif, **Little Lovelies Bunny Ring Rattle** (Manhattan Toy $ ○○○○). (800) 541-1345.

> **BABY MUSIC GAMES**
> **Sing, Sing a Song!** Okay, it doesn't matter if you sing off key or you don't know all the words. To your baby, you deserve a Grammy! Singing can soothe a crying baby or refresh and surprise a fussy baby. Go ahead! Add his name to the songs you sing and you'll really have a fan! Don't be afraid to do a little dancing—it's a great way to release your tension as well as baby's.

The Vertical Infant

What to Expect Developmentally
Once babies can sit up, they have a new view of, and fascination with, the world of things. Now they don't just grasp at toys, they use their hands and mouths to explore and feel objects. At

INFANTS • Birth to One Year

around 9 months, babies gain fuller control of their separate fingers and begin to use their index fingers to point and poke at openings. Now they can activate toys with spinners. It's also at this stage that babies can handle two objects at the same time.

Watch how your baby explores any toy, examining every angle. She looks at it, fingers it, tastes it. Using two hands, she bangs two blocks together, or spends many moments passing a toy from one hand to another. This is serious work, a way of discovering how things function and what she can do to make things happen.

During this exciting time your baby will begin to crawl and even pull himself up on his two little feet. Some babies may even take their first steps. In a matter of just a few months, your baby grows from needing others to play a game of patty-cake, to putting out his hands and leading others to play patty-cake with him.

Many of the toys from the horizontal stage will still be used. By now, however, the mobile should be removed from the crib, and other interesting playthings should be added gradually. As new toys are introduced, put some of the older things away. Recycle toys that have lost their novelty by putting them out of sight for a while, then reintroduce them or give them away. A clutter of playthings can become more of a distraction than an attraction.

Basic Gear Checklist for the Vertical Infant

- ✓ Rattles and teething toys
- ✓ Manipulatives with differing shapes, sounds, textures
- ✓ Plastic containers for filling and dumping games
- ✓ Cloth or sturdy cardboard books
- ✓ Washable dolls and animals
- ✓ Musical toys
- ✓ Soft fabric-covered ball
- ✓ Cloth blocks
- ✓ Rolling toys or vehicles
- ✓ Bath toys

🚫 Toys to Avoid

These toys pose choking and/or suffocation hazards:
- ✓ **Antique rattles**
- ✓ **Foam toys**
- ✓ **Toys with elastic**
- ✓ **Toys with buttons, bells, or ribbons**
- ✓ **Old wooden toys that may contain lead paint**
- ✓ **Furry plush dolls that shed**
- ✓ **Any toys with small parts**

These toys are developmentally inappropriate:
- ✓ **Shape sorters and ring-and-post toys—these call for skills beyond those of an infant**

Rattles and Teethers

Now is the time for manipulatives that encourage two-handed exploration while providing interesting textures and sounds, and safe, chewable surfaces for teething. You can't teach eye-hand coordination, but you can motivate exploration by providing toys that develop baby's ability to use hands and fingers in new and more complex ways.

■ Amazing Baby Teether Mirror Rattles 2007

(Kids Preferred $7 each ●●●●) Choose from a puppy-, kitten-, or bear-faced teether rattle. Each of the velour faces with stitched features is surrounded by petals of bold patterned fabrics with crinkle sound and textured teethers. Hang them in the stroller or car seat, or hand off for baby to explore for two-handed play. (866) 763-8869.

■ Asthma Friendly Rattle Teether Security Blanket 2007

(Kids Preferred $10 each ●●●●) Using fabrics and finishes to reduce allergens, this is one of a new line of toys designed to reduce the risk of asthma. Each critter (a bear, pup, or hippo) has chewy teethers attached to the velour flat body with baby-safe stitched features and soothing satin-backed blanket body. From top to bottom, a soft 11", and easy for baby to grab. Also

INFANTS • Birth to One Year

worth a look, **Pastel Rattle Teether Toy** ($9 ●●●●), a **Funny Bunny** with chewy teether ears or **Lucky Ducky** with teether arms. A satin-trimmed **Flower Rattle Baby Doll** ($9 ●●●●) is also cute, with stitched features and flowery trim. All have good rattle sounds inside, stitched features, and satin feet. (866) 763-8869.

■ Baby Cozies & Flatso Baby Cozies 2007

(North American Bear Co. $7 each ●●●●) Pick a duck, monkey, elephant, hippo, or frog in this velvety soft line of easy-to-grab toys. Each has an unstuffed body and small head with stitched features. Or, adapted from the BLUE CHIP Flatso line, small bunnies or bear with unstuffed bodies. These are the kind of soft toy that is likely to become a favorite "lovie." Also cute and not too loud, **Flatso 9" Rattles** ($10.50 ●●●●). (800) 682-3427.

■ Baby Toodles 2007

(Mary Meyer $5 each ●●●●) Easy to grab, soft to the touch, with quiet rattle inside, these pastel blue or pink elephants or giraffes come with a checked pattern that make them visually interesting. (800) 451-4387.

■ Cuddly Teether Blanket 2007

(Infantino $9 ●●●●½) Choose a terry cloth "blanket" (the size of a washcloth) with satin binding and teethers in each corner, topped off with a velour and satin head; new this year, a cow or mouse. We also like last year's frog or pup. A soft, safe, and interesting sensory toy. (800) 840-4916.

■ Earlyears Click & Play Triangles

(International Playthings $6.99 ●●●●) Ideal for two-handed play, these three-hinged triangles click as they are opened and closed. A central triangle has a small mirror and the textured triangles are fine for teething. Also fun, **Busy Bead Rattle** ($9.99 ●●●●); this hourglass-shaped toy has beads that drop from one cone to another. The cones turn with a quiet click and the colorful central ring has beads that turn. (800) 445-8347.

TOYS

■ Gummy Guppy 2007

(Sassy $2.99 ●●●●) Large enough to be safe, this multicolored fish-shaped teether has interesting textures and bends slightly for two-handed investigations. (800) 323-6336.

■ Tolo Abacus Rattle BLUE CHIP

(Small World Toys $5.95 ●●●●●) There are lots of moving parts to explore as they clack and move on this colorful plastic rattle for two-handed play. Also, still top rated, the **Tolo Roller Ball** ($5.50 ●●●●) with a small ball inside a larger ball and easy grip openings. Both beautifully crafted in sturdy, primary-colored plastic with interesting action for baby to manipulate. (800) 421-4153.

■ Whoozit Touch & Teethe

(Manhattan Toy $12 ●●●●½) An easy-to-hold, visually exciting rattle. The Whoozit face with a squeaky nose is on one side, and a mirror is on the other. A ring with hearts, stars, and other textured shapes surrounds the face and is ideal for two-handed exploration and teething. New for 2007, **Whoozit Grabbitz Ball** ($14.95 ●●●½) comes with six bulb-shaped grabbers with crunch sounds, teethers, and a squeaker. It's slightly heavy. Nice, but not a must-have. (800) 541-1345.

**SMART PARENT TRICKS:
Who's That?** Your baby in arms will be amazed to catch sight of herself and you in a mirror. Watch her surprise as she sees you twice—the real you and your reflection. Talk about what she sees and let her touch your face and your reflection. In time, you can play little games of "Where is my nose? Where is baby's nose?" Move baby in and out of the sight line of the mirror, playing yet another variation of peekaboo!

INFANTS • Birth to One Year

Floor Toys

Many of the toys here are truly "interactive"—and they're not electronic. They depend on an adult interacting with the baby to make something happen. Some testers complained that their babies did not know what do to with the stacking toy. True. Stacking, knocking down, and playing peek a boo are all the tricks you'll teach your baby. There is no button to push—you are the button! They also complained that the toy did not hold the baby's interest. Also true. You are the only plaything that will hold your baby's interest for long stretches of time. These toys are really just props for introducing games and being sociable. Especially at this stage of the game, interacting with your baby on the floor is more important than what toy you brought home. It is the dialogue you share with your baby that's key.

■ Bucket Buddies

(Infantino $20 ●●●●●) Three fabric buckets with happy stitched faces and crinkle ears can nest or stack. There are squeakers, rattles, and jingle sounds along with three crinkly soft play pieces to put in and take out of the buckets. Beautifully crafted in colorful patterned fabrics, a good toy for parent/child games of "knock it down" or "hide and find." PLATINUM AWARD '06. New for 2007, **Hula Hut** ($17.99 ●●●●) with a green roof is really much like a fabric block with an opening in the middle for an assortment of sea-inspired rattles to explore together. The new **Baby Mail** ($24.99 ●●●) is a fabric mailbox and is chock-full of important "mail" including a postcard, a gift, and a cupcake. Unfortunately, the postcard has water/gel in it that we don't care for. (800) 840-4916.

■ Lamaze Stack 'n Nest Birds

(RC2/Learning Curve $14.99 ●●●●½) There are four birds that can be stacked in a tower or nested one over the other. Three are done in fabric with zippy patterns, touchy-feely textures, and interesting sounds that rattle, crinkle, and squeak. The littlest bird is a funny-faced squeeze toy that can hide under all the others. Size order is built into the fun for peek-a-boo games of

"Where's the birdie?" 9 mos. & up. (800) 704-8697.

■ My Sound Cube 2007

(Latitude Enfant $20 ●●●●) A squeaky heart, a crackly leaf, a target graphic rattle and, best of all, two flower shapes, each with a beautiful bird song! Shapes fit inside a gaily patterned fabric cube. At first glance this looks like a shape sorter, but it is really a fill-and-dump toy with delicious sensory opportunities. CAUTION: toss the head-size plastic packaging! 8 mos. & up. (800) 544-9183.

First Blocks

We like the **Discover & Play Color Blocks** (Baby Einstein $12.99 ●●●●½), which have interesting textures on each side. One block makes a quacking sound that your baby will enjoy hearing long before she'll be able to make it happen. These are fun for stacking and knocking down. (800) 793-1454. We also still recommend **Earlyears Soft Busy Blocks** (International Playthings $15 ●●●●½), which have softer sides and corded piping, making them easier for baby to grasp. Colorful graphics and patterns and quiet sounds make these good floor toys for beginners. Also, **Earlyears Sweet Baby Blocks** ($10 ●●●●). Six soft, squeezable vinyl blocks, easy to grasp, with a colorful single image on each face of the cubes. Fun for stacking, knocking down, and tossing. (800) 445-8347.

■ Peek Rattle and Teethe

(Infantino $13 ●●●●½) Four easy-to-grasp hollow fabric blocks, each has a teether attached and interesting textures and patterns to explore. Best of all, one side of each block has a soft see-through vinyl "window" so baby can see and hear the bright plastic rings that are locked inside. Stack them, roll them, toss or taste them, these are a good choice for sitting-up babies. (800) 840-4916.

INFANTS • Birth to One Year

TWO-WAY BABY GAME Booom! Before baby starts stacking blocks, he'll like knocking them down. Use fabric blocks or a stack of big plastic ones. How high can you stack them before your little playmate makes them go BOOOOOOOOM? Baby loves the powerful feeling of making this happen, especially if you laugh it up.

Filling and Spilling Games

With their newly acquired skills of grasping and letting go comes the favorite game of filling and dumping multiple objects into and out of containers.

■ Baby's First Blocks and Snap-Lock Beads BLUE CHIP

(Fisher-Price $8 & $3.99 ●●●●●) Babies will enjoy these toys long before they can do what the boxes promise. **Baby's First Blocks** is technically a shape sorter, but the 12 blocks will be used to fill, spill, and throw long before baby can fit them into the four-place shape-sorter lid of the container. Put the lid away for now. The same is true of the lemon-sized **Snap-Lock** plastic beads that will be enjoyed for chomping on, picking up, tossing, and little games of fill and dump. Putting them together comes much later. Great for developing fine motor skills and the ability to litter the floor. (800) 432-5437.

■ Fill 'N Spill Fish *2007*

(Playskool $14.99 ●●●●) Designed as part of the "Let's Play Together" collection, this happy-looking fish rolls like a ball and can be opened for filling and dumping games. Three fabric cube-shaped "fish" crinkle, rattle, or squeak and can be used as finger puppets by a parent. 6 mos & up. (800) 327-8264.

■ Put and Peek Birdhouse

(Manhattan Toy $19.95 ●●●●) This cheerful fabric birdhouse is a parent-intensive toy with lots of possibilities for hamming it up. You can fly the four birds into the house (the roof opens wide, as does one side). Our nine-month-old tester favored holding (and tasting) the red bird as he watched his father fly the other ones about. 6 mos. & up. We found the new **Chimpanzee Jamboree** ($19.95 ●●●○) less inspired (smaller in scale). We'd stick with the birdies! (800) 541-1345.

> **How Many Socks? Game** The Put and Peek Birdhouse is a perfect prop to fill with all those unmatched socks you keep saving. Leave the wide door open and let some socks stick out of the other openings on the cube. This is almost as much fun to empty as a box of tissues, and much safer, since tissues fall apart when they are tasted. Strengthens hands and fingers while exploring textures, colors, and patterns.

Toys for Making Things Happen

Some of the best infant toys introduce babies to their first lessons in cause and effect. Such toys respond to baby with sounds or motion that give even the youngest players a sense of "can do" power—of making things happen! **What to Avoid:** toys that do too much. Most are overwhelming to kids and they end up watching rather than doing.

■ Classical Stacker

(Fisher-Price $10 ●●●●●) This former PLATINUM-AWARD winning stacker is back with new colors. The star rings fit on the post in any order (a plus). Post has magical lights that wink and play music when top is pressed. Sound quality is not excellent, but it is a long-term favorite. Says 6 mos. & up, we'd say 9 mos. & up. (800) 432-5437.

■ NooBoo Symphonic Stacker *2007* PLATINUM AWARD

(Manhattan Toy $29.95 ●●●●●) We tested a lot of fabric stackers this year but most were unforgiving—they didn't move easily on the post. These pleasingly soft patterned, textured, easy-to-grasp rings (they look almost like flowers) are fun to explore—they also activate "magical" sounds when stacked (although they don't always work 100% of the time). A good parent/child toy. (800) 541-1345.

INFANTS • Birth to One Year

■ Developlay Activity Center

(Tiny Love $44.95 ●●●●●) A two-sided activity center loaded with interesting challenges for the senses. A polka-dotted spinner reflects in a mirror; music plays with a press of the happy face; pull a ring to make a "hammer" rise and fall. Flip it over for musical buttons, knobs to turn, a gentle pop-up, and gears that spin. 9 mos. & up. PLATINUM AWARD '04. (800) 843-6292.

■ Discover Sounds Kitchen

(Little Tikes $40 ●●●●) There are multiple fill-and-spill activities built into the doors and chutes of this mini-kitchen. There are some noises but none that our parents found objectionable. In contrast, the **DiscoverSounds Workshop** (●●) was noisy, with limited playability. 9 mos. & up. (800) 321-0183.

■ Lamaze Clap with Me Monkey
2007 PLATINUM AWARD

(RC2/Learning Curve $19.99 ●●●●●) A purple-and-yellow monkey with geometric patterns and a jolly smile is ready to play and make music with. Squeeze Monkey's hand and you hear the familiar tune, "If you're happy and you know it, clap your hands!" Now, clap Monkey's hands or it stops making music. A playful way to learn about cause and effect. Also cute and PLATINUM AWARD-winning, **Giggle Bug** *2007* ($19.99 ●●●●●) plays "The Eensy Weensy Spider" when you squeeze its leg. There's a strap attached to the spider so you can move it, sing along, and give baby some tummy tickles along the way. (800) 704-8697.

COMPARISON SHOPPER
High Chair Toys

Fascination Station BLUE CHIP (Sassy $8.99 ●●●●●) Our favorite high chair toy on the market. Little testers can bat at this spinning toy that attaches to a tabletop with a stout suction cup. There is plenty to see, hear, and feel as the balls and clackers

with bold graphics and textures turn. 6 mos. & up. PLATINUM AWARD '99. If fish are your thing, **Fishy Fascination Station** ($8.99 ○○○○½) has spinners shaped like fish. This too converts to a handheld rattle with textures to explore and chewy ring for teething. (800) 323-6336. Also very interesting, **Earlyears Click N Spin Highchair Flower** (International Playthings $15.99 ○○○○½). This colorful flower suctions to the high chair tray. Petals have spinners, a mirror, textures, patterns, and sounds for sitting-up baby to activate. (800) 445-8347.

■ Lamaze Press n' Spin Safari Friends *2007*

(RC2/Learning Curve $19.99 ○○○○) You need to turn on the switch to activate this musical toy. A silly monkey and little lion laugh and spin under a palm tree until they stop. To make them spin again, baby must hit the top of the tree. This is a little lesson in cause and effect and making things happen. Package says 6 months & up; we think 9 months will understand it better. (800) 704-8697. Still one of our all-time favorites, **Lamaze Whirl & Twirl Jungle** (RC2/Learning Curve $19.99 ○○○○○). Three jolly creatures—a lion, an elephant, and a monkey—spin when placed on the colorful musical platform. A single big button activates the music and motion providing a little lesson in cause and effect. This innovative toy develops motor skills, visual tracking, and a powerful sense of being in charge. If we had to choose one toy in this category, this would be it. PLATINUM AWARD '06. Unlike the overly frenetic Fisher-Price's **Jungle Friends Treehouse** (○○), the Learning Curve animals here spin at a reasonable rate. 9 mos. & up. (800) 704-8697.

■ Melody Beads Piano

(Little Tikes $25.99 ○○) What should have been a basic gear kind of toy has missed a beat (sorry). Marked for 6 mos. & up, this musical toy has five musical keys and a bead-on-wire toy above. Sounds great in theory. We found the musical quality to be sub-par and, somehow, dogs barking music (the second sound option) seems more like music *depreciation* than *appreciation!* The greater problem with the

INFANTS • Birth to One Year

toy is that the lesson in cause and effect is lost since one touch of the button sets off tons of music. The older versions of this toy by all manufacturers used to give kids the option of playing one note at a time. The effect here is way too random. (800) 321-0183.

■ Roll-a-Rounds Drop & Roar Dinosaur

(Fisher-Price $35 ●●●●½) This is a ball run with multiple openings from which balls appear. Played with sounds and lights or in silence, it can be enjoyed by a sitting-down baby. That said, this is a large piece of green plastic and younger babies may have trouble fitting the balls into the holes on the front of the dino, rather than dropping them in—as they can in **Roll-a-Rounds Swirlin' Surprise Gumballs** ($17.99 ●●●●½). This is a much smaller ball drop with a lever that pops the gumballs out. It employs more direct cause and effect, although it tips over easily. Either is a better choice than the **Jungle Friends Treehouse** (●●), a frenetic ball drop with over-the-top sounds and twirling bases. (800) 432-5437.

First Toys for Crawlers

At around 7 months, most babies begin to creep. It takes a few months more before most are up on hands and knees and truly crawling. Rolling toys such as small vehicles and balls can match baby's developing mobility. Toys placed slightly beyond baby's reach can provide the motivation to get moving. But make it fun. Avoid turning this into a teasing time. Your object is to motivate, not frustrate. Games of rolling a ball or car back and forth make for happy social play between baby and older kids as well as adults.

■ Pull & Go Elephant Pal *2007*

(Sassy $9.99 ●●●●½) Give it a push, or pull the ring on the base to activate this little rolling polka-dotted cotton elephant with big stitched eyes and crinkly ears. A good choice for "go get the elephant" games with crawling babies, or for back-and-forth games for sitting-up-baby fun. 6 mos. & up. (800) 323-6336.

■ Baby Gymnastic Playwall

(Fisher-Price $54.99 ●●●) You need a good deal of space for this toy. There are three "walls": one with "chimes" that move and make electronic sounds; one with a curtained wall to crawl through; and the third with a hanging ball to hit. One tester loved this toy, but we'd recommend **Laugh and Learn Learning Home** (see p. 31), a more versatile play setting—also a much better choice than the wobbly **Activity Tunnel.** (800) 432-5437.

■ Lamaze Lights & Sounds Barnyard Crawl Toy

(RC2/Learning Curve $24.95 ○○○○○) Perfect for rolling back and forth, or set it in motion to motivate your beginning crawler to get moving. You can use this with sounds and lights off, or set the volume from low to high. Hourglass shaped, this has beads that rattle inside, colorful cloth knotties to feel, and bright patterns. Interesting to all the senses as well as to emerging locomotion skills. PLATINUM AWARD '06. (800) 704-8697.

> **SMART BABY TRICK:** If a young baby drops a toy she is holding, she will not look to see where it goes. Developmentally, at this stage, out of sight is out of mind. If she has a toy in one hand and you show her another, she will drop the first and reach for the offered toy.

■ Poppin' Push Car

(Sassy $6 ○○○○½) Push this little car forward and the popping beads (safely enclosed in the dome roof) make a pleasing sound. Pull the car back, and when you let go the car zooms forward. One of the best toys of the season! Just right for floor-time play. (800) 323-6336. **Safety note:** Hot Wheels and Matchbox-styled cars have small parts that pose a choking hazard for kids under 3.

■ Press N Go Inchworm

(International Playthings $12 ○○○○○) You can simply push this happy-looking Inchworm back and forth or press down on its back to make it zoom forward. There are little beads inside the domed wheels. A terrific toy that older siblings will love to demo for their little brother or sister. PLATINUM

INFANTS • Birth to One Year

AWARD '06. (800) 445-8347.

■ Sing & Go Choo Choo *2007*

(Fisher-Price $30 ●●●○) Big chunky, jointed elephant, giraffe, and monkey have built-in clicking sounds. Designed for sit-and-play fun, the engine will soon be used for move-along fun. Fun to load and unload, crawling tots can easily keep up, as the train takes off on its slow journey accompanied by sound effects and music. They say 6 months and up, we'd say more like 9–24 mos. (800) 432-5437.

COMPARISON SHOPPER
Fabric Balls *2007*

Nothing is more basic for this stage than a soft fabric ball that's easy to grasp, toss, and roll. A perfect toy for crawlers to chase and for early back-and-forth roly-poly social games. Our favorites:

Colorfun Ball BLUE CHIP (Gund $12 ●●●●●) A brightly colored ball done in soft velour. (800) 448-4863.

Amazing Baby Sound Balls *2007*

PLATINUM AWARD (Kids Preferred $17 ●●●●●) Three baseball-sized, brightly patterned fabric balls come packaged together in a see-through tote. A black-and-white ball with colorful swirls crinkles, an orange velour ball with stitched stars jingles, and a multicolored ball with bold patterns chimes. A classic toy for sensory exploration and active play. (866) 763 8869.

Toss the Taggie *2007* PLATINUM AWARD

(Taggies $19.95 ●●●●●) A big fabric ball with multiple patterns, ribbon taggies to grab, and a wonderful jingle inside is one of the best toys of the season. It's covered with soft velour but slightly understuffed to make it easier to grasp. (877) 482-4443.

SMART BABY GAMES: Roly-Poly Ball. Your sitting-up and crawling baby will love the back-and-forth fun of rolling a ball. Choose a soft fabric ball with jingle inside or a big beach ball that's slightly soft.

I'll Catch You and You Catch Me! Get down on the floor and take turns playing a crawling catch game. Say, "I'm going to catch you!" and crawl after baby. Or play it in reverse, telling baby to "Try and catch me!" Go slowly enough so baby can catch you. This can be a pretty exciting game!

Tub Time

Bathing a baby can be one of the scariest chores for new parents. (After all, once you take off all those layers, they're so small, and that doesn't even take into account the wobbly neck situation!) For your own comfort as well as baby's, make sure you have everything ready before you begin. The key is to remain calm, comforting, and prepared to get wet! For beginners, a small tub will be more comfortable for both bather and bathee. Little ones don't need much in the way of toys, but once they can sit securely, a few simple bath toys add to the fun.

SAFETY TIP: The Consumer Product Safety Commission reports 123 deaths since 1983 associated with baby bath "supporting rings," devices that keep baby seated in the bathtub. Never rely on such devices to keep baby safe. Going to answer the door or phone can result in serious injury, or worse, to babies and toddlers.

INFANTS • Birth to One Year

☞ **SAFETY TIP:** Avoid foam bath toys, which are often labeled in fine print, "Not for children under 3." Babies can choke on bits of foam that break off when babies chew on them.

First Huggables

Babies often receive tons of soft dolls that are too big, too fuzzy, and even unsafe for now. Although they may be decorative and fine for gazing at, fuzzy plush dolls with ribbons, buttons, plastic features that may pull out, or doodads that may be pulled off, are better saved for preschool years.

When shopping for huggables, look for:

✓ **Interesting textures**
✓ **Easy-to-grasp legs or arms**
✓ **Sound effects sewn safely inside**
✓ **Washable fabric such as velour or terry cloth**
✓ **Stitched-on features; no loose ribbons or bells**
✓ **Small enough size for infant to hold with ease**

■ Babipouce

(Corolle $10 & up ❍❍❍❍❍) Older babies are fascinated by dolls that look like real babies. The trick is to find dolls that are washable and safe enough for them to handle. Corolle has an assortment of dolls with all-fabric velour rompers in various colors and soft vinyl painted faces. Our favorites this season: **Puppet Blue,** with a tri-knottie hat, **Puppet Raspberry,** which is easy to grab with an un-stuffed body, or **Miss Grenadine,** with a bright red romper. PLATINUM AWARD '05. (800) 668-4846.

■ My Dolly & Sweet Dolly

(Gund $12 each ❍❍❍❍) These cloth dolls come with fabric clothes sewn on, stitched faces, and soft bodies that are easy to grasp. **My Dolly** wears polka dots. **Sweet Dolly** is in stripes and short plush. Both extremely cuddly but only available in Caucasian skin tones and pink clothing. (800) 448-4863.

TOYS

Best Travel Toys for Infants

Having a supply of several small toys can help divert and entertain young travelers, whether you're going out for a day or away for a week. Bring along a familiar comfort toy—a musical toy or doll that's like a touch of home. Pack a variety of toys with different sounds and textures and don't show them all at once; you need to dole them out. Select several very different toys, for example:

- ✓ Teether
- ✓ Highchair toy
- ✓ Musical toy
- ✓ Familiar quilt/playmat to rest on
- ✓ Handheld mirror
- ✓ Small huggable
- ✓ Books and pictures to share

■ Amazing Baby Developmental Blanket Teether
2007 PLATINUM AWARD

(Kids Preferred $11 ●●●●●) One of our favorite new toys of the year. Not really a blanket, this is about 12" of flat bear with crinkle body. It has chewy teether hands, easy-to-grab rings on its feet, and interesting patterns on its patchwork body. A variety of textures include plush head, satin foot, and velvety velour back. Likely to get a lot of touching moments. (866) 763-8869.

■ Amazing Baby Developmental Duck 2007

(Kids Preferred $12 ●●●●½) For starters, use this as a dangly gazing toy to hang in baby carrier. Pull down and the duck jiggles, press and it squeaks. Older babies will like chomping on duck's chewy teether "feet" that slide back and forth in its vibrantly patterned body with licks of black and white stripes. Also fun, **Developmental Butterfly** ($12); lots for eyes and hands to explore on this gaily patterned butterfly with crinkle-sounds wings, squeaky body, and many textures. A good take-along stroller toy. (866) 763-8869.

■ Car Seat Gallery BLUE CHIP

(Manhattan Toy $12 ●●●●●) Hang the four-way pattern pocket chart on the

INFANTS • Birth to One Year

back of the front seat of the car and use either the included graphic cards or your own photos! (800) 541-1345.

■ Lamaze Eli Elephant & Henry the Hippo 2007
(RC2/Learning Curve $12.99 each ●●●●)
Hook either of these zany-looking critters on the stroller where baby can explore their crinkles, satiny trims, and textured teething rings. (800) 704-8697.

■ Lamaze Traveling Mobile
(RC2/Learning Curve $14.99 ●●●●½) Three happy fabric critters hang from a ring that can be attached to either an infant carrier or stroller. Has a quiet sound and interesting textures for little hands to explore. (800) 704-8697.

■ Sing Along Spider 2007
(Playskool $19.99 ●●●●) A not-so-itsy-bitsy 15"-wide spider mat comes loaded with games of discovery for baby. Lift the peek-a-boo mirror for a see-through surprise. Each "arm" of the spider has interesting textures and colors, and one plays "The Itsy-bitsy Spider." You can detach the finger puppet spider, a roller rattle, and a little cloth book. All done in fabric, this is a good take-along for any trip. Part of the "Let's Play Together" collection, this is best enjoyed with an adult. 3 mos & up. (800) 327-8264.

Shakers

All our testers loved the toys that wiggle and shake. Most attach easily to a carseat or stroller. They'll usually buy you a little extra time! Here are our top choices:

■ Jittery Jungle Pal Zebra 2007
(Infantino $7.99 ●●●●½) You can attach this zebra to the car seat or stroller. His strong black-and-white pattern with bright yellow accents makes this a great gazing toy for younger babies, and older babies will enjoy pulling him down and making him jitter! Also fun, **Bee & Me** ($9 ●●●●½). Bee has a happy, featured face, satiny ribbons on its crinkly wings, and a bold yellow-and-black striped frame around the mirror. Soft and

TOYS

safe for baby to explore later, but perfect for early gazing. (800) 840-4916.

■ **Tolo Wiggly Jigglies Collection**
(Small World Toys $9.99 each ●●●●) Bring home either the **Ibis Bird** or the **Bug**. Both done in velour and satin with a pull cord that activates a wonderful jiggly sound! (800) 421-4153.

■ **Whoozit Starz Lights & Sound** *2007*
(Manhattan Toy $19.95 ●●●●) A fun new variation on the classic Whoozit—with a pull-down little Whoozit face that makes the whole thing shake. As with the original, there are a variety of dangling toys/teethers to explore. Still top rated, **Baby Whoozit** (Manhattan Toy $10 ●●●●) and the original big **Whoozit** ($20 ●●●●) (10½") with lots of dangly toys to tuck in and pull out. (800) 541-1345.

> **SAFETY TIP:** Links should never be made into a loop, or linked across a crib or playpen. We often see baby strollers draped with long lengths of links. Warning labels say that a chain of links should never be more than 12" long and should be used with adult supervision.

Best New Baby/Shower Gifts

Big Ticket ($40–50)	**ActiviTot Developmental Gym** or **Symphony in Motion Deluxe Mobile** (Tiny Love)
Under $40	**Sleepyhead Bunny** (North American Bear Co.)
Under $25	**Changing Table Flutterbug Musical Mobile** (Infantino) or **Wimmer-Ferguson Infant Stim-Mobile** (Manhattan Toy) or **Cuddly Pals** (Gund)

INFANTS • Birth to One Year

Under $20   **Me in the Mirror** (Sassy) or **Lamaze Whirl & Twirl Jungle** (RC2/Learning Curve)

Under $15   **Car Seat Gallery** (Manhattan Toy)

Under $10   **Fascination Station** (Sassy)

Under $5   **Snap-Lock Beads** (Fisher-Price)

Toddlers-in-Training Toys

Some of the early walking toys found in the following chapter may be ideal for infants who are seriously working on walking before their first birthday.

Looking Ahead: Best First-Birthday Gifts for Every Budget

Big Ticket ($50 or more)   **Push Cart** (Galt) or **Laugh and Learn Learning Home** (Fisher-Price)

Under $50   **Discover Sounds Kitchen** (Little Tikes) or **Roll-a-Rounds Drop & Roar Dinosaur** (Fisher-Price)

Under $25   **Read to Me Tot Tower** (eeBoo) or **Lamaze Whirl & Twirl Jungle** (RC2/Learning Curve)

Under $20   **Musical Stack & Play** (Tiny Love) or **Babipouce** (Corolle)

Under $15   **Colorfun Ball** (Gund) or **Roll-a-Rounds Swirlin' Surprise Gumballs** (Fisher-Price)

Under $10   **Poppin' Push Car** (Sassy) or **Books** (see Books section)

TOYS

Best Books for Babies 2007

At this stage, books are not merely for looking at. Babies and toddlers tend to taste, toss, and tear their books. Even sturdy cardboard books may not survive this search-and-destroy stage. Cloth and vinyl make good chewable choices. The mechanics of turning pages, pointing to pictures, and even listening make books among baby's favorite playthings and a key to language development.

For this year's PLATINUM AWARD-winning books, see page 177. For top-rated books with related easy-to-do activities and games, see our book, **Read It! Play It! With Babies & Toddlers.**

2 • Toddlers
Ones and Twos

What to Expect Developmentally

Ones and Twos. There is a tremendous difference between your one-year-old, whose focus is primarily on mastering and enjoying his new-found mobility, and your two-year-old, who is now running, jumping, and making giant leaps with language and imagination. Yet the second and third years are generally known as the toddler years. Many of the toys and games recommended for ones will continue to be used by twos in new and more complex ways. Since some toddlers will be steady on their feet earlier than others or talking and pretending at different times, you'll want to use this chapter in terms of your own child's individual development. This chapter is not arranged chronologically. You'll find toys and games for ones and twos under each of the following main headings: **Active Physical Play, Strictly Outdoors, Sit-Down Play, Pretend Play, Art and Music, Bath Toys, Basic Furniture, Travel Toys,** and **Birthday Gifts.**

Active Exploration. Anyone who spends time with toddlers knows that they are active, on-the-go learners. They don't visit long, because there are so many places and things to explore. Toys that invite active investigation are best for this age group. For toddlers, toys with doors to open, knobs to push, and pieces to fit, fill, and dump provide the raw material for developing fine-motor skills, language, and imagination.

Big-Muscle Play. Toddlers also need playthings that match their newfound mobility and budding sense of independence. Wheeled toys to push, ride on, and even ride in are great favorites. So is equipment they can climb, rock, and slide on. In these two busy years, toddlers grow from wobbly walkers to nimble runners and climbers.

Language and Pretend Power. As language develops, so does the ability to pretend. For beginners, games of make-believe depend more on action than on story lines. Choose props that look like the things they see in the real world.

Toys and Development. As an infant your baby was involved mainly with people. Now your toddler will spend more time investigating things. Some of the toys in this chapter, such as those for beginning walkers, will have short-term use. However, many of the best products are what we call bridge toys, playthings that will be used now and for several years ahead. While no toddler needs all the toys listed here, 1- and 2-year-olds do need a good mix of toys that fit varying play modes—toys for indoors and out, for quiet, solo sit-down times, and social run-and-shout-out-loud times. A variety of playthings (which may include a plain paper shopping bag or some pots and pans) gives kids the learning tools they need to stretch their physical, intellectual, and social development.

Your Role in Play. Playing (and keeping up) with an active toddler requires a sense of humor and realistic expectations. In order to satisfy their growing appetite for independence, select uncomplicated toys that won't frustrate their sense of "can do" power. For example, if your toddler does not want to sit down with you and work on a puzzle now, she may be willing in an hour, or she may be telling you that it's too difficult and should be put away and tried again in a few weeks.

Childproofing: Setting the Stage for Learning

Childproofing involves more than putting things out of reach. It involves setting the stage for learning by providing appropriate objects that children can safely explore. To avoid a constant monologue of "No! Don't touch!" remove treasures and objects that may be dangerous to handle. Touching is what toddlers do—it's how they learn. Toddlers who lack the freedom to explore get a negative message about learning. Your goal is to encourage their curiosity, not set up roadblocks to the world around them.

Many household items are the most interesting objects to explore. Toddlers need opportunities to discover how things work—knobs to pull, boxes to open, fabrics to feel, and containers to stack. A low cabinet in the kitchen with a stack of paper plates to explore will hold a toddler's interest. Pots and pans with lids to fit on and lift off will keep toddlers occupied while you are working in the kitchen. Toddlers love to take things off shelves. Why not put sturdy cardboard books on a low shelf so they can enjoy them independently?

Enlarging the Circle: Playmates

Your 1-year-old will play mostly with you and the significant people in her life. But 2s are ready to enlarge their social circle. Whether they go to a play group or the park or visit with neighbors, 2s begin to enjoy playing near and ultimately with other children.

A Word on Sharing. Lacking experience, toddlers live by the philosophy that what's mine is mine and what's yours is mine, too. It's not selfishness so much as not really understanding what sharing means. Toddlers consider their toys almost as extensions of themselves—not for sharing. How can you help? If you are having visitors over, keep visits relatively short. An hour is plenty for 2s—always leave them wanting more!

> ### Basic Gear Checklist for Ones
>
> ✓ Push toys
> ✓ Ride-on toy
> ✓ Musical toys
> ✓ Toy phone
>
> ✓ Pull toys
> ✓ Small vehicles
> ✓ Huggables
> ✓ Lightweight ball

- ✓ Fill-and-dump toys
- ✓ Manipulatives with moving parts

Basic Gear Checklist for Twos

- ✓ Ride-on/-in toy
- ✓ Big lightweight ball
- ✓ Climbing/sliding toy
- ✓ Big blocks
- ✓ Huggables
- ✓ Simple puzzles/shape-sorters
- ✓ Pull and push toy
- ✓ Shovel and pail
- ✓ Art supplies
- ✓ Table and chair
- ✓ Props for housekeeping

Toys to Avoid

These toys pose choking and/or suffocation hazards:
- ✓ Foam toys
- ✓ **Toys with small parts** (including small plastic fake foods)
- ✓ **Dolls and stuffed animals with fuzzy and/or long hair**
- ✓ **Toys labeled 3 & up** (No matter how smart toddlers are! The label almost always indicates that there are small parts in or on the toy.)
- ✓ **Latex balloons** (Note: The Consumer Product Safety Commission reports that latex balloons are the leading cause of suffocation deaths! Since 1973 more than 110 children have died from suffocation involving uninflated balloons or pieces of broken ones. They are not advised for children under age 6.)

These toys are developmentally inappropriate:
- ✓ Electronic educational drill toys
- ✓ Shape-sorters with more than three shapes
- ✓ Battery-operated ride-ons
- ✓ Most pedal toys

Active Physical Play

Between 12 and 15 months most babies start toddling. At first they sidestep from one piece of furniture to another. Soon, with

TODDLERS • Ones and Twos

arms used for balance, they take their first independent steps. In these first months of the second year they grow from those thrilling wobbly first steps to being sure-footed adventurers. Few toys lend the kind of security you give as you extend your hands to assure him you are there to catch him.

Beginning walkers will get miles of use from a low-to-the-ground, stable, wheeled toy. The products on the market are not all created equal. Here are some basic things to look for:

- Wobbly toddlers may use toys to pull up on, and most are tippable, so save push toys for true walkers.

- Try before you buy. Some ride-ons are scaled for tall kids, others for small kids.

- Toddlers do not need battery-powered ride-ons. Encourage foot power, not push-button action!

- Toddlers are not ready for pedals. Few have the coordination to use pedals before 2½. Four wheels and two feet on the ground are best.

- Toys with loud and constant sound effects may be appealing in the store, but can become annoying in tight spaces.

Walkers, Wagons, & Ride-ons for Steady-on-Their-Feet Toddlers

COMPARISON SHOPPER: *Plastic Push-Around Walkers*

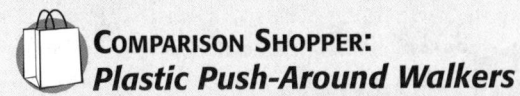

None of these are weighted the way they used to be made, so they are not for tots to pull up on. Testers gave high marks to two versions: **Stride-to-Ride Learning Walker** (Fisher-Price $34.99 ○○○○). This updated walker converts to a ride-on and has a shape-sorter car front end. Music can be turned off; and steering wheel, key, and gear shift are ready for pretend play. Best for steady-on-their-feet toddlers! (800) 432-5437. Little Tikes' **Wide Tracker Activity Walker** ($19.99 ○○○○) has a wider opening in the back so kids are less likely to trip themselves on the wheels! (800) 321-0183.

Top-Rated Wooden Push-Around Walkers

■ Baby Walker BLUE CHIP
(Galt $100 ●●●●○) This classic wooden cart is pricier than any of its plastic counterparts, but it is very stable for early walkers and a perfect first wagon for carting treasures. (800) 899-4258.

■ Classic Walker Wagon
(Radio Flyer $80 ●●●●) This updated version is heavier and slower moving than the original, better suited for new walkers to hold on to. Makes a quiet clicking sound as it moves about. PLATINUM AWARD '05. (800) 621-7613.

■ Pushing Car and Doll Pram
(Haba $159 and $130 ●●●●●) Our test family with three under the age of 4 got right into active pretend play with both of these beautifully styled push-about toys. The **Push Car** ($159 ●●●●●) is low to the ground and balanced enough so that a little sister or a big teddy bear could ride about as a larger child pushed. Furnished with seat cushions and pocket for treasures; made of varnished beech wood with rubber wheels, it maneuvers well, even in tight spaces. Equally well designed, a red and blue **Doll Pram** ($130 ●●●●●) comes with a cushion seat and accommodates several dolls. You can adjust the push bar as children grow, so this will grow into the preschool years. PLATINUM AWARDS '06. (800) 468-6873.

First Ride-Ons

Unfortunately, most ride-ons no longer have working steering ability, so kids need to move the whole vehicle with their bodies to change direction. Be sure to test-drive with your child before you buy. We found that kids with shorter legs had trouble getting on and off many models.

TODDLERS • Ones and Twos

■ Push Around Buggy

(Step 2 $44.99 ●●●○) Little toddlers can get into this vehicle without climbing. It is not a toy for them to run with foot power, it is more like a stroller for giving your tot a ride. It has a seat belt, push bar, and a storage compartment up front for treasures. Updated this year with an umbrella. Also in the "give me a ride" category is the new **Safari Wagon** ($129.99 ●●●○), with room enough for two with seat belts (a plus), and lots of storage under the seats and on the hard top (for your beverage!). (800) 347-8372.

■ Cozy Coupe II BLUE CHIP

(Little Tikes $49.99 ●●●●●) The classic ride-in toy that a generation of kids has grown up with is still basic gear and will be used into the next age group. One of the only ride-ons with a working steering wheel. They say 1½; we say more like 2 & up. (800) 321-0183.

> **SMART PARENT TRICK:** Ask your toddler what she's bringing as she rides by. Fuel her imagination by "opening" pretend packages she delivers. Modeling pretend games helps tots take the leap into fantasy play.

■ Retro Rocket

(Radio Flyer $60 ●●●●●) Our fifteen-month-old testers loved the push-button sound effects, lights, and vibrating motion on this low-to-the-ground ride-on. This vehicle is narrower and lighter than Radio Flyer's **Red Roadster,** and easier for tots to get on and off of. PLATINUM AWARD '05. (800) 621-7613.

Rockers

Low-to-the-ground rockers for toddlers are used for a short time, but match the young toddler's love of motion and repetitive action. These are low enough to the ground so that the older toddler can get on and off with independence, and they're slow enough to be soothing. Often promoted for older infants and young toddlers, these are a better choice for toddlers who are steady on their feet. (This was especially true this year where several of our contenders made the rounds with our testers—much like Goldilocks and the Three Bears . . . some testers found the rockers too small [and boring] and others found them too high. So our recommendation is to try before you buy).

■ Angel Fish Rocker

(Step 2 $49.99 ○○○○½) Reintroduced, this all-plastic fish has been an old favorite for toddlers. The seat is narrow and pretty easy to mount. Can be used indoors or out. But a warning: supervision is needed as rapid rocking can lead to spills. This is bigger than your average rocker and has been known to tip. (800) 347-8372.

■ Bounce & Spin Zebra *2007*

(Fisher-Price $45 ○○○○) Forget rocking horses, the 21st-century child rides a zebra that turns when the rider bounces on it. A spinner in the handle sets off random arcade sounds that (fortunately) can be turned off. Our 20-month-old triplets loved this toy, but some parents will find the sound over the top. (800) 432-5437.

■ Danny Dinosaur & Elijah Elephant *2007*

(Rockabye $109.99 each) These fabric animal rockers looked promising, but were not ready for testing. Choose either the low-to-the-ground soft musical Danny Dinosaur with squeaks, rattles and crinkles, or Elijah Elephant with crinkly ears and multipatterned seat. Designed for 9 months to 3 years, up to 50 pounds. (310) 631-2222.

■ Early Years Baby Dino Rocker *2007*

(International Playthings $99.99 ○○○○) This very low-to-the-ground rocker has little action. Designed for short toddlers and/or those who are not ready for wild action rides. Solidly built, this green dino has a satiny, colorful mane. No sound effects except for some crinkly sounds in the satin mane. They say 12 months; we'd say 18–20 months, and then adult help will still be needed. (800) 445-8347.

■ Surfin' Elmo Rocker *2007*

(Little Tikes $29.99 ○○○) Fans of Elmo may enjoy taking a ride on Elmo's back. Elmo also giggles and talks, but you can turn that feature

TODDLERS • Ones and Twos

off (thankfully). Some testers had trouble getting on and off by themselves 1 & up. (800) 321-0183.

Push and Pull Toys

Push comes before pull. Instead of holding someone's hand, young toddlers often find sheer joy in the independence of walking while holding on to a push toy. You probably started walking with Fisher-Price's BLUE CHIP **Corn Popper** ($8 ●●●●●) or **Melody Push Chime** ($8 ●●●●●). They are still great choices! (800) 432-5437. Pull toys are for older tots who are surefooted and can look over a shoulder without tripping.

■ IQ Preschool Follow-Along Frog

(Small World Toys $17 ●●●●) Here's a really old-fashioned-styled wooden frog that moves up and down as he's pulled. No sound here, just a pleasing motion. 18 mos. & up. (800) 421-4153.

> **SAFETY TIP:** Avoid pull toys with springs and beads that many toddlers will mouth. Old wooden pull toys from the attic may have dangerous levels of lead paint.

Balls

Big, lightweight balls for tossing, kicking, and chasing, or for social back-and-forth, roly-poly games are favorite pieces of basic gear. Twos are ready to play bounce and catch. Be sure the ball is lightweight so it won't hurt. Soft fabric balls or slightly deflated beach balls are the best choice for now. Avoid foam- and balloon-filled balls that can be a choking hazard.

■ Little Champs Sports Center

(Little Tikes $29.95 ●●●●) Toddlers like to imitate older siblings and this little sports set allows them to shoot baskets, hit a baseball, and spin a football. The basketball has a sound chip scoreboard that cheers them on and the baseball clicks as it turns on the post. 9 mos. & up. (800) 321-0183.

TOYS

■ Learning Hoops Basketball
(LeapFrog $24.95 ●●●) A small hoop for the type of repetitive play that toddlers love, but we could have done without the intrusive alphabet lesson. Making something happen is a big enough deal at this stage! (800) 701-5327.

■ Penguin Bowling *2007*
(Infantino $19.99 ●●●½) Cheerful and colorfully attired penguins are numbered and ready to be knocked down. Our parent testers had some difficulty getting the penguins to stand up before their kids lost interest in bowling. "Throwing" the penguins quckly became the name of the game. (800) 840-4916.

■ TotSport Bowling Set
(Little Tikes $16.99 ●●●●) More traditional than the Infantino set, these six see-through bowling pins with balls inside make a clattering sound when the lightweight bowling ball knocks them down. 2 & up. (800) 321-0183.

Strictly Outdoors

First Climbers and More
Climbers are great for big-muscle play for toddlers who are steady on their feet. We saw a number of low-to-the-ground climbers with open platforms and some that did not have secure enough sides once tots reached the top. Many looked like an accident waiting to happen. If you are shopping for a young or especially small toddler, stick to the lowest climbers. This is not a product to grow into. You will find climbers scaled for bigger children in the next chapter.

Playhouses
See Preschool chapter.

TODDLERS • Ones and Twos

COMPARISON SHOPPER
Big Climbers

Step 2's **Naturally Playful Woodland Climber** ($249.99 ●●●●), done in muted tones, comes with a small ladder up to the 27"-high platform leading to a slide on the other side. 2 & up. Step 2's **Naturally Playful Clubhouse Climber** ($599.99 ●●●●●) is still a great combo gym and playhouse for older toddlers and preschoolers with two towers, a slide, and a connecting bridge. One tower is outfitted with table, chairs, and props. PLATINUM AWARD '01. Little Tikes' **8-in-1 Adjustable Playground** ($399 ●●●●) with tunnels and two slides is packed with places to explore, but without the clubhouse features of Step 2's. Either is ideal for developing coordination, and both are big enough for several kids to share without quarrels! Step 2's towers and bridge were a big hit with our 2- and 3-year-old testers (tall 4s had to bend over to fit). Little Tikes' open-top design extends the age range of their set. Both are hard to assemble. Step 2 (800) 347-8372/Little Tikes (800) 321-0183.

■ Climb and Slide Castle

(Little Tikes $69.99 ●●●●) Designed for toddlers, this mini-castle-style climber has a low slide and steering wheel on top for dramatic play. It's 43" high. They say one and up; we'd say more like steady-on-their-feet toddlers—who are rarely younger than 18–24 mos. Requires supervision. (800) 321-0183.

SMART PARENT TRICK: Give 'em a Hand!

Toddlers love an appreciative audience—don't we all? When they finish a puzzle, dance a jig, or go down a slide, clap your hands together—give them a hand! Keep in mind that little children see themselves as you see them. During this often negative time, try to accentuate the positive.

Wading Pools and Water Tables

Our testers preferred inexpensive hard-vinyl wading pools to those that had to be blown up or filled with water to hold a shape (most of these had sides that were too high for younger toddlers to climb over by themselves). Prefab wading pools are also easier to lift, dump, and clean. You can find an adequate no-frills pool for under $20.

■ WaterWheel Table

(Step 2 $34.99 ୦୦୦୦) We had mixed reviews on this one. For stand-up water play this seems a great choice for the patio or terrace. It doesn't take up a lot of room and allows for spilling, filling, splashing, and getting good and wet! But be forewarned, there seem to be problems with leaks! The plugs on the table are not water tight, so you will have to refill this and not use it indoors. That said, this is also a toy that needs total adult supervision. (800) 347-8372. See Preschool chapter for sand table, p. TK.

■ Wagon Set with Bucket

(Small World Toys $17 ୦୦୦୦½) A toddler-sized red-and-yellow wagon that comes with everything needed for the beach or sandbox—a bucket, sand molds, rake, shovel, sieve, and watering can. 18 mos. & up. (800) 421-4153.

> **FREEBIE:** Toddlers love playing with soap and water and covering things with a sudsy lather. Washing kiddie cars, tabletops, and other surfaces is a favorite sport and a good way to cool off on a hot day. A small pail with soapy water and a sponge will pro-

TODDLERS • Ones and Twos

vide endless hours of entertainment! As with all water play, supervision is a must.

Sandboxes

While small boxes are good choices when space is a concern, keep in mind that a bigger box will give more than one child enough room to maneuver. We looked for smooth edges and strong sides that will support a child's weight. The motif is really a personal preference. See sand table in Preschool chapter, p. TK.

Our BLUE CHIP favorites: On the small side, **Frog Sandbox** (Step 2 $54.99) or **Turtle Sandbox** (Little Tikes $39). 1 & up. A bigger choice: **Crabbie Sandbox** (Step 2 $69.99). Step 2 (800) 347-8372/Little Tikes (800) 321-0183.

Sandbox Props: A basic bucket from any toy store will do—just be sure to check for smooth edges. To toddlers, sand is another opportunity for spilling and dumping. A simple sand mill or water wheel will have a lot of appeal! Many of the best props for the sandbox are in your kitchen: a plastic colander, empty margarine containers, strainers, squeeze bottles, etc.

Sprinklers

For toddlers ready to get wet, we'd recommend Little Tikes' **Playful Paws Sprinkler** or **Hook, Line & Sprinkler** ($10.99 each ●●●○). Both are designed to provide a smaller spray (in one position it's stationary; in the other position it will spin). A better choice than most bigger sprinklers that are often overwhelming. 18 mos. & up. (800) 321-0183.

■ No-Spill Bubble Tumbler BLUE CHIP

(Little Kids $6.95 ●●●●●) Toddlers love chasing bubbles, even though most are not able to blow their own. When they start, buy one of these no-spill containers that prevent the tears that used to come when the solution would spill! 18 mos. & up. (800) 545-5437.

TOYS

The Youngest Gardener

Unfortunately Little Tikes no longer makes their plastic gardening tools that we much prefer to metal sets since toddlers tend to toss and swing tools. Bring home a pretend mower such as Little Tikes' **Mulching Mower** ($19.99 ●●●●). Our all-time favorite Fisher-Price **Bubble Mower** is now replaced with the new **Mower** ($14.99 ●●●)—which works, but not nearly as easily as the original. Little Tikes (800) 321-0183/Fisher-Price (800) 432-5437.

Sit-Down Play

First Puzzles and Manipulatives

Toddlers enjoy toys that invite investigation but don't demand too much dexterity. Toys with lids to lift, buttons to push, and dials to turn give them satisfying feedback along with playful ways to develop fine-motor skills and eye-hand coordination. Once they understand how to use them, toddlers will enjoy many of the toys in this section independently, and that is very satisfying to the "me do it myself!" toddler.

First Puzzles

Start with whole-piece puzzles. Take the time to introduce a new puzzle or toy. Let your child take the lead, giving time to explore the pieces and experiment with them.

■ My Giant Floor Puzzle *2007*

(Alex $25 ●●●●) You will need to put this big 17-piece/36"-round puzzle mat together. Toddlers will have fun knowing and naming and helping you put the whole-piece puzzle parts into place. It has a cow, chick, flower, butterfly, tree, and other big pieces. For playtime together fun, roll a little car around and stop at the tree or the sheep or the bee. Use this colorful playmat for talking about colors and familiar objects. Also available with Three Bears House theme. Marked 0 & up, meaning it can be used as a playmat, but we think the pieces will be lost by the time an older toddler is ready for puzzle and play. We'd say more like 18 mos. & up. (800) 666-2539.

TODDLERS • Ones and Twos

■ Puzzibilities Sounds on the Go

(Small World Toys $16 ●●●●½) Four big puzzle pieces with easy-to-grasp wooden pegs—each vehicle makes a distinctive sound when placed in the frame. Also, **Sounds on the Farm**—this one moos, neighs, oinks, and baas. Also top rated, silent, giant, peg-handled three-piece **Shapes** or **Numbers** with bold patterns, or **Vehicles** and **Wild Animals** ($10 each ●●●●). 18 mos. & up. (800) 421-4153.

■ Big Shapes Puzzle Tote

(Lauri $9.99 ●●●●) Our testers enjoyed playing with this portable puzzle from Lauri, well known for their textured crepe rubber puzzles. Rather than having the traditional tray, this double-thick seven piece puzzle has a handle just right for travel and carrying about. Older 2s will be able to manipulate these whole-piece puzzles that 3s and 4s will continue to enjoy. (800) 451-0520.

Manipulatives

■ Learn-Around Playground

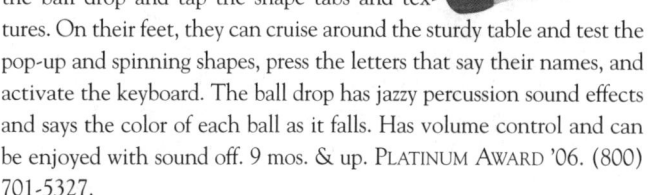

(LeapFrog $59.99 ●●●●●) This remains, hands down, the best activity table on the market because it invites kids to explore and make things happen. A great first birthday gift! Sitting down, tots can make the ball drop and tap the shape tabs and textures. On their feet, they can cruise around the sturdy table and test the pop-up and spinning shapes, press the letters that say their names, and activate the keyboard. The ball drop has jazzy percussion sound effects and says the color of each ball as it falls. Has volume control and can be enjoyed with sound off. 9 mos. & up. PLATINUM AWARD '06. (800) 701-5327.

■ Musical Stack & Play

(Tiny Love $19.95 ●●●●●) This cleverly designed elephant stacking toy has a place for dropping balls in its top. The balls come out at the base with some fanfare (lights/sound) but nothing over the top. Our testers also liked the soft fabric rings for stacking but really spent most of the time playing with the plastic balls. Marked

6 mos. & up, but will be most enjoyed by 1s and up. PLATINUM AWARD '05. (800) 843-6292.

■ Pop-Onz Pop 'n' Twirl Building Table

(Fisher-Price $29.99 ●●●●●) An activity table for the 18-month-and-older crowd that is exactly on target. The pop-ons are big chunky pieces that can be stacked easily on the plastic pegs. Great clear lesson in cause and effect: push the red button, and two parts of the table spin with a little music (volume control—a plus). PLATINUM AWARD '05. We skipped the **Pop 'n Musical Big Top** (●●), which didn't have as much play power as the original. (800) 432-5437.

■ IQ Preschool Pound-A-Ball

(Small World Toys $18 ●●●●) Most toddlers get to a stage when pounding is just the best! Here's a fun plastic variation with four balls that, once pounded, travel through a small see-through ball run. In the beginning you may need to hold the toy for over-eager pounders! If you prefer a wooden hammer toy, try **IQ Preschool Pound Around** ($16 ●●●●½), a six-sided pounding board with hammer and colorful pegs that don't come out. Just turn the board and start hammering again and again. Big toddlers love the powerful pounding action. 18 mos. & up. (800) 421-4153.

■ Rollipop Toddler Starter and Advanced Sets

(Edushape $19.95 & $24.95 ●●●●●) These are among our favorite toddler toys. Toddlers love to drop the oversized colorful plastic balls into the starter set (a tower) and track them as they go down. The balls also travel slowly down the advanced set (a bridge), making it an ideal toy for developing visual tracking. 18 mos. & up. PLATINUM AWARD '04. (800) 404-4744.

■ Super Spiral Play Tower

(International Playthings $32 ●●●●●) Toddlers love this marvelous toy that they quickly take charge of. Two weighted balls and a little penguin twist down the spiral and slide into different slots. PLATINUM AWARD '06. 18 mos.

TODDLERS • Ones and Twos

& up. (800) 445-8347.

■ Triple Track Tower 2007
PLATINUM AWARD

(Playskool $14.95 ●●●●○) Three little cars race down three parallel tracks that are like a giant slide. They can roll free, or be operated with the push of a button that also gives the sound effects of speeding vehicles. Kids can also turn the lever and stop them at the bottom. Good for repetitive action and dramatic play. Since the slides go straight down there is less tracking, or interest, than the typical ball runs with twist-and-turn action. 2 & up. (800) 327-8264.

First Construction Toys

Few toys have more long-term use or learning value than construction toys. Blocks give children a hands-on understanding of words such as *longer, taller, the same, more, less, bigger, and smaller*. These are basic math concepts built into the play. You can help your toddler connect words to these concepts by using language to describe the pieces or what he is doing. These hands-on experiences have much more educational value than electronic toys that try to teach symbolic numerals. Toddlers need to experience "two-ness" again and again before they make the leap to symbolic representation. Without taking over, get your child started by modeling ways to make an enclosure, or span two blocks with a third. By adding vehicles and small animals and people figures, you provide the ingredients for imaginative play.

■Kiddy Connects 2007 PLATINUM AWARD

(Edushape $12 ●●●●●) A drum-shaped zip-up bag comes loaded with 36 ball-shaped connectors with short arms that fit together in patterns or random shapes. A fun way to develop dexterity, color words, and even beginning counting skills, along with problem solving, as tots figure out how to fit the arms together. 2½ & up. (800) 404-4744.

■ Fill & Dump Wagon

(Mega Bloks $30 ●●●●) These are larger still than Lego Quatro, and fun to use. A tot-sized red wagon loaded with 50 oversized plastic pegged blocks is fun for making big, fast constructions. Pegs on side of wagon can be used for building up and over. New for 2007, **Build Off Lap Desk** ($9.99 ooo½). Nice idea that didn't work. Two wells at either side of the mini desk that serves as building surface—but there is not enough storage space for the 40 blocks that come with the desk. (800) 465-6342.

■ Lego Duplo Zoo 2007 PLATINUM AWARD

(Lego Systems $25 ooooo) The latest in the themed sets in the Duplo line, this comes with a sheet of eyes that you can add to the blocks to create your own animals (of course with a toddler, you'll need to help with this). Our testers really enjoyed placing the eyes on with help! Parents loved the green storage case. Still top rated, **Duplo Thomas Load and Carry Train Set** ($29.99 ooooo), easy-to-assemble tracks and environment including train, movable light signal, and cargo tower. 61 pieces. Our older toddler testers "looooved" this set! PLATINUM AWARD '06. 2 & up. For other more advanced Duplo sets, look at the Preschool chapter, p. 96.

■ My First Quatro Set 2007 PLATINUM AWARD

(Lego Systems $9.99 & up ooooo) Twos used to graduate to **Lego Duplo** bricks, but now there's a bigger brick (twice the size of Duplo and four times the size of standard Lego). This set comes with 20 pieces but here, "more is better," so we even suggest starting with the **Large Quatro Bucket** ($19.99/75 pieces). PLATINUM AWARD '05 1 & up. (800) 233-8756.

■ Peek-a-Blocks Bucket o' Builders 2007

(Fisher-Price $19.95 oooo½) Fifteen interesting blocks with see-though sides and interesting objects inside come in a large bucket with a textured lid. Each of the blocks has a bristle-like surface that fits into the lid and into each other. Fun for filling and dumping games, and for tossing and tasting, too. 1 & up. (800) 432-5437.

TODDLERS • Ones and Twos

■ EduBlocks 2007 PLATINUM AWARD
(Edushape $99.95 / 26 pieces ●●●●●) These peg-top blocks are bigger than Lego Quatros or giant-size Mega Bloks, and they are softer and more pliable. This makes them quieter and easier to manipulate for beginners. They come in four shapes and colors, and are ideal for making big constructions. They say 6 mos., we'd say more like 18 mos. Also new for 2007, **Soft Wood-Like Blocks** ($17.95 ●●●●½) Surprisingly pleasing light-weight blocks that look like the real thing, cut in standard unit block sizes of non-crumbly, super-dense, quiet foam. Set of 30 that will mix well with wooden blocks later. Also **Educolor Blocks** ($17.99 ●●●●½), a similar but smaller-scaled set in primary colors. (800) 404-4744.

How High? Use blocks to see how high a tower you can build together before it goes kaboom! Take turns adding one more piece—and keep a running count as you go. You can play variations of this game with empty frozen juice cans, wooden thread spools, or other collections.

■ Giant Constructive Blocks BLUE CHIP
(Constructive Playthings $18.99 ●●●●●) These big sturdy blocks (printed like red bricks) are lightweight but satisfyingly hefty for lugging about. Perfect for making tall towers and wide roadways for beginning builders. Strong enough to stand on, these are perennial classics that endure years of creative play. A dozen bricks, 12" x 6" x 4". #CP-626. (800) 832-0572.

Wooden Blocks
Older twos will begin to enjoy a beginner set of wooden blocks. We recommend **IQ Preschool Push-Along Block Cart** PLATINUM AWARD '03 (Small World Toys $46 ●●●●●) with 36 pieces, which older tots will enjoy lugging about. (800) 421-4153. For larger top-rated sets, see Preschool chapter, p. 93.

TOYS

Props for Blocks—See Preschool chapter, p. 94.

Wooden Train Sets

It's a great temptation to buy wooden train sets for older twos—but be forewarned, most have small figures and other small parts that make them dangerous for kids under three who still mouth their toys. See Preschool chapter for reviews of top-rated sets. To address this issue, Brio has introduced a new line of trains for toddlers.

First Stacking, Nesting, and Shape-Sorter Toys

What You Should Know. Classic stacking toys require the ability to see and arrange objects in size order—a skill that neither babies nor toddlers have. Such toys are often labeled 6 months & up, but there's nothing wrong if your child can't do it—the problem is with the label! Happily, there are more forgiving choices that introduce stacking without the need for size order. Toddlers will use them to taste, toss, and explore—just don't expect them to be expert stackers. As you play with your toddler, use color or size words to describe the pieces. Such concepts are learned with greater ease when they are part of everyday experiences.

Two good choices: **Lamaze Spin n Stack Rings** (RC2/Learning Curve $24.99 ●●●●) has four big plastic rings decorated with interesting textured fabric and ribbons that spin when the music in the post is activated. We thought the big ring would be too big for little hands, but our 10-month old tester loved it and soon figured out how to hit the post to activate music and make the base spin. (800) 704-8697. Still top rated, the **Classical Stacker** (Fisher-Price $19.99 ●●●●●) has a post with twinkling lights and sounds as each ring is put on. (800) 432-5437.

Nesting and Stacking Toys

Toddlers like the multiple pieces for pulling apart, banging, and stacking long before they can nest them. Stacking and nesting toys develop eye-hand coordination, size order con-

TODDLERS • Ones and Twos

cepts, and even counting skills. They provide hands-on experience with concepts such as *bigger, smaller, taller, inside, under, top,* and *bottom*—to name but a few. You can make the language connection as you play together.

Here are our top- (and not-so-top-) rated choices:

■ Read to Me Tot Tower

(eeBoo $19 ●●●●●) The latest in a handsome line of sturdy cardboard blocks with storybook-quality illustrations of images to know and name. 1 & up. PLATINUM AWARD '04. (212) 222-0823. We were disappointed by **Polar Bear Touch & Stack Blocks** (Small World Toys $25 ●●●) featuring the artwork of Eric Carle's classic book. Marked 18 mos. & up, we found that the ears of the elephant and the mouth of the hippo ripped off too easily, and the grommet inside of the hippo is an unnecessary small part for this age group. (800) 421-4153.

■ Stacking Shapes Pegboard

(RC2/Learning Resources $14.95 ●●●●½) A classic toy returns! Little hands will be busy with 25 easy-to-grasp, brightly colored chunky pegs that can be sorted by color or shape on the big 10"-square base. Pegs can be stacked and eventually strung like beads. Marked two & up, we'd say this is for slightly older twos and even threes. (800) 704-8697.

■ Tolo Stacking Activity Cubes

(Small World Toys $18 ●●●●) These three cubes can be stacked in any order; the shape fits under the cutout. Each block can be activated by cranking, spinning, or pushing a button. They take some finger power for the motion payoff. Introduce one at a time; once they have them all figured out, introduce the stacking aspect for multi-action surprise! 18 mos. & up. (800) 421-4153.

SAFETY NOTE: Plastic stacking cups should have air holes so they don't form a suction over baby's face. Most toymakers have updated cups, but some old-style products may still be on shelves. Check before you buy!

TOYS

Shape-Sorters

■ IQ Preschool Get-a-Grip Sorter

(Small World Toys $18 ০০০০) A triangular sorter that has a handle and a forgiving opening. Beautifully crafted in wood. A good parent-child toy. (800) 421-4153.

FREEBIE: Many sorters and nesting toys are too difficult for young toddlers. You can make your own. Cut holes in the lid of a shoe box for blocks to fall through. Or use a see-through plastic container so tots can see where their pop-beads or blocks have gone.

Pretend Play

As language develops, older toddlers begin their early games of pretend. So much of the real equipment tots see adults using is off-limits to them. Child-sized versions can (sometimes) offer a satisfying alternative and fuel the imagination of little ones, who love to mimic what they see you doing. Never again will sweeping and cleaning be more fun than to a toddler!

Dolls and Huggables

Both boys and girls enjoy playing with dolls and soft animals. For one-year-olds, velour and short-haired plush animals will hold some interest. Twos are ready for both oversized but lightweight huggables to lug about, and small dolls that fit in their fists. Toddlers often get attached to one huggable that becomes an inseparable "lovie." Having a tubbable vinyl doll may also do the trick for a reluctant bather. Since toddlers are still likely to chew on their toys, select uncomplicated dolls without doodads (buttons, long hair). If potty training is on the agenda, see the potty dolls in Preschool, page 84.

SAFETY NOTE: Do not leave large plush dolls or toys in cribs, as they can be stepped on and acci-

TODDLERS • Ones and Twos

dentally give tots a boost over the side. Toddlers should not have pillowlike dolls or toys to sleep with, or dolls with chewable doodads and features that pose a choking hazard.

Baby Dolls

■ Babicorolle *2007*

(Corolle $12 & up ●●●●) Corolle has beautiful dolls for every age group. For ones, we recommend soft huggables that feel big but are lightweight. **Babipouce** ($23 ●●●●), an old favorite, is now available with Asian and African-American as well as Caucasian painted vinyl faces and soft bodies. Their clothes are sewn-on velour and available in boyish as well as utterly pink choices. New and adorable, **Miss Grenadine** ($18 ●●●●●), done in deliciously bright hot pink and orange stripes with stitched features. 1 & up. Twos and up will enjoy Corolle's **Tidoo** collection ($32–$50 ●●●●), sweet 12" tubbable/floatable bald-headed dolls with beanbag bodies. Come dressed in knit outfits with Velcro. *Safety note:* Some Tidoo sets have small bottles, pacifiers, or fabric balls which we do not recommend for this age group. (800) 668-4846.

■ Götz Precious Day Mini Muffin Boy & Girl *2007*

(International Playthings $14 each ●●●●) These little 8" realistic dolls have painted eyes, bald heads, easy-to-hold beanbag bodies, and no small doodads. Dressed in striped rompers, they are light enough for older tots to carry and cuter in person than they appear online. 18 mos. & up. (800) 445-8347.

■ Little Mommy Newborn Twin Dolls

(Fisher-Price $14.95 ●●●●) These bald-headed dolls have no moving eyes or small accessories. They're truly toddler friendly. The realistic vinyl features are painted on. Heavily scented with soft bodies, and the rompers do not come off. Comes with a chunky molded bottle. Also available in African American as well as Caucasian dolls. Their new **Check Up Center** (oo) was not well designed. It had a lot of features that did not work. The scale was very hard, if not impossible, to move once it was attached to the table. Once the scale was on, you couldn't measure the baby, and the cardboard features fell off the back. We were really disappointed. 18 mos. & up. (800) 432-5437.

Dogs and Other Friendly Creatures

■ Asthma Friendly Puppy Dog 2007

(Kids Preferred $18 oooo ½) Choose a pink-and-white or blue-and-white spotted 12" floppy dog in this special fabric that reduces the risk of allergens. Soft filled, this is big enough for cuddling, yet lightweight for toddlers to hug, lug, and tug along. Stitched features make this safe and appealing. Also cute, **Comfort Cuddly** blue **Hippo** and yellow **Cow.** Both have dabs of satin trim and stitched features. Reduce the risk of asthma. (866) 763-8869.

■ Big Spunky

(Gund $59.99 oooo ½) Older toddlers love big dolls to lug about and flop down on from time to time. The trick is to find something large but light enough for these little ones. Big Spunky fills the order. He's 22" big and available in blue or pink soft plush with patches of white and stitched features for safety's sake. This is what you call a real armful that will get a lot of loving! For smaller but great choices, consider colorful 11" **Tutti Frutti** ($20 oooo) elephant, monkey, or cat, or the classic all-time favoite, **Snuffles,** a BLUE CHIP bear ($12 and $20 ooooo). (800) 448-4863.

■ Cosmo Club 2007 PLATINUM AWARD

(Mary Meyer $14 each ooooo) Select any one of these soft velour animals with stitched features. We especially love the giraffe and the moose. Just right to fill the bill as a first huggable for your toddler. (800) 451-4387.

TODDLERS • Ones and Twos

■ Flatopotamus, Flatofrog, Flatophant, Flatobearius 2007

(North American Bear Co. $17 & up ❍❍❍❍). These floppy, understuffed, under-structured huggables are oversized and totally appealing to toddlers who like their toys big! We've seen the hippo and bear before, but the lime green frog and pink elephant are new and very cute. These are 25" or 15" but light enough for toddlers to handle with ease. Or for another big armful to love, choose the velvety 22" **Creeper Sleeper Dog** ($17 ❍❍❍❍) in blue polka-dot jammies, or **Cat** with pink, with stitched details and nonremovable PJs. (800) 682-3427.

■ Latitude Enfant Grannimals Collection
2007 PLATINUM AWARD

(Pint Size Productions $5–$100 each ❍❍❍❍❍) Done in knitted fabric and stitched features, these are an unusual collection of machine washable soft dolls that are gender neutral. A real departure from the usual plush. Choose **Lucien** the rabbit, **Mona** the cow, **Sasha** the cat, **Marie** the mouse. The medium (8" $20) and large (16" $30) arrive in a special box that might well turn into a bed. The mini (5" $5) and giant (40" $100) come sans box. PLATINUM AWARD '06. New characters (available in only the smaller size) include **Lou** the wolf, **Leon** the Pig, **Theo** the Bear, **Hugo** the Hedgehog. Also new and extremely cute, parent/child pairs **Celestine** and **Celeste** (cats), and **Justin** and **Justine** (dogs). (800) 544-9183.

■ Rick the Frog & Friends

(Rich Frog $12 each ❍❍❍❍❍) These soft animal dolls with patterned cotton bodies and stitched features look like storybook characters and are not gender specific. Choose the bunny, elephant, duck, hippo, or frog. Also adorable, **Softies Collection:** a frog, bunny, elephant, and duck ($10 each). These are a little floppier and silky soft to the touch. Just the right-sized handful for toddlers. PLATINUM AWARD '06. (802) 865-9225.

■ Smushy Elephant 2007 PLATINUM AWARD

(North American Bear $25 & $49.95 ❍❍❍❍❍) You've heard of the three bears? How about three adorable pachyderms? In creamy white with pink or blue satin ribbons or powder blue, these fuzz-free huggables have high and low plush, turned up trunks, and floppy ears, and come in a 25", 17", or 11" cuddly soft armful. Very lovable! (800) 682-3427.

A few words about talking dolls for toddlers

Although soft huggable bears and dolls have long-term play value, interactive dolls that talk, dance, and sing are novelty items that may appeal. Don't be surprised, however, if your toddler is put off by a popular character that comes to life. Toddlers are still sorting out what is real and make-believe—so these "magical" dolls may have more appeal to adults than to the very young. The biggest news this year in this category will be the relaunch of Tickle Me Elmo, now called **Elmo T.M.X.** ($39.99). It was not ready for testing but builds on the same idea as the original. We'd pass on the **Bird's the word! Elmo** ($19.99 ⊙⊙) where Elmo wears a bird costume and tells jokes (way too derivative for a 2 year old). (800) 432-5437.

Doll Accessories

Most toddlers will try to get into doll furniture you buy. Most plastic doll furniture is very tippable. Better to wait until the preschool years for typical baby beds, highchairs, and strollers. Older 2s may enjoy a shopping cart they can push about and use for their dolls. We recommend:
Wooden Doll Cradle BLUE CHIP (Community Playthings $90 ⊙⊙⊙⊙⊙), a 29" solid maple cradle built to last and big enough for kids to climb in to play baby, or to put a family of dolls to sleep in. 2 & up. Item #C140. (800) 777-4244.
Shopping Cart BLUE CHIP (Little Tikes $25 ⊙⊙⊙⊙⊙): this bright yellow cart with baby seat is more gender free than most doll carriers. (800) 321-0183. See the **Doll Pram** from Haba, p. 38.

Vehicles

What to look for: Vehicles with clicky wheels, friction "motors," and passengers to load and unload provide sensory

TODDLERS • Ones and Twos

feedback. They are also great props for developing fine-motor skills and pretend play.

What to avoid: A fleet of vehicles with lots of electronic lights, sounds, and voices that will drive you crazy—and, worse, will do nothing to help tots develop language or imagination. Also, avoid small Matchbox or Hot Wheels cars; their small parts can be a choking hazard for kids under 3.

■ iPlay Zoom Around Garage 2007 PLATINUM AWARD

(International Playthings $59.99 ●●●●●) Our 2½ year old tester loved the levels of this multilevel garage and the elevator—his mom loved that the set comes with four cars (easier to share that way!) The chunky plastic cars can ride up the elevator and roll down the chutes and ramps with sound effects and flashing lights (not too loud). A fun setting for dramatic play. Cars can be played with separately or linked together with magnetic connectors. They say 1 & up—we'd say more like 18 mos. & up. (800) 445-8347.

■ Handle Haulers 2007

(Little Tikes $9.99 & up each ●●) New this year, a **Light & Go Thomas** version complete with flashlight and sound effects—sure to be a hit with Thomas fans. Here's the problem. Unfortunately most of this line is, in our opinion, mislabeled 12 months & up. For young toddlers, these are not stable enough to keep from flying into the child's face if he leans on the back or front of the handle for balance. The low rating reflects this age label problem. (The Thomas version is marked 18 mos. and up.) For twos and up, however, these are uncomplicated props for beginning pretend play. (800) 321-0183.

■ iPlay Farm Racers 2007

(International Playthings $8.99 each ●●●●) Push the little vehicles along and the dog, cow, or pig will bark, moo, or oink. Push the front bumper and it will sing its own silly "song." This novelty toy will either make you laugh or want to toss it. If you prefer less noise, these are not for you. 18 mos. (800) 445-8347.

TOYS

■ Mega Blok Lil' Cement Truck and Lil' Dump Truck

(Mega Bloks $9.99 ○○○○) These plastic vehicles are just right for 2s and up to enjoy spilling blocks from and refilling. They both come with a truckload of Mega Bloks, just right for pretend construction sites. While we liked the concept of the new **Lil' Copter** (○○○) and the plastic blades are neat, it is much harder to load than the trucks because of the angle of the cutaway lid. (800) 465-6342.

■ Little People Lil' Movers Airplane
2007 PLATINUM AWARD

(Fisher-Price $21.99 ○○○○○) Load the chunky Little People on and off through the top of the jolly looking white plane with licks of blue, red and green. Little People will not fit in the door/ramp, but not to worry; they fit through the open roof. There's a female pilot and two passengers that bounce up and down as kids push the plane along the floor. Push the pilot down in her seat and the music begins, a short little tune that is not too intrusive. A red handle makes it easier to "fly" the plane in the air. A toddler size prop for pretend. They say 1& up. We'd say more like 18 months & up. (800) 432-5437.

■ Little People Lil' School Bus 2007

(Fisher-Price $16.99 ○○○○½) Push down on the school bus driver and the lights flash, horn beeps, and music plays on this big yellow school bus. Kids can be loaded through the side door or the open roof. Bus includes a wheelchair but no ramp for getting it on and off. They say 1 & up. We'd say more like 18 months & up. Still fun, **Little People Cement Mixer Truck** (800) 432-5437.

■ Little People Lil' Kingdom Palace 2007

(Fisher-Price $20 ○○○) If you think this looks like last year's **Castle**—you'd be right. It's the same toy but it's pinker. Unfortunately, this means it no longer operates as a gender-free play setting. (The people still fall off the balcony.) We'd also skip the new **Little People Pirate Ship** ($20.99 ○○) since we don't believe toddlers need to be shooting cannons and walking the plank. The updatd **Little People Animal Sound Farm** ($34.99 ❍❍) is back, but now the inanimate gates say *moo* and *neigh* (not the animals). We also find the **Little People Dinosaurs** troubling since they come with a caveman. Apart from being factually incorrect, many of our older dino-enthusiast were alarmed by the concept of dinosaurs and people being around at the same time. We have been fans of this line but it seems that over the past two years the design group has lost sight of their very young audience. (All that said, look at the good rating for the **Little People Time-to-Learn**, p. 198.) (800) 432-5437.

Housekeeping Props

Older toddlers—both boys and girls—adore imitating the real work they see grown-ups doing around the house. Sweeping the floor, vacuuming, cooking, caring for the baby— these are thrilling roles to play. Many of the props for this sort of pretend play will be used for several years. They are what we call "bridge toys," which span the years. These toys are becoming harder and harder to find (a comment on our culture's view of domesticity?). We did receive vacuum cleaners that actually pick things up—but that also meant hair could get caught in the mix, too—so we passed on those. Fisher-Price took their classic vac out of the line, so your best bet is to sweep up with Schylling's red and yellow **Broom Set** ($7.99 ❍❍❍❍). 2 & up. (800) 541-2929.

> ☞ **SAFETY TIP: Buckets!** Beware of buckets used in the house for cleaning. Ever-curious toddlers have been known to fall into them and drown. Old buckets from building bricks also pose a problem. Most new play buckets have a safety bar halfway down to prevent tots from putting their heads all the way in.

Phones *2007*

Before you buy a play phone with sound, put the receiver to your ear. Many are alarmingly loud. The quietest of the bunch: the new **Take 'n' Talk Phone** (Sassy $7 ❍❍❍❍), a wonderfully chewy phone that opens up like a cell phone to reveal a hologram that changes as baby moves the phone. Push the buttons and you'll hear both English and Spanish. 6 mos. & up. (800) 323-6336. Still top rated, **Tolo Mobile Phone** (Small World Toys $12 ●●●●). (800) 421-4153.

For more bells and whistles: **Talk-to-Me Telephone** (Sassy $17.99 ●●●●). With an old-fashioned rotary dial on one side and push-button pads on the other, this yellow phone has lots of features for your toddler to explore. The phone counts from 1 to 9, and says "hello" and "goodbye" in English, Spanish, and French. 1 & up. (800) 323-6336.

> ☞ **SAFETY TIP: An old real phone may seem like lots of fun, but the cord and small parts pose a choking hazard to toddlers.**

> **It's for You! Game.** Older toddlers love talking on the phone. Use the power of pretend to "call" them when lunch is ready or it's time to go out. "Brrrinngggg! Brrrinngggg! Telephone! It's for you!" Transitions are often easier if you turn them into a game.

Toy Dishes and Pots

Finding a sturdy, gender-free set of plastic dishes isn't easy! Many sets we tested cracked, were too small for little hands, or were very, very pink! Stay away from sets with small parts and sharp cutlery, and of course, save the pottery and china for later.

There are more elaborate toy dish and cooking sets in the next chapter. For toddlers you want to keep it simple. Model pouring them a pretend cup of something delicious. Don't be afraid to ham it up: "It's too hot!" "This cake is yummy!" For this stage we recommend: **Little Helper's Dining Room & Pots and Pans** (Step 2 $14.99 ●●●●). White, magenta, and yellow 22-piece set comes with dishes,

TODDLERS • Ones and Twos

pots, and utensils. (800) 347-8372. 2 & up. ***Editor's Note:*** Many of the metal pot sets we looked at this year had rough edges—so check before you buy.

Toy Kitchens

Choosing which kitchen center to bring home is really a matter of style preference and space. There are sizes ranging from small single units to elaborate large units that need their own wall, if not room! Few of the sinks hold water, which is too bad. There is also a trend back to pink kitchens—we have noted our gender-free choices because we believe strongly that both boys and girls need to know their way around the kitchen.

■ Side-by-Side Kitchen 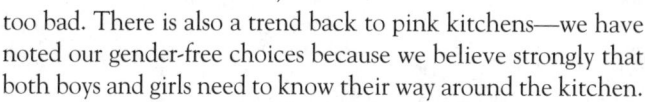

(Little Tikes $69.99 ●●●●) The corner style of this kitchen makes it a good choice for smaller spaces. We also liked the two work stations for two young chefs. Burner makes some sounds but nothing over the top. Also comes with small fridge, sink, oven, and phone. We prefer this to last year's **MagiCook Kitchen** ($79.99 ●●●) This high-tech kitchen will say 100 phrases in three different languages. Unfortunately there is no phrase: "Let's order in." While this may at first seem really neat, this type of directed pretend play robs kids of the pleasure of making their own original creations. 2–5. (800) 321-0183.

■ Lifestyle Dream Kitchen

(Step 2 $159.99 ●●●●) This combo kitchen with stove, oven, microwave, fridge, and phone (electronic) is 35½" long and is designed for the toddler who needs the dream kitchen (in plastic, of course). This one comes with wainscoting, crown molding, and simulated granite! For an even bigger version, there's the **Lifestyle Deluxe Kitchen** ($219/49" wide ●●●●)! Or if space is an issue, **Lifestyle Designer Kitchen** ($119 ●●●●), a smaller-scaled kitchen with "stainless" steel fridge and oven, copper-look hood. Has three electronic features: stovetop, light, and phone. (800) 347-8372.

TOYS

■ Small World Living Wooden Kitchen Appliances

(Small World Toys $130 & up each ●●●●●) Wooden sets usually cost a lot more. That's why we were thrilled to find these updated handsome individual pieces (a **sink,** a **stove/oven,** a **refrigerator**) or the **two-in-one sink & stove** ($180). Done in birch-toned wood with bright licks of red. Newest addition, a **BBQ Grill** ($130) with a set of tools. Best of all, the sinks are removable so that you can use "real" water. Most sinks no longer have this feature. These are gender neutral, a plus. They are a bit challenging to put together. PLATINUM AWARD '06. (800) 421-4153.

Pretend Settings

■ Laugh and Learn Learning Home

(Fisher-Price $59.95 ●●●● ½) For the get-about toddler, this "little house" is just the right size for active play and making things happen. It has a door that opens and shuts and is big enough to crawl through, lights that turn off and on, doorbell that rings, ball drop, and shape sorter, among other interesting features. A great first birthday gift to enjoy throughout this year and probably next. It is a big toy, but if you have the room, it's a good choice for solo or two-tot play! They say 6 months to 3. We'd say one and up would be a better bet. (800) 432-5437.

> **FREEBIE:** Empty, staple-free boxes are among the best toys known to toddlers. Great for sitting in, climbing out of, coloring on, lugging around, crawling through, or loading up.

Art and Music

Art Supplies

Give your toddler opportunities to explore colors and textures. This is not the time for coloring books and drawing within the lines. Scribbling comes before drawing, just as crawling comes

TODDLERS • Ones and Twos

before walking! Twos may give names to their drawings and creations after they are done. Finished products are not as important as getting their hands into the doing.

Even one-year-olds get a sense of "can do" power scribbling with big, easy-to-grasp crayons on blank paper. Older tots love the fluid lines they get with fat washable markers, but keep in mind that you'll need to replace covers or the markers will dry out. Twos also enjoy bright tempera paint with thick brushes, or play-dough and finger paints for lively hands-on fun!

You'll need to supervise and establish a place where art materials can be used. You don't really need an easel for now. A low table that children can stand at is fine. In fact, they have less trouble with paint rolling and dripping when they work on a flat surface. If your toddler persists in eating supplies or spreading them on floors or walls, put them away for a while and try again in a month or two.

■ Crayola Kid's Large Washable Crayons BLUE CHIP

(Binney & Smith $3 & up ●●●●●) These washable crayons are very big to match toddler's way of grasping with a whole fist. Save the smaller crayons, which snap in tots' hands, for their school days. 1½ & up. (800) 272-9652.

■ Crayola Color Wonder Paper & Markers

(Binney & Smith $8.99 ●●●●●) We thought this product should be called color magic! The marker has no color on the tip and will not "color" on normal paper, sofas, Grandma's wall (you get the idea!). But when you color on the special Color Wonder paper . . . voilà! Magically your design appears. We prefer the open-ended paper to the coloring books. Drawing at this age should be more about exploring the materials than worrying about lines or premade art. PLATINUM AWARD '02. We don't recommend **Color Wonder Finger Paints,** which require more finger pressure than most kids have at this age. (800) 272-9652.

■ Funky Artist 2007

(Alex $19.99 ●●●●) One step above finger paints, this set of three "funky" brushes is unlike anything you have seen before. One looks like a string mop, one like the soft brushes at the car wash, and one like a flower made of cloth. Each produces a different texture. Kit comes with three bottles of washable paint and flat dishes for paint. Fat handles make this easy for little hands to hold and bold colors will invite big arm movements as they experiment with spreading paints and mixing colors. There are little brushes included, but this is all about big strokes for little folks. 2 & up. (800) 666-2539.

Play Dough

Playing with premade or homemade dough is marvelous for twos who love pounding, poking, rolling, crumbling, and hands-on exploring. At this stage, the finished product is unimportant. The focus is on smashing a lump flat or pulling it apart into small pieces or mixing blue and yellow to get green. Dough should be used with supervision in a placed established for messy play.

> **Making Dough Game:** Save money by making your own dough with this homemade play-dough recipe. Kids will enjoy getting their hands into the bowl and helping to mix up dough, which can be stored in a covered container. Mix together 1 cup of flour, ½ cup salt, a few drops of vegetable oil, and enough water to form a ball. Food coloring or a splash of bright tempera paint can be added.

■ Play-Doh Case of Colors BLUE CHIP

(Hasbro $7 ●●●●●) Imagine a 10-pack with two-ounce lumps of 10 different colors. Don't let them see all the tubs; open one or two at a time at most. Add plastic dishes for added pretend! 2 & up. (888) 836-7025.

Paints and Easels

Older toddlers will enjoy painting either at a table where the colors won't run or at a standing easel. Start with three colors at most. Thick

TODDLERS • Ones and Twos

brushes and washable tempera paint are good choices available at most toy and art supply stores. Try to have the art supplies ready to go for whenever the creative mood strikes. See Preschool chapter for easels.

Musical Toys

Once they are steady on their feet, toddlers love to move to music. Play a variety of music for them to dance to or accompany with their "instruments." Aside from the usual music for kids, try some marches, ballet scores, or music from other cultures. Better yet, put on your dancing feet and shake, rattle, and roll along.

■ Bug Tunes Music Set

(Little Tikes $12.99 ●●●○) Get ready to shake, rattle, and boogie with this 6-piece set of bug-shaped maracas, tamborine, and jingler. Designed for younger players than the Lynn Kleiner set, below—this is more like a set of rattles shaped like instruments. Also fun, **Chimes the Caterpillar** ($14.99 ●●●○). Two classic musical toys—a xylophone and a keyboard—are combined in one buggy version. Forget the music on the box, the toy is more about exploration than playing a tune. Skip the **Jungle** (●●) sets with mallets that are more like traditional drumsticks. Our testers tasted all the mallets—so you're better off with the bigger rounder heads. 18 mos. & up. (800) 321-0183.

■ Lynn Kleiner Babies Make Music Set

(Remo $40.25 ●●●●½) Many musical instruments for young kids make noise, not music, and many are basically unsafe. Strike up the rhythm band with these instruments that are well crafted with both sound and safety in mind. This set includes a jingle shaker, wrist jingle, small drum, and scarf (all safe enough for toddlers who still mouth their toys). 2 & up. (800) 525-5134.

■ Neurosmith Music Blocks

(Small World Toys $45 ●●●●●) Welcome back! Comes with five colored plastic blocks, each side making a different sound. Match the shapes on the blocks or play them in random order—there's no right or wrong way. The "composer" allows you to record and play back your composition. Comes with one jazz cartridge; we'd suggest bringing home the classical cartridge ($15), too. PLATINUM AWARD '06. (800) 421-4153.

TOYS

■ Neurosmith Together Tunes Block

(Small World Toys $60 ●●●●●) Also reintroduced this year, an active musical toy for young toddlers. Just a turn of the oversized fabric block activates a familiar nursery tune along with peek-a-boo surprises built in. Songs include "Wheels on the Bus" and "Old MacDonald." A good choice for cruising toddlers. PLATINUM AWARD '04. (800) 421-4153.

■ Tolo Baby Concerto

(Small World Toys $28 ●●●●½) Toddlers will like lifting the little yellow bear off his sleek red platform or putting him back and watching as he spins to the music. Tots can use the five big key pads to make single notes, or activate one of five melodies by Mozart, Handel, Bach, and Vivaldi. An empowering toy for making things happen. 1 & up. (800) 421-4153.

> **Follow the Leader Toddler Game.** Use a full-length mirror to play a "can-you-do-what-I-do?" game. Use big and little motions from faces to toes. Getting kids to copy what you are doing is more than fun. It helps kids begin to focus on details and translate what they see into actions. Demonstrate a sequence of two motions—pat your head and then your tummy. Can your toddler remember two motions? How about three?

Bath Toys

For young bathers, the tub is just another locale for learning and play. Working up a lather, trying to keep a slippery soap from slipping away, discovering how water spills from a cup, drips from a washcloth, and splashes when you hit it—these are a child's way of finding out how things like soap and water work.

> **☞ SAFETY TIP: A lot of parents have raised the issue of bath toys that retain water and possibly e.coli bacteria. We saw a lot of toys this season**

TODDLERS • Ones and Twos

with squirters, tubing, and squeezable parts that produce seemingly appealing water play. But the safety of these toys represents a reasonable concern and we are not recommending them—even though they are really, really cute.

■ Rub a Dub Jungle Waterfall Bathtub Set *2007*

(Alex $17.50 ●●●●½) Arrange the many suction cup pieces on the wall of the tub and get ready for action. Pour the water in at the top and the pieces will spin and splash. Hands on lessons in physics for toddlers. 2 & up. This works a lot better than the Whistling Hippos (below) that our testers liked but found disappointing due to their limited sound effects. (800) 666-2539.

■ Whistling Hippos *2007*

(Alex $14.99 ●●●) Four colorful hippos float in the tub. Hit them gently on their heads and each one makes a quiet whistling sound. You can play a color matching game, matching the hippos and rings. Our testers liked playing with the hippos but were very disappointed with the limited sound effects. 18 mo. & up. (800) 666-2539.

■ Baby Einstein Bath Puppets

(Kids II $8.99 each ●●●●½) There's a blue octopus, a two-toothed teal hippo, and a friendly green dragon all done in terry cloth. Use these for playtime in or out of the tub. These are designed with loops for hanging and drying after the tub fun is done. (800) 793-1454.

■ Bathtime Kitchen Sink

(Sassy $15.99 ●●●●½) Now tots can tub with everything including the kitchen sink! This floating "sink" has a net basin to hold scooping, squirting, and straining props. Squeeze the squirting spigot for a shower or pour water through the sieve. A clever toy for tubtime. Still top rated, **Sassy's Car Wash** ($15.99 ●●●●) with three little cars that roll down ramps and get "cleaned" by a big yellow shower head nozzle that squirts tub water. They say 9 months; we'd say both are better toddler

TOYS

toys for 18 mos. and up. (800) 323-6336.

> ☞ **SAFETY TIP: Bath toys need to be completely drained and dried between baths to prevent harmful bacteria and/or mold collecting in them. Squeeze toys, although a lot of fun, are particularly susceptible to this problem.**

■ Froggies in the Tub
(Sassy $11 ●●●●½) More like a good piece of equipment than a toy, this happy-faced frog goes over the faucet to protect active toddlers from bumping into metal spout. It comes with a suction-cupped frog with net holder for all those tub toys that make happier tub time for toddlers. (800) 323-6336.

■ Bathketball
(Little Tikes $7.99 ●●●½) Suction cups hold the hoop securely to the side of the tub. This comes with three squirty balls. The bottom of the net cinches shut for storage. If you are worried about squirty toys in the tub harboring bacteria, pass on this one. We passed on the **Little Tikes Bathtime Band** ($14.99 ●●). This requires 3 AA batteries. Add water to each of the instruments and they play Calypso music. We do not like the idea of battery-operated toys for the tub. Their new **Bathtime Toy Waterfall** (●●) also did not work well. (800) 321-0183.

■ Tolo Animal Water Slide
(Small World Toys $25 ●●●●) Part shape sorter, part pour and spill, this fun bath toy attaches to the tub with big suction cups. Pull a lever to make shapes slide down chutes and splash into the water. Comes with three shaped pourers to fill and spill. They say 1 & up—we'd say more like 18 months & up. (800) 421-4153.

Basic Furniture

Table and Chairs
These are basic pieces of gear that will be used for years of snacks, art projects, and tea parties. Best bets are going to have steady

TODDLERS • Ones and Twos

legs and a washable surface. After that, it's a matter of budget and style to fit your home. Check the underside of tables and chairs for smooth finishes that won't snag little fingers. Twos also enjoy a rocking chair or armchair scaled to their size. 2 & up.

Some basic safety and design questions you may want to ask:

- Can your child get on and off chairs/bench easily?

- Is this a set that will work when your child gets a little bigger?

- If you're looking at a wooden set, are there exposed screws or nuts (check the underside) that can cut your child?

- Is the table surface washable and ready for abuse? (A beautiful painted piece will be destroyed by paint, playdough, crayons, etc.)

Best Travel Toys For Toddlers

We ask almost the impossible from toddlers when we travel by car. Sitting still for long stretches is physically stressful for this age group. Having a plan before you get in the car may help make the transition a little bit easier. The most obvious tip would be to try to plan your car travel to happen at nap time. Of course, that's not always possible. While some kids find the movement of the car soothing and fall asleep easily, others seem to feel the need to co-drive the car—staying alert the entire way!

It's at this age that kids do that straightening-of-the-back trick when being put into their car seats. It will help if you:

- Give your child a heads-up about getting ready to go into the car.

- Leave a special toy in the car that she can look forward to playing with only in the car.

- Bring along favorite tapes to listen to in the car.

- Bring snacks and drinks—especially good if you get caught in traffic!

- Bring along a favorite huggable and/or blanket.

- Bring big washable crayons and pad of paper in a travel sack small enough to fit into a diaper bag or glove compartment.
- Bring an inflatable ball for out-of-the-car breaks and when-you-get-there fun.
- Bring small cardboard books he can handle himself when in his car seat.
- Bring a small set of big plastic blocks or the "favorite toy of the week" for extended stays, one you know she'll be happy to play with while you're unpacking!

A Present for Me! Game One of the best tips we have for toddlers is to wrap small items for them to unwrap. They don't need to be new—little books, a tape, a box of cereal, or a small toy. Don't show your bag of tricks all at once. Dole them out as you go! Toddlers love surprises, and the unwrapping process is part of the fun and a real time burner.

Best Second-Birthday Gifts For Every Budget

Over $100   **Wooden Blocks** (various makers) or **Playhouse / Large Climber** (Little Tikes / Step 2) or **Toy Kitchen** (Step 2 / Small World Toys) or **Doll Pram** (Haba)

Under $75   **iPlay Zoom Around Garage** (International Playthings) or **Neurosmith Music Blocks** (Small World Toys) or **Retro Rocket** (Radio Flyer) or **Sandbox** (Little Tikes / Step 2)

Under $50   **Super Spiral Play Tower** (International Playthings) or **Cozy Coupe** (Little Tikes) or **IQ Preschool Push-Along Block Cart** (Small World Toys) or **Smushy Elephant** (North American Bear Co.)

TODDLERS • Ones and Twos

Under $30	**Lego Duplo Zoo** (Lego Systems) or **Latitude Enfant Grannanimals** (Pint Size Productions) or **Giant Cardboard Blocks** (Constructive Playthings) or **Jumbo Jungle Animals** (Learning Resources)
Under $25	**Little People Lil' Movers Airplane** (Fisher-Price) or **Rollipop Advanced Set** (Edushape)
Under $20	**Toy Dishes** (various makers) or **Puzzibilities Sounds on the Go Puzzle** (Small World Toys) or **Asthma Friendly Puppy Dog** (Kids Preferred)
Under $15	**Triple Track Tower** (Playskool) or **Rick the Frog & Friends** (Rich Frog) or **Tolo Mobile Phone** (Small World Toys) or **Kiddy Connects** (Edushape)
Under $10	**My First Quatro Set** (Lego Systems) or **Crayola Color Wonder Paper & Markers** (Binney & Smith)
Under $5	**Play-Doh** (Hasbro)

A Word about Balloons. Despite the fact that latex balloons are considered unsafe for children under 6, people continue to give them to kids in stores and parks, and at parties. The problem is that kids can suffocate on pieces of latex if they bite and/or inhale a balloon that they break or try to blow up. Yes, they are an old tradition—but a dangerous one. Why take the risk? Stick to Mylar!

TOYS

Books for Toddlers

Reading to your toddler is not just a bedtime thing. Books provide a wonderful way to make the transition from active play to quiet together time. Books with rhyme, rhythm, and repetitive patterns invite tots to chime in with the telling and stretch their own blossoming mastery of language. Keep one shelf of books accessible for "independent" reading. Our new book, **Read It! Play It! With Babies and Toddlers** suggests 50+ books and activities for this age group. Look for past winners and current Gold and Platinum winners on our website at Toyportfolio.com. For our PLATINUM AWARD 2007 books, see page 177.

3 • Preschool
Three to Four Years

What to Expect Developmentally

Learning Through Pretend. Preschoolers are amazing learning machines! Watch and listen to them at play and you can hear the wheels of their busy minds working full tilt. From sunup to sundown, preschoolers love playing pretend games. Playing all sorts of roles gives kids a chance to become big and powerful people. Providing props for such play gives kids the learning tools to develop language, imagination, and a better understanding of themselves and others.

Social Play. Your once-happy-to-be-only-with-you toddler has blossomed into a much more social being. He enjoys playing with other kids. Sharing is still an issue, but there's a budding understanding of give and take.

Solo Play. Unlike the toddler who moved from one thing to another, preschoolers become able to really focus their attention on building a bridge of blocks, working on a puzzle, or painting pictures.

Toys and Development. Although preschoolers love to play at counting and singing, or even at trying to write the alphabet, informal play is still the best path to learning. Building a tower with blocks, they discover some very basic math concepts. Digging in the sand or floating leaves in puddles, they make early science discoveries.

TOYS

Big Muscles. Threes and fours also need time and space to run and climb and use their big muscles to develop coordination and a sense of themselves as able doers.

Your Role in Play. A child who has shelves full of stuffed animals or every piece of the hottest licensed character may seem to have tons of toys, but the truth is, no matter how many trucks or dolls a kid has, such collections offer just one kind of play. Take an inventory of your child's toy clutter to see what's really being played with and what needs to be packed away or donated.

> ### Basic Gear Checklist for Preschoolers
>
> ✓ Set of blocks and props (small vehicles, animals, people)
> ✓ Trike
> ✓ Dolls and/or soft animals
> ✓ Dress-up clothes
> ✓ Housekeeping toys
> ✓ Transportation toys
> ✓ Matching games
> ✓ Picture books
> ✓ Sand and water toys
> ✓ Art materials—crayons, paints, clay
> ✓ Simple puzzles (eight pieces and up)
> ✓ Tape player and music and story tapes

> ### Toys to Avoid
> These toys pose a safety hazard:
>
> ✓ Electric toys or those that heat up with lightbulbs, which can burn
> ✓ Toys with projectile parts that can injure eyes
> ✓ Toys without volume control, which can damage ears
> ✓ Two-wheelers with training wheels
> ✓ Latex balloons
>
> These toys are developmentally inappropriate:
>
> ✓ Complex building sets that adults must build while children watch
> ✓ Teaching machines that reduce learning to a series of right or wrong answers
> ✓ Coloring books that limit creativity

PRESCHOOL • Three to Four Years

Pretend Play

This is the age when pretend play blossoms. Some kids pretend with blocks, trains, and miniatures they move around as they act out little dramas. Others prefer dressing up and playing roles with their whole being. Either way, such games are more than fun. They help children learn to stretch their imaginations, try on powerful new roles, cope with feelings and fears, and develop language and social skills.

Housekeeping Tools

Both girls and boys use props for cleaning, cooking, and childcare. Few toys will get more use by both boys and girls than a mini-broom or -mop. This is an inexpensive favorite that you'll find in most toy supermarkets. Kitchen toys are used for playing house and running restaurants. As children's experiences broaden, so does the scope of their games of make-believe.

■ **Crank 'N Glow Flashlight** 2007

(Playskool $9.99 ●●●◐) Kiss the batteries goodbye! Here's a "magic" flashlight that you wind, and the faster you crank it, the brighter it glows. This is a novelty item that kids may enjoy for a few minutes and then it will turn into a piece of equipment. 3 & up. (800) 327-8267.

COMPARISON SHOPPER
Hamburger, Anyone? Grills 2007

Both Little Tikes and Step 2 get high marks this year for gender-free pretend cooking sets with an outdoor twist. The **Inside Outside Cook n Grill Kitchen** 2007 (Little Tikes $149 ●●●●) is a combo unit right on the mark for "pretend" cooking with a kitchen on one side and an outdoor grill on the other. (800) 321-0183. With an even more outdoor feel, **Bistro Grille** (Step 2 $99.99 ●●●) comes with a cook surface, counter, and stool. While we like the design of the Bistro very much, the lower rating reflects the plastic hot dogs that are unnecessarily small and should be removed for kids who still mouth their toys. (800) 347-8372. For more kitchens, see Toddlers chapter.

■ My First Stove

(Alex $19.99 ●●●●) Big kitchens are in the toddler chapter, but this mini-kitchen (12" x 11" x 11") fits on a table top; ideal for tight spaces. A painted wooden stovetop with colorful knobs and drawer that opens to store utensils. Companion to **My First Sink.** Don't be fooled by the picture on the box—no pots or dishes in the package! 3 & up. (800) 666-2539. For more kitchens, see Toddlers chapter.

COMPARISON SHOPPER
Dishes *2007*

There are three high quality dish sets: **Kitch 'n Carry Sets** (Alex $14.99 & up ●●●●)—testers loved the brightly colored kitchenware. They are gender specific, however, with lots of pink. (800) 666-2539. For gender-free sets, we recommend: **Pretend & Play Dishes** (Learning Resources $12.95 ●●●●) Service for four includes sturdy plastic cups and saucers, octagonal plates, and cutlery in primary colors. 3 & up. (800) 222-3909. **Cooking Essentials** *2007* (Step 2 $17.99 ●●●●½)

A handsome 7-piece set of enameled blue pans includes a large and small saucepan with lids and a sauté pan with wooden handle plus two pot holders. Their **stainless steel set** ($24.99 ●●●) with tea kettle, colander, sauce pots, sauté pan, and pot holders would have been a top winner but for the tea kettle's handle, which is roughly finished. We pass on the **bake set** ($17.99 ●●●) because the measuring cup, marked as a cup,

PRESCHOOL • Three to Four Years

is short of a true cup. It seems silly to be inaccurate. 3 & up. (800) 347-8372.

■ Pretend & Play Teaching Telephone BLUE CHIP

(Learning Resources $29.95 ooooo) You can program in any phone number and leave a message. When your child calls that number they hear your message. A great way to teach important phone numbers and the concept of 911. Even the concept of taking messages is built into the pretend. 4 & up. (800) 222-3909.

Dress-Up Play and Let's-Pretend Props

Old pocketbooks, briefcases, jewelry, hats, or a homemade badge are often all that's needed to transform young players. Below are a few specialty items you may want to buy:

■ Get Real Gear *2007*

(Aeromax Toys $49.95 & up ooooo) We were impressed with this company's themed jumpsuits: new for *2007*, an astronaut's white suit and an amazing helmet ($43.95) that comes with audio commands for a "lift off"—really for 4s and up. Past favorites: **Jr. Air Force Pilot** and **Jr. Championship Racer.** Come in sizes for kids 3–12. PLATINUM AWARD '05. They have new gender-specific doctor outfits (not our speed). (877) 776-2291.

■ Giggle Gear Magical Unicorn *2007*

(Cranium $19.95 oooo) White plush with a silver horn and lavender mane fit on child's head without covering eyes. Touch the unicorn and it makes a magical sound (happily, volume control is built in). Comes with furry hooves with their own cloppity magical sound as child runs. Newest addition to award-winning **Roaring Dinosaur, Clippity Clop Horse,** and **Get-up Fairy.** 3–6. (877) 272-6486.

■ Let's Pretend Careers *2007*

(Small Miracles $29.99 & up ooooo) Handsome enough to wear as real clothes, the newest items in the career line are an **Astronaut** (oooo½), and an **ER Worker** (oooo½) with green scrubs, stethoscope, and other tools. Forget the stereotypical **Teacher** (oo) costume with black glasses and old-fashioned red smock with white lace. Still top rated, **Chef** (with coat, hat, and tools); in the fantasy line, a **Pirate** (outfit comes with a felt hat). Past winners include: **Doctor, Pilot, Equestrian, Firefighter, Construction Worker,** and **Police.** PLATINUM AWARDS '02 & '04. 3–8. (888) 281-1798.

■ Little Pretenders

(Chenille Kraft $24.99 each oooo) A line of costumes made of wipe-able vinyl provides the most affordable choice. Each theme comes with accessories (stethoscopes, extinguishers, etc.) and appropriate headgear. Other costumes include **Veterinarian, Hair Dresser** (the pretend blow dryer makes a great sound), and **Doctor.** 3 & up. (800) 621-1261.

■ Pretend & Play Doctor Set

(Learning Resources $24.95 ooooo) The "black bag" we grew up with is gone, but then again so are house calls. This set comes in a large plastic case with 19 pieces including a stethoscope with heartbeat and cough, a beeper, a cellphone, and other chunky tools. PLATINUM AWARD '04. (800) 222-3909. Also available, **Fisher-Price's Medical Kit** (Fisher-Price $10 oooo) comes in a smaller plastic case with almost the same basic gear as their original "black bag." (800) 432-5437.

■ Pretend & Play Office 2007

(Learning Resources $29.99 oooo) A briefcase loaded with 75 items is full of props for playing office. Few of the props are electronic except for the calculator and cell phone. Kit includes a kid's checkbook, blank calendar, wipe-off chart, and very skinny laptop (just a piece of cardboard that opens like a book cover with screen and keyboard printed). 3 & up. (800) 222-3909.

■ Super Star Sing-Along Vanity

(Little Tikes $47 oo) "Mirror, mirror on the vanity, will I be part of the future American Idol insanity?" We're not big on vanities that come loaded with a karaoke mirror, a wireless microphone (the hairbrush) . . . and an applause button (honest!). Not available for testing. 3 & up. (800) 321-0183.

PRESCHOOL • Three to Four Years

Dolls and Huggables

Preschoolers love soft animals and dolls as huggable companions for bedtime and playtime. At this age, playing with dolls gives both boys and girls a chance to try out new roles and language.

■ Baby Stella *2007*

(Manhattan Toy $24.99 ●●●●½) Younger preschoolers will enjoy tending to this all-fabric baby doll that comes in two skin tones with a few strands of yarn hair. New this year are a fun bouncy seat and outfits for Stella. (800) 541-1345.

■ Butterscotch My FurReal Pony *2007*

(Hasbro $250) It will be interesting to see how kids respond to this very large pony that has animatronics . . . it will whinny, move its head, and rock a bit, but will not walk or trot or gallop away! Not ready for testing. (888) 836-7025.

■ Bebe Do with Moses Basket
2007 PLATINUM AWARD

(Corolle $70 ●●●●●) A very special-looking present that comes with a 14" baby doll in a charming pink fabric-lined carrying basket with quilt, toy bunny, bottle, and baby book! There is an **African American Bebe Do** version but unfortunately not with the basket. (800) 668-4846.

■ Jules

(Corolle $60 ●●●●●) Finding a boy doll is not easy, yet it's a great gift, especially when there's a new baby in the family. Meet Jules, a 17" bald baby doll in blue romper with bottle, bib, and pacifier. He cries, laughs, and babbles. 3 & up. PLATINUM AWARD '06. New for *2007*, **Baby Chou Twins** ($34.95 ●●●●), soft-bodied 11" bald boy and girl dolls in knitted rompers and hats with sleep eyes and tethered tiny teethers (not for kids who still mouth their toys). (800) 668-4846.

■ Trixieville 2007 PLATINUM AWARD

(Manhattan Toy $19.99 each ●●●●●) From the makers of Groovy Girls comes Trixieville—a more sophisticated collection of dolls that come with jointed hips and shoulders. First collection: **Zayla** (redhead), **Avena** (blonde), and **Elonia** (brunette) have a modern fairy look. Think Tinker Bell goes Vogue (with wings, of course). The furniture, including the **Leafy Lounger** ($19.99 ●●●●●) and accessories for this line, are equally whimsical and fun. Our only regret is that these are not multicultural fairies. (800) 541-1345.

Multicultural Dolls

Just a few years ago, there were few options that reflected our diversity. Now, there are so many more great choices.

■ Miss Corolle Collection: Doucette 2007

(Corolle $24.95 each ●●●●) We love this multiethnic collection of soft-bodied dolls with silky hair, bright knitted striped outfits, and charming faces with painted-on features. Other multicultural collections: **Bebe Do** ($50 ●●●●), a charming 14" baby doll available in two skin tones (in pink or blue romper); **Chouquettes** ($44.95 ●●●●½), 14" girl dolls where the emphasis is age-typical hair play (they have very silky locks)—new this year, a beautiful Asian doll; and **Les Minis Calins** BLUE CHIP ($16 each ●●●●●), small baby dolls that come in Caucasian and Asian skin tones. (800) 668-4846.

■ Götz Precious Day Muffin Collection 2007

(International Playthings $29.99 ●●●●½) 13" dolls with soft cuddly bodies; brown, green, and blue sleep eyes; and long rooted blonde, red, or black hair done up in two ponytails. Available in African American and Caucasian skin tones. 3 & up. (800) 445-8347.

PRESCHOOL • Three to Four Years

■ Groovy Girls and Groovy Boys 2007 BLUE CHIP

(Manhattan Toy $14.95 & up ○○○○○) This continues to be a BLUE CHIP collection of soft 13" multi-ethnic dolls with stitched features, yarn hair, and groovy clothes. Happily, there is a boy doll in this line. Also new for 2007, **Melina** with sea green hair, plus a sea horse in her arm to go with her mermaid body. The new **Groovy Girl Beachy Keen Sand Buggy** ($40 ○○○○½) would make a special present for a GG fan (even though the wheels don't roll!). Still the superlative gift, consider **Supersize Yvette** or **Gwen** ($50 each), a 40" child-sized fabric doll that's like a pretend play pal. We found the new **Groovy Girls' PetRageous** ($16.99 ○○○) disappointing. If you didn't see the hangtags you wouldn't know they were from the same folks—they lack the wonderful design quality and spirit of the dolls. 3 & up. (800) 541-1345.

■ Love Me Chou Chou 2007

(Zapf Creation $49.99 ○○) This crying babbling doll disappointed our testers, who thought she was "too heavy . . . it had a seam on her head—looked like she had a brain surgery." New for 2007, **Talking Chou Chou** ($34.99), a 19" baby doll available in Caucasian or African American skin tones, which promises to speak both English and Spanish but was not ready for testing. **My Little Baby Born** ($14.95 ○○○) is a 13" tub-able baby doll, Caucasian or African American, who does whatever your child imagines (a plus). *Editors' note:* the lower rating reflects our concern that the doll is labeled 1 & up but has an attached pacifier that poses a choking hazard. (877) 629-9273.

Talking Dolls

These novelty dolls often get a lot of media attention. Some are worth the buzz, others deserved silence. For example, **Bird's the Word Elmo** 2007 (Fisher-Price $19.99 ○○) features our pal Elmo dressed up like a bird, telling jokes and singing. It's just too derivative and remote for kids. The big news is really **TMX Elmo,** a refreshed version of Tickle

TOYS

Me Elmo that hopes to recapture the magic of the craze. It was not ready for testing.

■ Language Littles

(Language Littles $35 ○○○○) Each of these 16" fabric dolls with yarn hair speaks in English and another language (each says 25 words and phrases). Will they make your child bilingual? Of course not, but they are a place to start. Choose Italian, Greek, French, Chinese, Hebrew, Russian, German, Spanish, or Japanese. 3 & up. (212) 535-8122.

COMPARISON SHOPPER
Drink-and-Wet Dolls

Our testers gave thumbs up to **Bébé Do Emma** or **Paul Fait Pipi** (Corolle $40 each ○○○○½), anatomically correct girl or boy 14" doll with all-vinyl tubable body. Comes with potty, bottle, and diaper for pretend play. (800) 668-4846. In the novelty doll category, **Potty Elmo** (Fisher-Price $19 ○○○○○) is amazing. Give Elmo his sippy cup and you'll hear him drink; if you don't get him to the potty, he says, "Oops, Elmo didn't get to the potty. Accidents happen," and if he makes it, "Elmo can do it and so can you!" One of the best and most polite interactive dolls we've ever tested. PLATINUM AWARD '05. (800) 432-5437. We pass on Zapf Creations' **Baby Born** ($39.99 ○○), who got low marks from our testers because they had difficulty getting the pretend poop out (no joke). (877) 629-9273.

Bears of the Year *2007* PLATINUM AWARD

Goober (Gund $30 & $50 ○○○○○), a pot bellied bear that you'll just want to hug. He's two-toned with a really distinctive big nose—very endearing. (800) 448-4863. Still very special, **Great Big Creamy Bear** (Mary Meyer $130/36" ○○○○○) Remember the oversized bear you always dreamed of winning at the fair? This one is much better, because he's totally huggable, soft, and delicious! 36" big, this memorable bear will be great to talk to and lean on. PLATINUM AWARD '06. (800) 451-4387.

Best of Show: Dogs of the Year 2007
■ **Lucky the Incredible Wonder Pup**
   2007 PLATINUM AWARD

(Zizzle $49.99 ooooo) "Works right away," noted our parent tester. Lucky is a two-toned dog that responds to 15 different commands including "speak," "come here," "lie down," and "shake hands." Very clever and gets high marks for really being well trained. 5 & up. (866) 494-9953.

Past Favorites: **Doogie Dog Flip Flops** (Mary Meyer $15 oooo) Extremely soft and huggable, this 12" pooch has interesting markings, soft body, velvety nose, and beanbag feet. (800) 451-4387. Or, in the floppy, understuffed, and very shaggy dog class, our vote goes to 22" and 18" **Fluffies** (Manhattan Toy $20 & $40 oooo). With corduroy noses and weighted paws, these come in two sizes in either pink or white. They shed just like the real thing! (800) 541-1345. **Puppies for Sale** (North American Bear $13 each oooo½) Choose from an adorable, snuggly **Black & White Springer Spaniel, Beagle,** or **Cocker Spaniel** with curly ears. (800) 682-3427.

Miscellaneous Stuffed Critters
■ **Yakety Squeeze Me Critters** 2007

(Mary Meyer $10 each oooo½) These are perfect stocking stuffers—soft animals that each make a unique sound when squeezed. Just the right size to fill a child's fist and take along. New favorites: **Yakety Donald Donkey, Brant Bull;** our old favorites: **Floyd Frog, Nell Cow, Luke Lion,** and **Doug the Pug.** (800) 451-4387.

Notable Doll Accessories 2007
Budget and taste will go into making the choices here. Just like real equipment, there are doll carriers for the silver-spoon set and more practical models for your average doll. New for

2007: Corolle's PLATINUM AWARD-winning **Play Crib** ($36 ●●●●●) looks most like a portable crib done in pink and white. Still top rated: American Girl's yellow and blue **Collapsible Stroller** ($34 ●●●●), designed for their 15" Bitty Baby Dolls. Also special, **Bitty Twins Double Stroller** ($48 ●●●●). (800) 845-0005. Community Playthings' BLUE CHIP **Wooden Doll Cradle** ($95 ●●●●●) is made of solid maple and built to last. The large 29" model is big enough so kids can climb in and play baby or put a family of dolls to sleep in. 2 & up. #C140. (800) 777-4244.

Puppets and Puppet Stages

Through the mouths of puppets, kids say things that they might not otherwise speak about; so puppets provide a way of venting feelings and developing imagination and language skills. Young puppeteers replay stories, create original tales, and develop skills that link to reading and writing. See Early School Years chapter for more puppets and stages.

■ Animal Puppets 2007

(Gund $16 each ●●●●) Good news! Gund has reintroduced their beautifully made hand puppets. Choose from some of their classic bears such as **Manni,** or other animals, such as **Luke the Lion** or **Bamboo Panda.** (800) 448-4863.

■ Center Stage Puppets 2007

(Mary Meyer $13 each ●●●●) Just right for lively reenactments of your favorite stories. There's a wide assortment of animals: bear, dog, frog, horse, monkey, lion, moose, and wolf! (800) 451-4387.

■ Puppet Theater

(Alex $79.99 ●●●●½) This has a clock for show time and eye-appealing graphics! This stable floor model is 48" high, with painted trim on one side and a chalk surface for messages. Their tabletop model looks like a fairytale castle and comes with two felt puppets. ($50 ●●●●½). 3 & up. (800) 666-2539. For more stages and puppets, see Early

PRESCHOOL • Three to Four Years

School Years chapter.

> **FREEBIE: Do it yourself.** A large appliance box can be turned into an excellent puppet stage, and so can a cloth-covered card table that kids can hide behind. Another great option is a spring curtain rod and length of fabric that can be used in any doorway.

Pretend Settings:
Doll Houses, Castles, Garages, & Cruise Ship

Some of the mini-settings listed in the Toddlers chapter will be used in more elaborate ways now. Here are descriptions of recommended settings that are more complex:

Dollhouses

Dollhouses should be kept simple for little hands. Plastic or wood, it really comes down to personal preference. Here are our top picks:

Plastic Dollhouses

■ **Calico Critters Townhome** 2007
(International Playthings $79.99 ●●●●●) Our testers have loved the characters and furnishings from this line for years. Now the Townhome, in molded plastic, has a woodland look with red tile roof and lights that plug in and turn on with a switch. The **animal critter families** ($19.99 a set) are like storybook characters. The house opens for play and closes for storing all those little play pieces that kids adore. PLATINUM AWARD '06. New for 2007, **outdoor furniture** ($24.99 ●●●●) complete with sandbox! 4 & up. (800) 445-8347.

■ **Twin Time Dollhouse**
(Fisher-Price $69.95 ●●●½) This big eight-room house has a patio, garage, a mom and dad and twins, plus 10 pieces of furniture and accessories. It opens to a spacious setting that folds up after playtime is done. The color scheme screams plastic, but a good value for the price. 3 & up. (800) 432-5437.

TOYS

Wooden Dollhouses

■ Ryan's Room Home is Where the Heart Is Dollhouse

(Small World Toys $105 ●●●●●) This is a three-stories-high house with lots of room for pretend play. PLATINUM AWARD '03. Or consider the smaller **Home Again, Home Again A-Frame** ($125 ●●●●●), which can be enlarged with an add-on basement and stairs ($74 ●●●●). Also fun, a two-story **Backyard Clubhouse** with "cable car" that connects dollhouse to clubhouse. Multicultural families and interesting furniture collections available; and **Multimedia Mania** ($15 ●●●●) with a flatscreen TV, of course. (800) 421-4153.

■ My Dollhouse BLUE CHIP

(Alex $169 ●●●●●) Done in a bright-colored, patterned palette, this house has three floors with 22 pieces of furniture. (800) 666-2539.

■ Smart Living Holiday Home

(HaPe $79.95 ●●●●) Of the three recommended, this is smaller in scale with a tower shape. You build the four-level home complete with spiral staircase with your child. An ultra-modern look with furniture and people. (800) 661-4142.

Dollhouse Accessories

■ Groovy Girls Minis *2007*

(Manhattan Toy $4.99 & up ●●●●½) Best props for dollhouse play are long-term, multi-ethnic favorites: Groovy Girls, done as "minis" in molded plastic with various hairdos, groovy clothes, pets, and funky home furnishings. New for *2007*, **Reese, Gwen, Lourdes** and **Leticia.** These little 4" dolls can stand on their own two feet and are pose-able for active pretend. (800) 541-1345.

Other Pretend Settings

■ Ryan's Room Adventures Ahoy

(Small World Toys $99.99 ●●●●●) Yahoo! Get ready for imagination to set sail with Captain Hook and two of his mates aboard this magnificent wooden ship with working sails, rigging,

PRESCHOOL • Three to Four Years

hatches, anchor, crow's nest, and even a plank to walk! A stunning gift for years of dramatic play. 34" w x 24" h. 4–8. PLATINUM AWARD '05. Also special from the same line, **Ryan's Room Majestic Castle & Mighty Knights** ($100 ✪✪✪✪✪), a truly majestic wooden castle, 20" x 20", with working drawbridge, movable staircases, four towers, and walls that can be arranged in different configurations. Comes with four knights and a horse. Easy to assemble, this play setting might become an heirloom. 4 & up. PLATINUM AWARD '04. (800) 421-4153.

■ Deluxe Tumble Treehouse & Skycoaster

(Maxim Enterprises $99 ✪✪✪✪✪) One of our favorite pretend settings! With pulleys and stairways, this furnished treehouse has lots of pretend power and action. A **Sky Coaster** can be added for vehicles ($30). A gender-free setting that will mix well with block structures. An outstanding value! 4–8. PLATINUM AWARD '05. (888) 266-2946.

Trucks and Other Vehicles

Preschoolers are fascinated with all forms of transportation. The real things are out of reach and on the move, but toy trucks, cars, boats, jets, and trains are ideal for make-believe departures, both indoors and out. Choose vehicles with working parts to use with blocks, in the sandbox, or at the beach. BLUE CHIP choices such as Funrise's **Tonka Trucks** or Little Tikes' **Construction Trucks** are perfect gifts for now. So are **Matchbox** or **Hot Wheels** cars, which are now appropriate and are often the first "collectible."

■ Automoblox

(Automoblox $32 each ✪✪✪✪✪) A new collection of sleekly designed cars destined to be a bestseller in museum shops for their handsome design, and a hit with kids for their playability. Each wooden car comes apart (making it part vehicle, part puzzle). The plastic connectors have shape receptors. For parents looking for "cool design" for the playroom, look no further. 4 & up. PLATINUM AWARD '06. (973) 364-8090.

■ Bendos My First RC Buggies

(Kid Galaxy $19.95 each ✪✪✪✪✪) Our testers loved this new line of

TOYS

remotes designed with preschoolers in mind. Choose a **Bumble Bee** or a spotted **Ladybug** with simple one-button control. These have plenty of action; even when the remote is not pressed, they spin. PLATINUM AWARD '06. Still top rated, **Old Tyme R/C Bumper Cars** ($49.99 ●●●●½). (800) 816-1135.

■ Bob the Builder Follow Me Scoop 2007

(RC2/Learning Curve $39.95 ●●●●) Point the play figure and push the buttons on Bob the Builder and kids can activate Scoop, the bright yellow earthmover/excavator. Bob fans are going to love controlling the voice commands, music, and action. Label says 2; we'd say more like 3 and up. (800) 704-8697.

■ Rugged Riggz 2007

(Little Tikes $9.99 & 14.99 ●●●●) We're big fans of this updated collection of basic trucks. Among our favorites are a **Helicopter Hauler**, a **Sports Car Hauler** with two cars, and a **Garbage Truck**. Still top rated, **Motorcycle Hauler**, and the classics (**cement, dump,** and **hauler**). New for 2007 are **Haulers,** Ford or Chevy trucks that haul racing cars. Also neat, **Spark Racerz Hummers** ($5 ●●●●), smaller-scaled, pull-back vehicles. All are just right for the 3 & up crowd. (800) 321-0183.

■ Tonka Toughest Mighty Crane 2007

(Hasbro $29.99 ●●●) Our tester thought he had broken the crane when a piece came off in his hand and he could not put it back on. Although he loved the crank action, it did not hold his interest for long and was soon classified as "broken." Sadly, this is not up to the classic name of the Mighty Tonka! 3 & up. (888) 836-7025.

First Trains and Track Toys

What They Learn

A nonelectric train is a classic toy that will keep growing in

PRESCHOOL • Three to Four Years

complexity as you add working bridges, roundhouses, and other extras. Note: Preschoolers are not ready for electric trains, except to watch!

Trains are really open-ended puzzles with no right or wrong answers. Making the track work often becomes more important to many kids than actually playing with the trains.

Many stores display their trains on tabletops with the track glued down, but much of the open-ended play value is lost when you do that at home. Making ever-changing settings is half the fun. Skip the table and invest in more tracks and bridges.

Editors' Note: First, we know from many testing families that toddlers are playing with wooden trains. Be forewarned that the trains have small parts and that many of the accessories are also very small and pose a choking hazard. Second, as a sign of the times, some of our four-year-old testers were overheard discussing that they don't want to play with the trains that they have to "push" (preferring the battery operated trains). Sad.

Wooden Train Sets

■ **Thomas & Friends Water Tower Figure 8 Set** *2007*

(RC2/Learning Curve $39.99 ○○○○½)
This 25-piece set is a great buy and gives beginners a great place to start. Includes Thomas, a cargo car, water tower, and stone bridge for a figure 8. New for *2007*, **Edward the Great Set** ($79.99,
29 pieces ○○○○½) features Edward & Spencer with Duke and Duchess Coach Car and Furniture Car; we'd pass on the **Rheneas & the Roller Coaster Set** ($129.99, 32-piece set ○○○) which looks great but the trains are hard to maneuver; **Storm on Sodor Set** ($179.99, 35-piece set) with tunnel, tumbling trees, breakaway shed, and collapsing windmill was not ready for testing. Still top-rated, **Deluxe Aquarium** themed set ($299 ○○○○½). Call in the grandparents! (800) 704-8697.

Plastic Train and Track Sets

■ **Geotrax All About Trains Motorized Starter Set**
  2007 **PLATINUM AWARD**

(Fisher-Price $24.99 ○○○○○) A classic 20-piece figure-8 set with 13 pieces of track, motorized engine and trail car, yield sign, crossing sign, gantry with crate, coal loader and crossing gate. Comes with a wonderful live-action DVD (see p. TK for fuller review). A great value! Still top rated, **GeoTrax Workin' Town Railway** ($39.99 ●●●●) This 30-piece set comes with a bridge, station, and windmill. Our testers found that it is possible for the train to get caught in a loop and fitting the tracks together is more challenging than with wooden tracks, since these only fit right side up. That said, kids liked the many features of this set and the flexibility of extending the system with other settings, such as the **GeoTrax Coastal Winds Airport** ($24.99 ●●●●½). Marked 2½—we'd say it's a true preschool set. (800) 432-5437.

■ Shake 'N Go Speedway

(Fisher-Price $39.99 ●●●●●) This is a closed system with looping tracks, but the upside is kids can use the cars off the track, too. Kids love the two innovative cars in this racing set that have to be shaken to make them go. Does this mean no batteries? Sorry, Charlie! Still, this is going to make a memorable gift and a better choice than electric trains for this age. 4 & up. PLATINUM AWARD '06. (800) 432-5437.

Best New Wooden Train Props

New accessories can inspire fresh layouts and keep interest chugging along. These were among the best of the new toys this season!

■ Thomas & Friends Load & Sort Recycling Center / Echo Tunnel / Sodor Fire Station
2007 PLATINUM AWARDS

(RC2/Learning Curve $49.99 & up ●●●●●) Three pieces of cargo slide through the **Recycling Center** ($49.99) and magically drop down the can, paper, or glass chutes and onto a waiting truck. Clever use of technology with a built-in message! Also great fun, **Echo Tunnel** ($49.99). Our tester loved speaking into the tunnel and hearing his own words echo back! There are also a train whistle and rackety track sounds that echo as trains run through the small tunnel that fits into any track set-up. One parent noted: "The ability to record one's voice is so much fun for this age." Also won-

PRESCHOOL • Three to Four Years

derful, **Sights & Sounds Deluxe Fire Station** ($69.99 ●●●●●). An alarm activates lights and sounds of the fire crew with their fire truck and fire train. Switches above the doorways turn on lights and sounds, and open the double doors. 3 & up. (800) 704-8697.

■ Brio Double Suspension Bridge

(K'nex $25 ●●●●½) This is the longest bridge in the line—three and a half feet long! Can also be used side by side for two-way traffic.  Our tester liked the **Stop & Go Station** ($16.50 ●●●●); with a simple push button the train is locked into the station and then released to go. (800) 822-5639.

Construction Toys

If there's one toy no child should be without, blocks are it! Few toys are more basic. Stacking a tower, balancing a bridge, setting up a zoo—all call for imagination, dexterity, decision making, and problem solving. Built into the play are early math and language concepts that give concrete meaning to abstract words such as *higher, lower, same,* and *different*. Best of all, blocks are wonderfully versatile—they build a space city today, a farm tomorrow.

Kids will enjoy both wood and plastic types of blocks, which encourage different kinds of valuable play experiences. Choosing blocks depends largely on your budget and space. Although many of these sets are pricey, they are a solid investment that will be used for years to come.

Wooden Blocks

Unit blocks come in many shapes and lengths and should be carefully proportioned to each other. Many catalogs offer unit blocks in sets of different sizes. Parents are sometimes disappointed when kids don't use the small starter sets they buy. Keep in mind that kids really can't do much with a set of 20 blocks and no props. This is one of those items where the more they have, the more they can do.

🛍️ COMPARISON SHOPPER
Unit Blocks

No two companies have the same number of blocks or shapes in any set, so there are small differences among all the sets listed. The cost of shipping will vary depending upon where you live and the weight and price of the item. Our best suggestion is that you call around and compare. Here's a sampling of what a good basic set will run:

Back to Basics set of 82 blocks in 21 shapes. #2728. $175.99 (800) 356-5360.

Constructive Playthings set of 82 pieces in 12 shapes. #KRP-U312L. $79.99 (800) 832-0572.

Small World Toys' IQ Preschool 120 Unit Blocks of Fun ($120); Also **IQ Preschool Block Party** ($30) a 60-piece set of small-scaled colorful wooden blocks. (800) 421-4153.

Foam Blocks *2007*

This year we saw more foam blocks and, unlike earlier forms, they do not have a foul smell or crumbly finish. Colorful foam blocks are less pricey than wood and quieter when they fall. They are not for kids who still mouth their toys and may chew off small bits of foam. See more Foam Blocks in Toddler chapter.

■ Soft & Sturdy Deluxe Blocks *2007*

(Step 2 $44.99 ○○○○½) This is a 64-piece set of multi-colored blocks that come in 17 shapes and are scaled to each other, although they are not in traditional unit block sizes. The set comes with a big zip bag for storage. 3 & up. (800) 347-8372.

Props for Blocks

Providing a variety of props such as small-scale vehicles, animals, and people enhances building and imaginative play. Here are some props designed to inspire young builders. Our favorites:

■ Flocked Animal Sets

(Melissa & Doug $14.95 & up ○○○○) Set of nine **Barnyard Friends**

PRESCHOOL • Three to Four Years

(or nine **Prehistoric Pals,** or **Pasture Pals,** 12 different horses), are perfect for block play. Sets come in wooden display storage boxes that make order out of preschool chaos. 3 & up. (800) 284-3948.

■ Jumbo Jungle Animals *2007* PLATINUM AWARD

(Learning Resources $25.99 ●●●●●) Perfect props for pretend, a set of five jungle animals—a 13" giraffe, an elephant, a lion, a tiger, and a gorilla. Handsomely finished with realistic colors. Little hands will find lots of ways to use these with and without blocks. 2 & up. Still top rated, **Jumbo Farm Animals** ($22.95 ●●●●½) Seven farm animals, a horse, cow, pig, goat, sheep, goose, and rooster sized proportionately to each other. 3 & up. (800) 222-3909.

■ Mega T-Rex *2007*

(Fisher-Price $30 ●●●●) Two colorful articulated dinosaurs with eyes that light up, tails that move, necks that turn, and mouths that open, came roaring into the office as we went to press. To many a young dino lover, T-Rex will be a dream come true; for others, a true nightmare. 4 & up. (800) 432-5437.

■ Windows and Door Blocks BLUE CHIP

(Constructive Playthings $16.95 ●●●●●) Scaled to standard unit blocks: a five-piece set of four windows and one door. #PCR-62L. (800) 832-0572.

■ Woody Click

(HaPe $4.99 & up ●●●●½) Part construction, part pretend, the Woody Click line has many wooden vehicles; sold individually or as parts of sets. They are ideally scaled for unit blocks, but will require adult assistance to assemble. Choose from colorful construction vehicles, fire trucks, and a helicopter with small flexible play figures. There are several pricey but handome mini-settings ($99 each) such as a hospital, fire station, and police headquarters. (800) 661-4142.

SMART PARENT TRICK: Playful Cleanup. Preschoolers often need help cleaning up. You can get some learning in by saying, "I'll find the trucks, you pick up all the cars," or "Let's find all the smallest blocks first." Set up open shelves for blocks and baskets for props to avoid having a constant jumbled mess!

Plastic Blocks

Plastic building sets call for a different kind of dexterity. Here's what you should look for:

> Beginners are better off with larger pieces that make bigger and quicker constructions.
>
> Encourage beginning builders to experiment rather than copy or watch you build.

■ Mega Bloks BLUE CHIP

(Mega Bloks $10 & up ⚬⚬⚬⚬⚬) These oversized plastic pegged blocks are easy for preschoolers to take apart, fit together, and assemble into B-I-G constructions with a minimum of pieces. Select a set with wheels and angled pieces for more flexibility. (800) 465-6342.

■ Kid K'nex Wild Ones 2007

(K'nex $9.99 ⚬⚬⚬⚬½) These up-sized K'nex look related to your old Tinkertoys—our testers especially like the "crimpy pieces." Fitting the pieces together can be challenging and requires finger strength as well as visual discrimination. Comes in a fun "wild one" carry case. Marked 3 & up, but we'd say more like 4 & up. (800) 543-5639.

■ Airport Action 2007 PLATINUM AWARD

(Lego Systems $49.99 ⚬⚬⚬⚬⚬) One of the most satisfying Duplo sets of the year (no matter how old you are). Your preschooler will need a lot of help putting this set together but he will love playing with it! Comes with a plane, airport with tower, and ground crew! Still top rated, last year's PLATINUM AWARD-winning **Fire Station** ($29.99 ⚬⚬⚬⚬⚬), which can be built as a tower or horizontally. Past winners include: **The Big Farm Set, Bob the Builder,** and **Dora the Explorer** sets. We also highly recommend a **big**

PRESCHOOL • Three to Four Years

bucket ($19.95) for open-ended creations. 3 & up. (800) 233-8756.

Comparison Shopper
Magnetic Building Sets 2007

This year we heard tragic news about toddlers who swallowed the small round magnets from sets designed for older children. If you have mixed aged children, this kind of toy will need super supervision! The good news is that there are larger rod and magnet sets designed for younger kids who still mouth their toys. Last year's **Jumbo Magneatos** (Guidecraft $30 & up ooooo) are still a great choice for younger children because they are oversized primary-colored plastic rods and balls, safe and easy to manipulate. Comes in 36 ($30), 72 ($50), or 144 pieces ($100). 2 & up. PLATINUM AWARD '06. New for 2007, **Magneatos Intermediate PLATINUM AWARD** (Guidecraft $15–$100 ooooo). Smaller in scale than the jumbo set, these colorful magnetic rods and balls can be mixed with the Jumbos and are the right size for kids from 4–7. They are big and chunky compared to sets for older kids, but the short rods do fit in a choke tube and are not appropriate for kids who still mouth their toys. An open-ended building toy that develops dexterity and problem solving skills. 4–7. (800) 524-3555. Also worth a look, **Magtastik** 2007 (Mega Bloks $29.99 oooo)—oversized magnetic balls and rods that are less pricey than Jumbo Magneatos, but set includes some smaller pieces that fit in a choke tube. Not for kids under 3 or those who still mouth their toys. (800) 524-3555.

■ Superstructs Big Builder 2007

(Waba Fun $35.95 & up oooo) Looks a lot like your old Tinkertoys, but brighter. Made of bright-colored plastic rods and connectors, this is an open-ended building set. Comes with directions for making many kinds of vehicles, but allows for kids' original creations, as well. The **Big Builder** set has 126 pieces; or consider the 230-piece set. (303) 926-0848.

Early Games

Preschoolers are not ready for complex games with lots of rules or those that require strategy, math, or reading skills. Best bets are games of chance such as lotto and picture dominoes, and classics such as Candy Land, where players depend on luck of the draw rather than skill. Taking turns is often hard, and so is the concept of winning or losing. We've selected games that can be played cooperatively and those that are quick and short so there can be lots of winners.

Active Games

■ Air-powered Action Stadium 2007 PLATINUM AWARD

(Hasbro $49.99 ●●●●●) Scaled just right for preschoolers to enjoy the fun of playing air hockey complete with a friendly sports announcer and some (but not too many) lights and sounds. Converts into a pinball game that is also not over-the-top frenetic—just on the mark for this age group. 3 & up. (888) 836-7025.

■ Egg and Spoon Race

(International Playthings $12 ●●●●½) Four big plastic spoons are loaded with bright eggs to balance as kids race for the finish line. But watch out—if you drop the egg, it cracks and a yoke falls out! A classic game with fabric yokes that are less messy, and there's no risk of salmonella! They say 3 & up; we'd say more like old 4s and 5–6s. Great for a party! (800) 445-8347.

■ Pin the Tail on the Donkey

(Eeboo $10 ●●●●) This classic game is printed on a sturdy reusable poster and comes with a bandanna blindfold and two sets of 16 self-adhesive tails—no tacks needed! A good party prop for several years of play. 4–8 (212) 222-0823.

PRESCHOOL • Three to Four Years

Color, Counting, & Other Concepts

■ Caterpillar Race 2007 PLATINUM AWARD
(EduShape/PlaySound $12.95 ●●●●●) Two caterpillars are racing to the finish line. The way they get there is with a roll of the dice, players move the matching piece of the caterpillar's body forward. Okay, so there are some body integrity issues here, but it's really fun to play and a fresh new twist on color concepts! (800) 404-4744.

■ CooCoo the Rocking Clown! 2007
(Blue Orange Games $19.95 ●●●●½) CooCoo the Clown rocks on big green shoes as players take turns putting the "balls" on his arms and head. Watch out! Do not let them fall! There are lots of opportunities to win and lose this classic balancing game. 3 & up. Still top rated for kids working on counting skills, **Zimbbos!** ($19.95 ●●●●½). Roll the die and stack the number of elephants shown. Can you do it without having the pyramid fall? Not exactly easy, but fun. 3–6. (415) 252-0372.

■ Dora the Explorer Candy Land
(Milton Bradley $9.99 ●●●●½) Fans of Dora will enjoy this variation of the classic color matching game that incorporates Dora and her friends. Still top rated, **Duck Duck Goose** ($19.99 ●●●●●) —a fun, easy-to-learn, color concept game. PLATINUM AWARD '05. (888) 836-7025.

Matching and Memory

Prereaders match pictures before they match words. These games provide playful ways to develop vocabulary, memory, and visual skills. While there are lots of choices, many sets either have too many images or are not sufficiently distinct for young players. We found the following to be graphically clearer for kids to follow. Here are our top picks:

■ Animal Bingo 2007 PLATINUM AWARD
(eeBoo $12.95 ●●●●●) Award-winning ilustrator Kevin Hawkes designed the graphics on this simple matching game. It is more

like a lotto game than bingo, with six animals on each playing board and matching animal chips that players pull from a cloth bag. A game of chance that is good for language development. Still top rated, **I Never Forget A Face Memory Game** ($12.95 ○○○○). Our almost-five-year-old tester proclaimed this the best memory and matching game ever. 3 & up. (212) 222-0823.

■ Feed the Kitty *2007*

(Gamewright $11.99 ○○○○½) Roll the dice and try to keep your mice out of the "kitty" (a.k.a. a bowl). The arrow icon means pass one of your mice to the person on your left; roll the "bowl" icon and in goes one of your mice. Player holding the last mouse wins. Memory, visual discrimination, and turn taking make this a fast, easy game of chance. 4 & up. Still fun, **Hisss,** with snake parts—head, body, and tail that players "build" to collect the most snakes. 4 & up. (800) 638-7568.

■ Spinnerific Bye-Bye Balloons & Animal Pairs Games

(International Playthings $6.99 each ○○○○½) Here is a new spin on concentration. Quick and easy to learn, each game comes with a deck of cards and a domed spinner. Push the dome and it tells what color balloon you must find. In **Animal Pairs** the spinner will tell you to turn over two, three, or four cards and find matching animals. Our four-year-old tester loved beating us every time, and wanted to play again and again . . . the best sign of success. 3–5. (800) 445-8347.

■ Tea Party Game *2007* PLATINUM AWARD

(eeBoo $15 ○○○○○) Our three-and-a-half-year-old tester loved the big playing pieces and the tablecloth that add to the pretend part of this simple game. Players use a spinner to collect the pieces of the tea set needed for their party. There are no skills involved in this luck-of-the-draw game. Graphics are beautiful and the game is on target for the preschool set. **Picnic Game** ($15) uses the same idea with a few ants thrown into the mix! Both are winners! 3 & up. (212) 222-0823.

> ### COMPARISON SHOPPER
> ### Dominoes 2007
>
>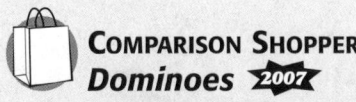
>
> Dominoes are great for developing matching skills that are needed for reading. Some are made with dots for counting, others with images. Either way, they develop visual skills and turn taking. Here are some of the best choices: **WonderFoam Dominoes** (Chenille Kraft $15.49 ●●●●). These oversized foam dominoes with traditional dots were a favorite of our testers. Our tester said that the "chunky play pieces were easy to pick up" and it "was a game he came back to again and again." (800) 621-1261. Very special, **Counting Bugs Dominoes** 2007 (Mudpuppy $14 ●●●●), 28 jumbo reversible dominoes with bug pictures on one side and dots on the back. Also top rated, **Color Dominoes** (eeBoo $12.95 ●●●●). This handsomely designed, sturdy cardboard set of dominoes focuses on colors and matching shapes (stars, moon, train, heart, blueberries) rather than on traditional numbers or dots. 3 & up. (212) 222-0823.

A Word About Electronic Quiz Toys for Preschoolers

For the past few years, we have objected (loudly) to many of these platforms because they did not use real books as a foundation and because the games were really nothing more than drill and practice. We are happy to report that things are changing—you'll find that well known storybooks are now being used, and that the games are more open ended. These toys are attractive to preschoolers, who generally love pressing buttons, making things happen, and working on learning their numbers and letters. That said, preschoolers still learn best through concrete experiences and should have a rich diet of playing games, working on puzzles, and listening to great stories. Here are our top picks:

■ Fridge Phonics Magnetic Letter Set *2007*

(LeapFrog $17.99 ●●●●½) For the 21st-century child, magnetic letters that talk! Put the "magnetic phonics reader" onto the fridge and play one capital letter at a time. They say and sing each letter's name and sing each letter's "sounds." New for *2007*, **Lowercase Letters** ($17.99 ●●●●) that will play on the same platform as the uppercase letters. Add them slowly and have kids match upper- and lowercase letters free-standing on the fridge door. Also new, **Fridge Phonics Word Whammer** ($24.99 ●●●●) Can be used for letter name and sound recognition, but this goes on to directing kids in spelling simple three-letter words and is more age-appropriate for early school years, although it is labeled 3 & up. Still fun, **Fridge Farm Magnetic Animal Set** ($14.95 ●●●●½): five animals, each in two pieces; match front and back, and they say their names. (800) 701-5327.

■ TeleStory *2007*

(Jakks Pacific $34.99) An interactive reading platform that includes an electronic book that plugs into the A/V jacks of any television—no DVD player required. The book can also be used on the go without the TV by using the included headphones. What looked really promising, too, is that kids can follow along with ot without help. So far the titles seem to be pretty licensed fare (Dora, Winnie the Pooh, Sponge Bob). Not ready for testing. (877) 875-2557.

■ Read With Me DVD

(Fisher-Price/Scholastic $34.99/$14.99 each DVD ●●●●●) Nothing short of a breakthrough—because it marries technology with great storybooks! Kids interact with a wireless controller that allows them to "play" real picture books and games on your TV. The DVDs "read" stories or, on play mode, you can interrupt the story to ask questions. Some of the workbook-ish games are rough going for 3s

PRESCHOOL • Three to Four Years

and 4s, but on target for 5s and up. That said, this is a story machine for younger kids and a slow-paced game machine for 5–7s. Packaged with *Where the Wild Things Are*, we suggest *The Little Engine That Could* and *Chicka, Chicka, Boom Boom!* as better choices for 3s and 4s. Does it replace reading with your kids? No. We applaud Fisher-Price for their great book selections. 3–7. PLATINUM AWARD '06. (800) 432-5437.

■ V.Smile

(Vtech $59.99 ●●○) A console that also plugs into the TV and specializes in drill-and-review games that usually borrow from arcade formats. While seven year olds often enjoy reinforcing what they know, the pace of this product is way too fast to "learn" from and certainly way beyond the preschool crowd (its targeted audience). New **Art Studio** and **Dance Mat** were not ready for testing. (800) 521-2010.

Puzzles

A word about puzzles: Preschoolers gradually move from whole-piece puzzles, to simple puzzles that challenge them to see how two or more parts make a whole. For kids with no previous experience, start with five to seven pieces in a frame. Children's skills vary, so take your cue from the child. Some 4s can handle 20 to 30 pieces, while others are still working on 10 to 15 pieces. Large pieces are easier for little hands. A word of warning: with some notable exceptions listed below, many of the wooden puzzles that came our way continued to be badly finished and were rife with splinters.

■ The Very Books Block Puzzle *2007* PLATINUM AWARD

(Mudpuppy $13 ●●●●●) Nine cubes can be turned to create six different images from several beloved Eric Carle books such as *The Very Hungry Caterpillar*, *The Very Quiet Cricket*, *The Very Lonely Firefly*, and others. These images are painterly. Also noteworthy and PLATINUM AWARD-winning in Carle's exuberant style, **1, 2, 3 to the Zoo Great Big Puzzle** ($15 ●●●●●). A 24" x 36" floor puzzle with 24 big pieces. Carle's picture book animals are on their way to the zoo by train. Count the creatures from 1 to 10 and don't forget to find the mouse that is hiding on every train car. 3 & up. Still top rated in this line, **Our World** ($15 ●●●●), an oversized 24-piece floor puzzle (24" x 36") with each of the continents, is illustrated with animals, people, and landmarks. Mudpuppy's storybook puzzles are objects of beauty, celebrating the best in picture book art! They say 3; we'd say more like 4 & up. (800) 670-7441.

■ Beginner Pattern Blocks

(Melissa & Doug $19.99 ●●●●½) Ten wooden scenes are ready to fill with triangles, circles, squares, rectangles and ovals. Part puzzle/part shape sorter, all beautifully crafted with wooden storage box. 2½ & up. (800) 284-3948.

■ Rhyming Words *2007*

(eeBoo $14 ●●●●) Twenty-five puzzle sets of rhyming pairs such as *cake* and *rake*, *house* and *mouse*. Each pair is color coded and illustrations are easily recognizable objects to know and name. Rhyming games are useful for prereaders. 4 & up. Still top rated, **Baby Animals** ($14 ●●●●), pairs of mother and baby animals. We recommend starting out with five pairs at a time rather than the whole set. 3 & up. (212) 222-0823.

■ Lauri Puzzles *2007* BLUE CHIP

(Lauri $7.99 ●●●●●) Lauri's puzzles come with rubber pieces and a pattern printed in the container/tray for beginners to follow. For building confidence, these are the perfect place to start. New for *2007*, a 22-piece **Race Car.** Past favorites include: a 13-piece **T-Rex,** a 16-piece **Farm Scene, Birthday Cake,** and **Airplane.** 3–7. (800) 451-0520.

■ Magnetic Dinosaur Puzzle

(The Orb Factory $14.99 ●●●●) Dino fans will love working with this circular puzzle with magnetic pieces featuring 15 dinosaurs. The puzzle board gives a little hint by showing the skeleton of the dino and the shape of the puzzle piece (a little creepy but a big hit with testers). Puzzle also comes with a huge dino

PRESCHOOL • Three to Four Years

poster full of info. (800) 741-0089.

■ Puzzibilities Sound Puzzles

(Small World Toys $16 each ●●●●●) Six raised pieces are easy to lift, and when they are put back in the puzzle board, each makes a rip-roaring sound. Choose **Wild Animals, Dinosaurs,** or **Under Construction.** 2½ & up. PLATINUM AWARD '05. Also noteworthy, bilingual puzzles: **Colors and Shapes** 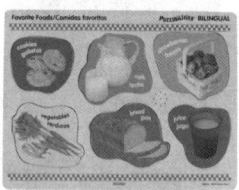 (●●●●), and **Count 1–10** (●●●●). The latter uses nontraditional forms of numbers 9 and 4, which may be confusing for some beginners. Still top rated, **Puzzibilities** (●●●●): nine-piece puzzles with small red knobs (themes: transportation, snapshot wild animals, or community vehicles). (800) 421-4153.

■ Where's My Tail? 2007

(Infantino $12.99 ●●●●) Twenty-two-piece puzzles that develop matching skills as well as language. Front and back ends of 20 animals to fit together. 3 & up. Still top rated, **Alphabet Boat Puzzle** ($12.99 ●●●●): each boat has a letter in upper- and lowercase painted on the side and an object that starts with the sound of the letter; and **I Spy My House Puzzle** ($12.99 ●●●●), with objects in the frame to "spy" in the puzzle. This is more challenging. (800) 840-4916.

Lacing Games

Kids dive right into lacing activities without knowing they're a great way to develop the fine-motor skills they'll need for writing. Our favorites:

Musical Friends and **Fairies of the Field** (eeBoo $14.00 each ●●●●), beautifully illustrated sturdy cards that kids will love to work on. Marked 3 & up, but will be most enjoyed by 4s. (212) 222-0823. New for 2007, **Farm Lacing and Tracing Set** (Lauri $6.99 ●●●●) with pig, horse, sheep, cow, hen, barn, and farmer on a tractor, plus colorful laces for "sewing." (800) 451-0520. **Editors' note:** Alex has introduced attractive new lacing sets that are charming. But the

age labels are misleading. We cannot give them an award since they are labeled for 18 months and 2; these will be right for preschoolers and even kindergarteners who are just gaining the kind of dexterity needed for such activities. This is not a skill important for toddlers and strings around toddlers must be completely supervised.

Science Toys and Activities

Floating a leaf in a puddle, collecting pebbles in the park, making mud pies in the sandbox, watching worms wiggle—these are a few of the active ways children learn about the natural world.

■ Mighty Magnet

(Learning Resources $6.50 ●●●●½) A jumbo 8" horseshoe-shaped magnet that can hold up to four pounds! They also have a set of **Six Mighty Magnets,** 5" horseshoes that can be used for hunting up how many places kids can make them stick ($17.95 ●●●●). 4 & up. (800) 222-3909.

■ Live Butterfly Pavilion

(Insect Lore $29.95 ●●●●) Kit includes a 3'-long windsock-like habitat where ten Painted Lady caterpillars (which they mail to you) are transformed. A coil allows the habitat to pop up, stand on a table, and fold away for future use. Take pictures of the metamorphosis, or encourage your child to draw the changes and keep a log. Great for preschoolers as well as early school years. Company also makes a **Ladybug Land** ($16.95 ●●●●) where you hatch ladybugs! (800) 548-3284.

■ The Mixed-Up Chameleon Maze Board 🏆2007

(Small World Toys $24.99 ●●) This should have been a PLATINUM AWARD winner . . . it's a color matching magnetic toy maze, where you pull small colored balls into the right color spot on the chameleon. Here's the drawback: the magnet isn't strong enough so it's quite frustrating to move the balls about. Really disappointing. (800) 421-4153.

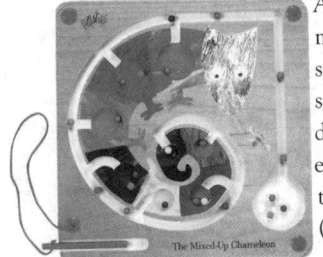

PRESCHOOL • Three to Four Years 107

SMART PARENT TRICK: Give your preschooler a magnet and a sheet of peel-off stickers to put on anything she finds that the magnet sticks to. Or give kids a bag full of household items to sort into two baskets. Have them put all the things that are attracted to the magnet in one basket and all the rest in another.

Garden Work

Preschoolers love the magic of seeing things grow. If you're looking to get a young gardener started, we recommend plastic **Garden Tools** (Little Tikes $2 each for small tools/$13 for a set of three larger tools. (800) 321-0183). **WHAT TO AVOID:** For preschoolers, stay clear of metal tools. An accidental swing in the wrong direction with plastic will not mean a trip to the ER. They also don't have splintery handles as some metal tools do, and won't rust when they are inevitably left outside.

Sand, Water, & Bubble Toys

Sand and water are basic materials for exploring liquids and solids, floating and sinking, sifting and pouring. An inexpensive pail and shovel are basic gear along with a sand mill for sandbox or beach. Older preschoolers will be delighted with a set of turrets and tower molds for building beautiful sand castles—kids will add moat, imagination, and who knows what else! Some other sand tools are also worth considering.

■ Naturally Playful Up & Away Sand Table 2007

(Step2 $79.99 ●●●●½) This oversized table is low enough for older toddlers to stand at and big enough for three or four children to enjoy together. It has a crane that pivots and scoops sand and other treasures. An umbrella provides shade and lowers to cover sand. 2 & up. (800) 347-8372.

TOYS

■ Castle and Bucket Set

(International Playthings $12.99 ○○○○) A castle-shaped bucket doubles as a mold and comes with a watering can, three stout digging tools, and sand/water mill. 3 & up. (800) 445-8347.

■ Car Wash

(Alex $23.99 ○○○○½) After a day in the sandbox, it's tough to deal with the "don't wanna take a bath" preschooler. But this floating car wash with spritzer, conveyer belt, and turning gate might just change some minds. Comes with four little cars and miles of play power. Takes some hand strength and fine motor tuning to operate. 3 & up. (800) 666-2539.

■ Super Spiral *2007*

(Little Tikes $11.99 ○○○) Looks like great fun for the backyard on a hot day, but our testers found that the balls often got stuck in the chute. 3 & up. (800) 321-0183.

Bubbles *2007*

Blowing bubbles has come a long way since the small plastic containers of pink liquid with the small, sticky wand. Leading the way in innovative bubbles is Little Kids with their no-spill containers. New this year, **Super Scoop Bubble Wand** ($3.49 ○○○○), a little drippy but provides a constant flow of bubble solution on the wand. Also fun, their **Little Kids' Super Size Bubble Wand** ($7.99 ○○○○) for super duper bubbles. (800) 545-5437.

> **FREEBIE:** For superlarge bubbles, mix 1 cup of Dawn liquid detergent with 3 tablespoons of Karo syrup in 2½ quarts of cold water. Stir gently. Leftovers (if you have any) need to be refrigerated. Ideal for large groups.

PRESCHOOL • Three to Four Years

Active Physical Play

Active play builds preschoolers' big muscles, coordination, and confidence in themselves as able doers. It also establishes healthy active patterns for fitness, relieves stress, and provides a legitimate reason to run and shout. Agreeing on the rules of the game and taking turns promote important social and cooperative skills.

■ 2 in 1 Hitting Trainer Hit-a-Way Jr. 2007

(Coop Kids $29.99 ○○○○) Our baseball players-in-training can work on their swing with the well designed low-tech hitting machine. The ball is tethered so that you don't have to run after every hit. Be sure to load the base with water for added stability. (760) 931-5733. New for 2007, **ESPN Grow to Pro Baseball** (Fisher-Price $24.99 ○○○○½). Starts as T-ball, converts to pop-up pitch, and converts again to pitch three balls up to 10 feet away. (800) 432-5437.

■ Crawl N Fun BLUE CHIP

(Playhut $25 ○○○○○) Testers giggled their way through this 6'-long tunnel as they crawled along! Also top rated: longer and more spacious **Yellow School Bus, Red Fire Engine,** and a blue **Deluxe Train** engine. These each easily accommodate two kids for pretend fun. 3 & up. (888) 752-9488.

COMPARISON SHOPPER
Basketball Hoops 2007

You really can't go wrong with either the **ESPN Grow To Pro Basketball** 2007 (Fisher-Price $39.99 ○○○○) or the **Easy Score Basketball Set** (Little Tikes $29.99 ○○○○). Both adjust to many different heights to grow with your slam dunker. Here you can go with the best price offered. Both need to be filled with sand or water for added stability. 2 & up. Fisher-Price (800) 432-5437. For big preschoolers, consider the **Adjust & Jam** ($35 ○○○○), a hoop that starts at 4' and grows to 6'. (800) 321-0183.

TOYS

■ 100 Hoops 2007

(LeapFrog $29.99 ★★★★½) Hang this electronic counting hoop on a doorknob, drawer, or chair. Set the counter to count by ones. For older kids, set it to count by 2s, 5s, 10s, or backwards and they are ready to start shooting baskets. Kids can set a goal and the payoff comes with special music. Counts in English or Spanish and, even better, it also has a volume control. 3 & up, up, up. (800) 701-5327.

■ Gertie Balls BLUE CHIP 2007

(Small World Toys $5 & up ★★★★★) Preschoolers need soft, lightweight, easy-to-catch balls that will not bend back a finger or hurt when they hit. Gertie Balls are gummy and soft enough for kids who may be scared of big heavy balls coming toward them. New for 2007, **Supersized Gertie Balls** ($13), really oversized and great fun for this age group and next. 3 & up. (800) 421-4153.

■ Hopping Sport Balls

(Franklin $14.99 each ★★★★) Our testers liked the sports theme of these classic 18" ball hoppers. Comes

as either a basketball, baseball, or soccer ball. Comes with its own air pump. (800) 225-8647. For bigger kids, consider **26" Hoppity Ball** (Small World Toys $21 ★★★★). (800) 421-4153.

■ Jungle Toss Bean Bag Game 2007

(Alex $23.99 ★★★★½) Our three- and five-year-old testers like this so much their mom had to put it against a wall so they wouldn't break anything. It's great for getting little ones up and moving. Throw the five bean bags to get them into the lion's, hippo's, or gator's mouth and score your shots. A little math, a lot of motion! (800) 666-2539.

■ Mini Golf

(Alex $19.99 ★★★★) Our four-year-old testers thought this circus-themed miniature golf set was loads of fun. Comes with two clubs (with foam heads), two balls, and 6 illustrated targets. 3 & up. (800) 666-2539. For a basic plastic set of clubs, **TotSports Golf Set** (Little Tikes $20 ★★★★)

comes with a pull cart, two clubs, and three balls. Says 2 & up; we'd say 4 & up. (800) 321-0183.

> **SAFETY TIP: Do little kids really need helmets? More than 500,000 people are treated annually in U.S. emergency rooms for bicycle-related injuries. Data show very young riders incur a higher proportion of head injuries. A helmet can reduce risk of head injury by up to 85%!**

Wheel Toys: Trikes and Other Vehicles

Preschoolers will still use many of the vehicles featured in the Toddlers chapter. Vehicles with no pedals remain solid favorites. Older preschoolers are also ready for tricycles and kiddie cars with pedals. The battery-operated vehicles that go 5 mph look tempting, but they won't do anything for big-muscle action. Here's what to look for in a three-wheel drive with pedal action:

- Bigger is not better. Don't look for a trike to grow into. Take your child to the store to test-drive and find the right-size trike. Kids should be able to get on and off without assistance.
- Preschoolers need the security of a three-wheeler, which is more stable than a two-wheeler.
- A primary-colored bike can be reused by younger sibs regardless of their gender.
- See Safety Guidelines section for safety standards for helmets.

■ Liberty

(Radio Flyer $120 ᴏᴏ) A classic style spring rocker with plastic horse and yarn mane was difficult to put together, and the frame was so big that you'd need to be more like six or seven to get on it without making a parent wince. Their smaller horse (with safety seat) requires a parent to lift the child in and out to ride and we found that the seat required a pretty slim child. (800) 621-7613. Our prior favorites from Mamas and Papas have lost their US distributor (too bad).

TOYS

Wheeled Toys

■ Ride & Rescue Cozy Coupe — 2007 PLATINUM AWARD

(Little Tikes $79 ●●●●●) A twist on the classic ride-in, comes with firefighter's handheld gizmo for turning on flashing lights and seven siren sounds built into electronic microphone. Still runs on good old-fashioned foot power! Also refreshed, **Tikes Patrol Police Car** ($75 ●●●●) now done in new colors. 3 & up. (800) 321-0183.

■ Fold 2 Go XL Trike

(Radio Flyer $60 ●●●●) Our tall four-year-old tester had trouble with her long legs on other trikes. According to her mom, "The minute I put her on this one, she took off. This one is easy for her to steer and pedal, it's stable because of the wide base at the back, and it folds up nicely . . . the best one yet!" She did note that the parent push bar was not as sturdy as the one on their **Ultimate Family Trike** ($80 ●●●●●) but her daughter found this one easier to ride! Also worth a look, the **Twist Trike** ($60 ●●●●). You can twist the body of this trike from trike to low-to-the-ground "chopper." Our tester enjoyed the dual mode of the trike, although her mom noted that the turning radius wasn't as good as other Radio Flyer trikes. (800) 621-7613.

■ Kiddo Supertrike

(Kettler $80 ●●●●) This gender-proof primary-colored trike has a stroller bar and high back bucket seat (seat belt available), storage bin, and air-filled tires. Well built, this has an adjustable four-position frame for growth. Kettler trikes tend to run small and fit younger preschoolers only. (757) 427-2400.

■ PlasmaCar

(PlaSmart $69.95 ●●●●●) Our testers from ages 4 to 12 could not get enough of this new ride-on which, according to the manufacturer, runs on "inertia, centrifugal force, and friction." Sounds like a lot of serious scientific principles—but this is sheer fun rolled up into one zippy vehicle! There are no pedals, or batteries needed. Rotate the steering wheel and you're off on any smooth surface. One mom suggested the manufacturer should add bumpers to the front and back to protect the walls. 4 & up. PLATINUM AWARD '05. (877) 289-0730.

PRESCHOOL • Three to Four Years

Stand-Alone Climbers

■ **Little Tikes Playground** BLUE CHIP

(Little Tikes $699 ●●●●●) This top-of-the-line climber is part playhouse, part climber. It does not provide the kind of big-muscle climbing, dangling, and jumping that classic monkey bars do, but kids had no complaints. They loved the multiple play areas with mini-tunnel, slides, and platforms for imaginative play. Expensive, but a solid investment. 3 & up. (800) 321-0183. For other climbers, see Toddler chapter.

> **SHOPPING TIP:** Little Tikes suggests using a little liquid detergent or cooking oil on the connecting pieces of their toys if you are having difficulty putting them together.

Playhouses

A playhouse is the ultimate toy for pretend that will be used for years of solo and social play. Kids as young as two love the magic of entering their own domain—being the owner of a space that's scaled to size. Children love opening and closing the door, looking out the windows, or playing with the toy kitchen (in some models). You'll find houses to fit a variety of tastes and budgets.

■ **Naturally Playful Welcome Home Playhouse**

(Step 2 $500 ●●●●●) This oversized 66" high house will accommodate growing children and has bay windows, full kitchen, doorbell, and room for multiple children. "She loves playing peek-a-boo and having her own special space," wrote our tester's mother. PLATINUM AWARD '06. (800) 347-8372.

■ **Endless Adventures Tikes Town Playhouse**

(Little Tikes $200 ●●●●●) An innovative design with four different themed sides on this 55"-tall structure: firehouse/schoolhouse, gas station, grocery store/bank with ATM machine (of course), and a sports wall complete with hoop. For grander housing, consider the **Playcenter Playhouse** ($499 ●●●●), 78" high with kitchen, bay window, deck, slide, and optional ($99.99) swing set. (800) 321-0183.

■ Dive, Dodge 'n Slide Bouncer
2007 PLATINUM AWARD

(Little Tikes $299 ●●●●●) The neighborhood that tested this 16' x 7' x 7' bouncer raved. It requires lots of space but delivers a great deal of play value. "Larger kids were able to enjoy it too," "easy to blow up with built in pump." Kids have to make their way through the obstacle course and then down one of two red slides. As with any inflatable toy, lots of parental supervision is a must. There are larger inflatables in this line (notably a rock wall that looks like fun, but we are concerned about smaller children climbing and potentially falling awkwardly). Still top rated, last year's **Jump 'n Slide** ($200 ●●●●½). 3 & up. (800) 321-0183.

■ Megahouse

(Playhut $39.99 ●●●●) This is one big fabric pop-up playhouse with a roll-up window and a doorway. Five feet tall and almost as wide, this is a big enough play setting for several kids to enjoy. Best suited for indoor use. A good gust of wind would send it flying! We couldn't put it back into its case. (888) 752-9488.

■ My Playhouse/Theatre BLUE CHIP

(Alex $200 ●●●●●) Here is imagination central! A giant 60"-high combo playhouse, puppet stage, and store. Sure to be the focal point of any playroom, this sturdy wood-and-laminated play center is done in Maisy-like primary stripes and dots. It has a shelf for a puppet stage, side-window "ticket" office, front and back curtains, and a working door. 3 & up. PLATINUM AWARD '00. (800) 666-2539.

> **FREEBIE:** For temporary indoor housing, don't overlook the charm of a big cardboard box with cutout windows and door or a tablecloth draped over a table for little campers to use as a tent. A great way to overcome rainy-day cabin fever.

Art Supplies

Markers, crayons, chalk, clay, and paint provide different experiences, all of which invite kids to express ideas and feelings, explore color and shapes, and develop the muscles and control needed for writing and imagination. A supply of basics should include:

Big crayons
Glue stick
Finger paint
Tempera paint
Washable markers
Safety scissors
Colored construction paper
Plain paper
Molding material such as Play-Doh or plasticine

Paints and Brushes

Tempera paint is ideal for young children because of its thick, opaque quality. Watercolors are more appropriate for school-age children. Young children will have more success with thick brushes than skinny ones, which are harder to control. To reduce the number of spills, invest in paint containers sold with lids and openings just wide enough for a thick paintbrush. Buying paint in pint-sized squeeze bottles is more economical than buying small jars of paint that will dry out. Look for both nontoxic and washable labels on any art supplies you buy.

■ Aquadoodle 2007

(Spinmaster $24.99 ●●●●½) Our four-year-old tester looked up and said, "Even if I get it on the floor, it won't show, will it?" Indeed, this is a mess-free and semi-magical oversized mat for drawing with water! Using the "water pen," blue drawings appear on the surface and disappear once they are dry. Great for developing hand and arm movements needed for writing without restrictive lines. New for 2007, a **Sing 'n' Doodle Mat** ($34.99 ●●) that plays Old MacDonald and silly sound effects as you draw. Our testers found it confusing and distracting. Stay with the original—less is more! (800) 622-8339.

TOYS

■ Crayola Color Wonder Paper & Markers

(Binney & Smith $8.99 ●●●●) Our three-year-old tester couldn't get enough of making pictures "appear"! These are washable markers sans color to stain wallpaper and clothing! We prefer the open-ended paper to the coloring book so kids can make their own designs. Forget the new "magic" finger paints; they don't work well because they require more pressure than kids can exert. 2 & up. (800) 272-9652.

COMPARISON SHOPPER
Collage Materials 2007

You can't go wrong with either of these big containers full of craft materials. **Colossal Barrel of Crafts** (Chenille Kraft $39.99 ●●●●●) is like a giant jar of treats in an old-fashioned candy store. But the jar is plastic for safety and loaded with a mammoth supply of pom-poms, craft sticks, beads and string, foam shapes, pipe cleaners, googly eyes, glitter, metallic spangles, cutters, and plasticine. Add glue, scissors, and imagination for many crafty sessions! 4–8. PLATINUM AWARD '02. (800) 621-1261. Similar but with less "stuff" (and also less expensive) is the **Giant Art Jar** (Alex $ 24 ●●●●½). 3 & up. (800) 666-2539.

■ Finger Painting Party 2007

(Alex $20 ●●●●½) Roll up those sleeves and get ready to make squiggles, swirls, and other delicious patterns with the tools that come in this bucket along with six jars of fingerpaint. Assorted tools with chunky handles add new dimensions to the messy whole-hand fun of finger paints! New for 2007, Alex introduced a **No-Mess Finger Paint Tray** ($12.99 ●●●●), which keeps the mess confined to one easier-to-clean-off space. 3 & up. (800) 666-2539.

■ Magna Doodle Color Plus 2007

(Ohio Art $17.99 ●●●½) There's a new twist to your old Magna Doodle. Use one side of the stylus and you get a bluish line; use the other side and you get a reddish line. It says red or blue on the package, but it's neither.

PRESCHOOL • Three to Four Years

Unlike previous color versions, this does erase with three or more swipes of the "eraser" and there is a wide blade tool that can turn the red to blue. But in all honesty, the original **Magna Doodle** ($14.99 ○○○○○) is a BLUE CHIP that works better and remains a classic. 3 & up.

■ Nature Barrel of Beads

(Bead Bazaar $19.99 ○○○○) A huge bucket of wooden beads that are big enough for small hands to string. Includes natural and colored strings, ten wooden charms, and rings for keychains. There are enough packets of colored beads for ten or more kids to use as an activity for a party. They say 3 & up; we'd say more like 4–7. (800) 838-1769.

> **SMART PARENT TRICK: Magic Painting** is great fun. Have child draw on paper with a piece of wax or a white crayon. Then water down a bit of tempera and have child paint over his invisible drawing. Abracadabra! The drawing appears!

Easels

A flat table may still be easier for young preschoolers, since the colors won't run. Older preschoolers are better able to adjust the amount of paint they load on brushes, and many enjoy painting at an easel. Avoid watering down paint; thicker paint is easier to control. Having an easel set up makes art materials accessible whenever the mood moves young artists.

Plastic Easels

Depending on your space and needs, the following are top-rated choices: **Double Easel** (Little Tikes $50 ○○○○) or **Easel for Two** (Step 2 $40 ○○○○); both come with chalkboard on one side. The Step 2 easel comes with magnetic letters that attach to the magnetic board. You can't go wrong with either. Little Tikes (800) 321-0183/Step 2 (800) 347-8372. **Safety note:** While easels can be enjoyed by 2s, the magnets that come with this set are small and can come out of the plastic, so they are unsafe for kids under 3.

■ Crayola Grand Canvas *2007*

(Binney & Smith $69.99 ○○) Our testers all thought this was a great concept but very poorly designed. "Putting it together is not that hard,

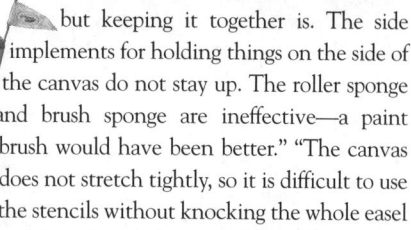

but keeping it together is. The side implements for holding things on the side of the canvas do not stay up. The roller sponge and brush sponge are ineffective—a paint brush would have been better." "The canvas does not stretch tightly, so it is difficult to use the stencils without knocking the whole easel down." Another complained that the whole thing "kept falling over," even with water in the base. For **Crayola Color Cyclone** ($19.99 ✺✺), another family wrote: "the paint came out either in clumps or extremely watery" and the **Super Brush** ($9.99 ✺✺) was also "cool" in concept but did not work well and was "frustrating." (800) 272-9652.

■ SparkArt Creativity System *2007*

(Fisher-Price $99.99 ✺✺) Imagine an easel that tells you what to do! Its so-called "magical technology" "gets kids' creative juices going with audio prompts, inspiring them to use colors, sounds, objects, and the alphabet." In other words, it tells your child what to draw. Where's the creativity in following audio prompts? While the technology may be amazing (it has over 600 word combinations and sound effects), we don't believe that kids should be standing at an easel waiting for instructions. From a developmental point of view, we want kids to be able to explore their own imagination and make their own sounds. Was not ready for testing, but the concept is misguided. 3 & up. (800) 432-5437.

Wooden Easels
■ Super Rolling Art Center

(Alex $129.99 ✺✺✺✺✺) You need a lot of room for this generously sized art cart that has two easels and place for storing your child's creations and supplies in between. The wheels gives this good-looking piece of equipment some portability. It does require a fair amount of assembly, which was not always easy. That said, it looks like it belongs in a Pottery Barn catalog. PLATINUM AWARD '06. If space is an issue, consider the **BLUE CHIP Tabletop Easel** ($40 ✺✺✺✺✺). Folds flat for convenient storage. (800) 666-2539.

Modeling Materials

These totally pliable, unstructured materials invite kids to use their hands and imagination to shape something from nothing. Fun for pounding, stretching, kneading, and rolling—three-

PRESCHOOL • Three to Four Years

dimensional experiences that preschoolers love. Older preschoolers may name what they make after the event. Few set out to design something in particular. The focus here is on the process, and not on making something realistic. Some of our favorite materials:

■ Crayola Model Magic Bucket

(Binney & Smith $11 ●●●●) Our toy testers love working with Model Magic for school projects and just playing around. We recommend the bucket, which comes with four 8-oz. packages, now in natural, assorted, or neon colors. 2 & up. (800) 272-9652.

■ Dough Party

(Alex $17 ●●●●) Comes in a newly designed see-through canister with six bright colors, a roller, cutters, plus a mat to work on. 4–7. (800) 666-2539.

■ Play-Doh BLUE CHIP

(Hasbro $2 and up ●●●●●) Play-Doh is one of those products you either love or hate as a parent. We are long-time fans—the product can be used to build hand strength. 3 & up. (888) 836-7025.

> **FREEBIE: Cookie cutters, rolling pins, baby-bottle rings, and other items around your kitchen make great tools for molding clay.**

Music and Movement

Many instruments for children have such poor sound quality it's hard to call them musical. And kids at this stage are not ready for reading notation. It's more an exploration of sound, rhythm, and movement that makes good sense for preschoolers.

■ Hokey Pokey Musical Skirt 2007 PLATINUM AWARD

(Acting Out $32 ●●●●●) Following the success of last year's winning **Swan Lake Musical Dress** ($32 ●●●●½) and **Nutcracker Sugar Plum Musical Skirt** ($26 ●●●●½) that gave little ballerinas an orchestra they could activate as they danced, this season dancers can turn themselves around as they do the Hokey Pokey in a polka-dotted skirt with motion-activated music. All make magical gifts to stir active imaginative performances. 3 & up. (877) 727-0222.

■ Lollipop Drum BLUE CHIP

(Remo $21.99 ❂❂❂❂❂) Preschoolers can easily hold onto the handle of this 10" lollipop-shaped drum. Makes a pleasing sound, according to both kid and parent testers. Still top rated, **Maracas Shakers** ($5 ❂❂❂❂), small maracas with great sound and perfect fit for little hands. (800) 422-4463.

■ Woodstock Band

(Woodstock Percussion $29.99 ❂❂❂❂½) Beat out that rhythm with this six-piece set with wooden tambourine, recorder, maraca, egg shaker, castanet, and sleigh bell jingler with big wooden handle. Solid-sounding instruments. (800) 422-4463.

MP3s for the Preschool Set *2007*

One of the big trends in toyland this year was musical equipment for the preschool set. We have no problem with the concept—kids love having scaled-down versions of adult equipment. Here's the problem: they didn't fare well with our testers. They got poor marks for the music selection, the quality, or, most disturbing, the volume level. We remain very concerned, as does the League for the Hard of Hearing, with constant noise at high volumes for children of all ages.

Dance Along MP3 *2007*

(Playskool $14.99 ❂❂) The LCD screen on this machine looks crude with only black graphics. Comes loaded with 100 songs to "download," making their own play lists but the music quality is very tinny and unpleasant. (800) 327-8267.

Kid-Tough FP3 Player *2007* PLATINUM AWARD

(Mattel $69.99 ❂❂❂❂❂) Parents can download songs and stories to the preloaded player designed for preschoolers. Add your own music or selections from the Fisher-Price Song & Story Content Store. (Software PC compatible only.) In contrast to the Star Station On-the-Go Player (next page), the FP3 has a volume control and limiter to protect young ears! Comes with a 1.4" LCD screen that displays titles and visual icons for pre-readers. 3 & up. (800) 524-8697.

PRESCHOOL • Three to Four Years

Star Station On-the-Go Player *2007*
(Fisher-Price $19.99 ○) Player comes equipped with headphones and cartridge with three Kidz Bop songs (not our favorite, but we know they're popular). Here's the problem: the on/off dial is also the volume control. If you go the wrong way you can really get blasted. The top volume level is just way too loud. (800) 432-5437.

On-the-Go-Microphone ($14.99 ○○) comes with a cartridge that plays three Kidz Bop songs that our testers found very difficult to sing along with (an adult male and kids singing such odd choices as: "I Like It (like that)," "Absolutely," and "Purple People Eater"). The microphone on its own is wireless (a plus) but in order to get enough amplification, your voice sounds fuzzy. (800) 432-5437.

SMART PARENT TRICK: Use a drum to beat out someone's first name. For example, Sa-man-tha would get three beats. Take turns guessing whose name is being marked.

Preschool Furniture Basics

Table and Chairs
These convenient pieces of basic gear will be used for artwork, puzzles, tea parties, and even lunch. You'll find many choices in both plastic and wood. This is a decorating choice as well as a functional one.

■ My Creative Center *2007* PLATINUM AWARD
(Alex $159.99 ○○○○○) You'll need lots of room for this oversized wooden table (49" x 29.5" d) that eclipses their previous **Super Art Table** ($179 ○○○○○) in size. Rounded on one end with a storage container, this table comes with a chalk surface and a paper roller/cutter and two long benches. Done in the same cheerful primary "Maisy-like" color scheme as the other tables in the collection. For a smaller round table with same style, consider **My First Table** (Alex $100 ○○○○½). 3 & up. (800) 666-2539.

TOYS

Best Travel Toys

Preschoolers can entertain themselves for short periods of time with toys and art supplies. A well loved soft doll or mini-setting with multiple pieces makes for cozy pretend play. At this stage, a piece of home, whether it's a toy or a blanket, is still important. One of the best ways to make time fly is to bring along a tape player with favorite songs or stories to enjoy. For restaurant stops, pack a plastic baggy filled with simple games, cards, or crayons and paper to fill time before the bread basket arrives. Bring along a handful of paperbacks to share and for independent "reading." Here are some of our favorites:

■ Construction Activity Pack

(Lauri $14.99 ●●●●) Loaded for dramatic play, with lacing and tracing figures, workers and tools, 20 stringing pieces, dump truck, roadway and sawhorses. Plenty of activity here for developing fine motor skills along with pretend play. Also top rated, **Fire & Rescue** or **Space Odyssey Pack.** 4–7. (800) 451-0520.

■ Wikki Stix Curious George Activity Books 🏆2007

(Wikki Stix $14.95 each ●●●●) Choose from three different themes (school, birthday, or circus), which come with a colorful pack of wax-coated bendable stix that can be used to trace geometric shapes, follow the dots, do puzzles, trace mazes, or circle the "answers" to questions. A little workbookish, but an entertaining parent/child activity. 3 & up. (900) 869-4554.

■ Matchbox Construction Zone Pop Up Adventure Set 🏆2007

(Mattel $14.99 ●●●●½) Ideal for travel, this slim case, close to 10" square, pops up into a play setting with crane, ramps, and plenty of action for dramatic play. Comes with just one vehicle. This is likely to make a great birthday party gift or take-along toy. Also available in **Harbor Patrol** and **Auto Center** settings. Says 3 & up; we'd say more like 4s and more. (800) 524-8697.

PRESCHOOL • Three to Four Years

■ Penelope Peapod 2007 PLATINUM AWARD

(Penelope Peapod $40 ●●●●●) Imagine a drawstring pocketbook made of a basket with fabric top, that opens into a bassinette and has a sweet little doll inside, dressed in a matching romper. Perfect for pretend on the go. Dolls come in various ethnicities, with cotton prints (including our favorite with Pucci-inspired fabric). Additional dolls also done for Kate Spade (but you'll need to add $10 to the price). (877) 352-1035.

■ Woodkins

(Pamela Drake $12–$25 ●●●●) These wooden "paper" dolls come with fabric choices that stay in place with a "frame" that lifts and closes over the edge of the doll. Also fun, a charming collection of fairies to dress in gossamer and glittery fabrics plus a necklace for the "designer." Perfect for quiet pretend time. 4 & up. (800) 966-3762.

■ Fascinating Creatures 2007 PLATINUM AUDIO AWARD

(Frances England $12.97 ●●●●●) Once in a while a new and distinctive voice arrives with songs that are bright and clever and totally on the mark for young listeners. This is one of those! England's indie-rock style will pass the car test and you may even find yourself tapping your foot and singing along. A keeper! Francesengland.com

Best Third and Fourth Birthday Gifts for Every Budget

Big Ticket $100 Plus	**Set of wooden blocks, trains, playhouse,** or **dollhouse** (various makers), **table and chairs**
$100 & under	**Wooden train set or easel** (various makers) or **Ride & Rescue Coupe** (Little Tikes) or **Color Pixter** (Fisher-Price)
Under $75	**Leapster L-Max** (LeapFrog) or **Stroller** (American Girl) or **Supersized Groovy Girl** (Manhattan Toy)
Under $50	**Lucky the Incredible Wonder Pup**

(Zizzle) or **Thomas & Friends Echo Tunnel** (RC2/Learning Curve) or **Penelope Peapod** (Penelope Peapod)

Under $40   **Bob the Builder Follow Me Scoop** (RC2/Learning Curve) or **Automoblox** (Automoblox) or **Colossal Barrel of Crafts** (Chenille Kraft) or **Pretend & Play Teaching Telephone** (Learning Resources) or **Baby Chou Twins** (Corolle)

Under $25   **Jungle Toss Bean Bag Game** (Alex) or **Pretend & Play Doctor Set** (Learning Resources) or **Lollipop Drum** (Woodstock Percussion)

Under $20   **Bendos My First RC Buggies** (Kid Galaxy) or **Our World** (Mudpuppy Press) or **WonderFoam Dominoes** (Chenille Kraft) or **Fridge Phonics Magnetic Letter Set** (Leap Frog)

Under $15   **The Very Books Block Puzzle** (Mudpuppy) or **Rugged Riggz** (Little Tikes) or **Tea Party Game** (eeBoo)

Under $10   **Bendos** (Kid Galaxy) or **Birthday Cake Puzzle** (Lauri) or **Dora the Explorer Candy Land** (Milton Bradley) or **Model Magic** or **Color Wonder Paper** (Crayola) or **Super Size Bubble Wand** (Little Kids)

Under $5   **Gertie Ball** (Small World Toys) or **Hot Wheels Cars** (Mattel)

PRESCHOOL • Three to Four Years

Books for Preschoolers

Preschoolers are ready now for stories with a lively plot and playful language. Nothing can build a readiness for reading better than a daily time spent reading aloud to your child. Choose books with a playful use of language and pictures with more details to discover. Preschoolers enjoy stories about real children as well as animal stories that are about "children-in-fur"—just one step removed from reality. Encourage your child to retell in her own words the story in a familiar picture book, using the illustrations to guide the telling. Build a little library of books that she can enjoy looking at independently. Our book, **Read It! Play It!** suggests 50+ books and activities for this age group. Look for past winners and current Gold and Platinum winners on our website at Toyportfolio.com. For our PLATINUM AWARD 2007 books, see page 177.

4 • Early School Years
Five to Ten Years

What to Expect Developmentally

Learning Through Play. During the early school years as children begin their formal education, play continues to be an important path to learning. Now more-complex games, puzzles, and toys offer kids satisfying ways to practice and reinforce the new skills they are acquiring in the classroom.

Dexterity and Problem-Solving Ability. School-age kids have the dexterity to handle more-elaborate building toys and art materials. They are curious about how things work and take pride in making things that can be used for play or displayed with pride.

Active Group Play. These early school years are a very social time when kids long for acceptance among their peers. Bikes and sporting equipment take on new importance as the social ticket to being one of the gang. Children try their hand at more-formal team sports where being an able player is a way of belonging.

Independent Discovery. Although these are years when happiness is being with a friend, children also enjoy and benefit from solo time. Many of the products selected here are good tools for such self-sufficient and satisfying skills.

Basic Gear Checklist for Early School Age

- ✓ Sports equipment
- ✓ Craft kits
- ✓ Musical instruments
- ✓ Water paints, markers, stampers
- ✓ Two-wheeler with training wheels
- ✓ Lego and other construction sets
- ✓ Electronic game/learning machines
- ✓ Dolls/soft animals
- ✓ Board games
- ✓ Tape player and tapes

Toys to Avoid

These toys pose safety hazards:
- ✓ Chemistry sets that can cause serious accidents
- ✓ Plug-in toys that heat up with lightbulbs and can give kids serious burns
- ✓ Audio equipment with volume controls that cannot be locked
- ✓ Projectile toys such as darts, rockets, B-B guns, or other toys with flying parts that can do serious damage
- ✓ Superpowered water guns that can cause abrasions
- ✓ Toys with small parts if there are young children in the house

The following is developmentally inappropriate:
- ✓ An abundance of toys that reinforce gender stereotypes; for example, hair play for girls and gunplay for boys

Pretend Play

School-age kids have not outgrown the joys of pretending. They like elaborate and realistic props for stepping into the roles of storekeeper, athlete, or racing-car driver. For some, mini-settings such as puppet theaters, dollhouses, and castles are a preferable route to make-believe. This is also the age when collecting miniature vehicles and action figures can become a passion. Such figures generally reflect the latest cartoon or movie feature. Nobody needs all the pieces, although many kids want

EARLY SCHOOL YEARS • Five to Ten Years

them all. At this stage, owning a few pieces of the hottest "in" character represents a way of belonging.

Dollhouses, Castles, and Other Pretend Environments and Props

Kids are ready now for finer details in house and furnishings. Specialty dollhouse shops and craft stores sell prefabs and custom houses for all budgets. Some of the settings recommended here require construction skills and a great deal of adult involvement. Anticipate that you'll be doing most of the constructing, but then you have a wonderful playsetting for your child.

COMPARISON SHOPPER
Dollhouses

For premade dollhouses, see Preschool chapter, p. 87. For houses you have to construct, Playmobil offers several models: The **Grande Mansion** PLATINUM AWARD '06 ($129.99 ○○○○○) has two stories and a usable attic; this yellow house has an old world charm. Playmobil's **Family Vacation House** ($49.99 ○○○○), smaller than other houses, is relatively easy to put together. Playmobil's **Modern House** ($119.99 ○○○) did not test well; the roof collapses easily! (800) 752-9662.

PLAY TIP: Build these large structures on a board or table that they can remain on. Moving them later is an impossible dream!

COMPARISON SHOPPER
Castles

Playmobil's **Knights' Empire Castle** (Playmobil $179.99 ○○○○○) uses the company's new SystemX, which is designed for shorter assembly time and durability. Comes with a working gate and dungeon and looks like the classic friendly Playmobil settings of years past. PLATINUM

AWARD '06. By comparison, **Rock Castle** ($79.99 ●●●●) has a more sinister feel to it. Suggested add-on, the **Red Dragon** (because you always need a dragon), is sold separately. Projectile cannons sold separately. Also darker in feel than their previous castles is Lego's new **Vladek's Dark Fortress** ($99 ●●●), which comes with catapults. Most kids love the action of projectiles until one hits them. 8–12. (800) 233-8756.

■ **Lego Pirate Ship**

(Lego Systems $39.99 ●●●●●) We tested this with 4- and 5-year-olds and they all loved it, even though most needed help putting it together. While one parent wrote that the "pictorial directions were (blessedly) easy to follow," another complained that their 4 year-old son had a hard time conceptualizing the 3-D instructions. That child put the ship together with his Dad and he liked the poster and extra pieces. "This has been front-and-center since the 5 year-old put it together and is used for storing pirate treasure." Marked 4 & up but will need assistance. PLATINUM AWARD '06. New for , **Playmobil Skull Pirate Ship** ($29.99 ●●●½) is big and showy, but our tester had trouble connecting the deck and hull securely. Kids will need help attaching the "nets" that clamp the ship together, and once done, it will not be convenient for storage. Lego (800) 233-8756 / Playmobil (800)752-9662.

> 🛍 **COMPARISON SHOPPER**
> **Soccer** 2007
>
> Both Playmobil and Lego introduced new soccer sets this year that scored high with our testers. Playmobil's **Soccer Match** ($39.99 ●●●●½) comes with six players with kicking action and an oversized 38" x 26" soccer mat that you build the frame around. Comes with a suggested scoring game, which our testers tried; then they made up their own games.

EARLY SCHOOL YEARS • Five to Ten Years

The **Lego Grand Soccer Stadium** (Lego Systems $49.99/386 pieces ○○○○½) is an updated version that is much improved, with greater stability in the core playing field. The goalies have the greatest mobility and two players are also on slides to cover more of the field. Other players can kick (our testers thought two of them should also be on slides for great coverage). Much smaller and different in feel from Playmobil's—our testers thought both were fun. Younger builders will need help putting both together. 7 & up. Lego (800) 233-8756/Playmobil (800) 752-9662.

■ Zoo

(Playmobil $99.99 ○○○○○) "The Zoo took a long time to build but has plenty of play value," wrote our adult tester. PLATINUM AWARD '05. Also top rated, a **sea lion pool** ($16.99 ○○○○). For construction-minded kids, check out the incredible, large **Crane** PLATINUM AWARD ($69.99 ○○○○○) which moves up, down, and around! One of the coolest toys around. PLATINUM AWARD '06. Previous award-winning **Airport** ($54.99 ○○○○○) and **Fire Station** ($69.99 ○○○○○) have been scaled down in price and size. 5 & up. (800) 752-9662.

Props for Pretend
See Preschool chapter for this year's best costumes.

■ My Picnic Basket

(Alex $20 ○○○○) We liked the sturdiness of this 18-piece set that comes with blue enamelware including plates, cups, spoons, forks, and tablecloth. Great for real picnics or pretend tea parties. 5 & up. (800) 666-2539. For an older child who is ready for more delicate tea sets, consider **Angelina Ballerina Party Time Picnic** or **Tea Sets** (International Playthings $TK & TK ○○○○). 8 & up. (800) 445-8347.

■ Smoby Star Party Duo Mix Set *2007*

(International Playthings $59.99 ○○○○) A set of mikes perfect for American Idol wannabes and host. Unfortunately, very gender specific in pink and lavender. For a solo mike there's **Star Party Micro Star**

($39.99 ●●●●). Both have applause sound effects. 5 & up. For the full disco effect, check out **Smoby Star Party Disco Bubble and Light** ($64.99 ●●●●). You might just need this faceted-mirrored disco ball that turns on a platform with an automatic bubble maker and spotlight. Not exactly a toy, this is more like a piece of equipment to add a twinkle to parties. 5 & up. (800) 445-8347.

Money, Money, Money

Teaching kids about money will cost you. . . . Here are our favorites:

■ Ceramic Allowance Bank

(Creativity for Kids $14.99 ●●●●) A chubby white ceramic pig, ready to paint and hold spare change or allowance. It has an easy-to-pull-out rubber stopper, so kids don't need to break the bank when they want to spend some of their savings! Includes a "chores" booklet with star stickers . . . the idea being that they earn their allowance. We have mixed feelings about paying kids for chores . . . but we do like the idea of encouraging them to save their pennies. In contrast, our testers gave poor ratings to Alex's new **Piggy Ballerina Bank** ($12 ●●●) because the tutu did not go on easily and did not stay. Still top rated, **Wake Up! Alarm Clock** (Creativity for Kids $17.99 ●●●●)—on the theory that time is money!? Both 7 & up. (800) 311-8684.

■ Teaching Cash Register

(Learning Resources $44.95 ●●●●●) A clever way to combine math skills with pretend play! When kids play store with this smart new register they learn to use a calculator, make change, use coupons and charge cards, and even check the customer's credit! It has a pretend scale plus a three-level coin game that asks kids to deposit specific amounts. PLATINUM AWARD '04. (800) 222-3909.

■ YOUniverse ATM Machine

(Summit Inc. $39.95 ●●●●½) After setting the ATM with your name and PIN, you can make deposits and withdrawals and check your balance. The machine recognizes the coins and adds them to

EARLY SCHOOL YEARS • Five to Ten Years

your total automatically. Depositors need to let the bank know how many bills they are putting in or withdrawing. We also love the less complicated **Amazing Money Jar** ($12.99 ●●●●)—coins only, but still very neat. (205) 661-1174.

Dolls

Now's the time when girls often get heavily invested in dolls with tons of paraphernalia. Although 5- and 6-year-old boys often find ways to play with a cousin's or sister's doll or dollhouse, they are more likely to choose action figures for this kind of play. Both boys and girls continue to enjoy soft stuffed animals—the zanier the better.

For many years, the only kinds of dolls around were blonde with blue eyes, but happily, more manufacturers today are creating dolls that reflect our cultural diversity. Here are some of the best:

■ **American Girl Emily** *2007* PLATINUM AWARD

(American Girl $87 doll w/book ●●●●●) In the American Girl collection of dolls, each comes with a book that introduces girls to a bit of history through stories. Emily is in fact not an American girl, but an English girl, an auburn-haired beauty evacuated during WWII from London, to live with Molly and her family. Still top rated, any number of historic dolls from various times in our history. Last year's winner was also an English girl, **Elizabeth,** from a prominent Loyalist family (and best friend of well-known Felicity). She's 18" tall with long blond hair and blue eyes. PLATINUM AWARD 06. Still top rated, **Nellie O'Malley** (Samantha's best friend). PLATINUM AWARD '05. 7 & up. (800) 845-0005.

■ **Barbie** *2007*

(Mattel $15.99 & up) New for *2007*, **Barbie Fairytopia** now transforms . . . are you ready? . . . from a fairy to a mermaid! Just fold down her wings and clamp her fin on and there she is! The big news in Barbie Land is **Let's Dance Barbie!** *2007* ($54.99). Barbie can follow your dance moves or teach you a new move. Comes with a motion-sensor bracelet and shoe clip for the child to wear to direct Barbie's movements. Was not ready for testing. (800) 524-8697.

■ Les Cheries

(Corolle $35 each ooooo) Thirteen-inch dolls that are purposefully not fashion dolls; they are meant to look like girls of today. Think Olson twins before they discovered make-up. New for 2007, **Clara,** redhead with knit sweater, floral skirt and **Camille,** blonde with denim ruffled skirt and pink plaid shrug. We pass on Camille with pink streaks in her hair. 4–8. PLATINUM AWARD '03. See preschool chapter for **Lili** dolls that were a hit with early school girls, as well. (800) 668-4846.

■ Only Hearts Club Collection 2007 PLATINUM AWARD

(OHC Group $15 each ooooo) These 9" dolls have bendable bodies, delicately etched faces, and charming accessories, as well as small books that relate to typical problems of girlhood. Girls will need considerable dexterity to get the little shoes and clothing on and off. Unlike most fashion dolls today, these have outfits that would be acceptable to well-heeled parents and grandparents. They are dressed like girls—not funky streetwalkers in training. Our testers were thrilled with the **Ballet Studio Theater** ($60) and **Stable** ($85). New for 2007, a **Sleeper Sofa** ($19.99)—a first in Toy Land! And **Sleeping Bags** ($9.95), a clever tie-in to a favorite activity, sleepovers! We'd pass on the My Little Pony-inspired **Fantasy Pet** collection (ooo) of plush animals that includes lavender horses and dolphin riding mermaid—just not our thing. (805) 456-0241.

■ Tiptoes Touche Mediterranean Madge
2007 PLATINUM AWARD

(Manhattan Toy $19.99 ooooo) The latest in one of our favorite lines of plush—they're fun and funky, and come with plenty of attitude. You can select Madge the pig in her new polka dot bikini or her pink boa, or Gladys the cow with hot pink shoes. (800) 541-1345.

EARLY SCHOOL YEARS • Five to Ten Years

Puppets and Puppet Stages

Puppets provide an excellent way for kids to develop the language and storytelling skills that are the underpinning of reading and writing. Kids who can tell a story have less trouble writing a story. Many of the puppets and stages in the Preschool chapter will get lots of mileage now. Older kids may also become interested in marionettes or making shadow, stick, or hand puppets of their own.

■ Royal Treatment Theatre Set 2007

(Manhattan Toy $35 ✪✪✪✪) A royal blue brick velour tabletop stage has a foldout platform on which finger puppets can perform. Or consider **Puppettos Theatre Stage** (same idea but done in teal with a red curtain—not our favorite color combo, but that's a personal preference). Top-rated puppets include the new-for-2007 **Finger Puppets Under the Sea,** and **Paws at Play** (dogs and cats) collections. Still top rated: **Metropolicity Community** worker types, **Birthday Belles,** and **Royal Rumpus Finger Puppets.** 4 & up. (800) 541-1345.

■ Puppet Palace

(Enchantmints $100 ✪✪✪✪) Built for hand puppets or marionettes, this wooden 42" x 36" tabletop theater is laminated with graphics, and has six backdrops and a curtain that hides stand-up puppeteers. A handsome choice for 7 & up. (888) 440-6468.

Favorite Hand Puppets

■ Elephant 2007

(Folkmanis $36 ✪✪✪✪½) An oversized floppy-eared grey elephant with a clever two-ring mechanism that raises and lowers the trunk, this full-bodied puppet is sure to take over the show! On a more domestic scale, there is also an adorable 13" brown **Tabby Cat** ($22 ✪✪✪✪), the favorite of one of our toddler testers! Still charming, a 30" honey-colored **Golden Retriever** ($60 ✪✪✪✪). (800) 654-8922.

TOYS

■ Emergency Rescue Squad Puppets BLUE CHIP

(Learning Resources $19.95 set of 4 ●●●●●) Multicultural workers—doctor, paramedic, police officer, and firefighter—with vinyl heads and cloth bodies. 4 & up. (800) 222-3909.

■ Farm Puppets Lacing Craft Kit

(Lauri $12.99 ●●●●½) The latest in the wonderful collection of precut felt puppets (among other themes: bunnies, bugs, circus animals). Kids lace them up and use them for storytelling. Kits come with yarn and big plastic needle for sewing (which develops fine-motor skills kids need for writing). 5 & up. (800) 451-0520.

■ Magical Mystique Puppets

(Manhattan Toy $10 each ●●●●) These hand puppets are perfect for fairy tales: a splendid new dragon, a unicorn, and a pup who's dressed as a wizard. Still top rated, **Knightingtales Puppets** ($10 each ●●●●). You need all five fingers to make the most of these velour royals—a king, queen, and knight. (800) 541-1345.

Track Sets 2007

Here's the deal. Our testers always want these tracks. They do have great novelty appeal but they are not the Hot Wheels that we grew up with—these tracks are much more closed-ended. **Hot Wheels Terrordactyl Track Set** 2007 (Mattel $49.99 ●●●½) Our kid testers like the two interlocking tracks (over 19' of track) so that two players can launch their cars at the same time. The game play is to get the large red Terrordactyl to launch. "For the money, they could have included two cars so that two kids can play as intended," and "it took almost 30 minutes to put together" noted one parent. We liked that kids have to launch their cars manually instead of just watching a battery-operated track move the cars along. If your child has his face directly in front of the Terrordactyl, he could potentially get hit in the face with it. The other big set this year is **Hot Wheels Turbo Glo** 2007 (Mattel $49.99 ●●●½). After counting to ten, you release your special Turbo Glo car (specially designed with lights on its underside) and the car goes through the clear turbo loop (you can see the lights

EARLY SCHOOL YEARS • Five to Ten Years

as it goes through). It did take a certain amount of finesse to get the car to stay on the track. ("We had more fun when it didn't stay on," noted one tester). Concerns: There are projectile parts that fly off, though they do not fly with great force (keep younger siblings away). "We wish it came with more than one light-up car." "Not easy to put together and the instructions are limited." Both 5 & up. (800) 524-8697.

Remote Control Cars and Other Vehicles

■ Air Hogs Hydro Launcher *2007*

(Spinmaster $99.99) Promises to take flight from the water! Marked appropriately 14 & up (the propellers have a potential to really hurt). Equally neat looking, **Air Hogs Helix Helicopter** ($69.99)—a small-scale copter designed for indoor use. If this works, it will be great. No assembly required. 8 & up. Neither ready for testing. (800) 622-8339.

■ Hot Wheels Flashfire *2007*

(Mattel $89.99 ●●●●½) Newest from the Pro Power Series, this oversized RC is an all-terrain racing car that can splash through water, leap over rocks, and thrill young drivers. It has an 8 multi-channel system that means you can race up to 8 cars at once—pretty cool! (800) 524-8697.

■ Mindstorm NXT *2007* PLATINUM AWARD

(Lego System $249.99/517 pieces ●●●●●) This is "so amazing"—the resounding comment we got back from a 13-year old builder and his dad. "You have to build everything and there are lots of pieces but there's a demo which gets you started." Once it's together, you can program it using either a PC or a Mac. "Even cooler, you can use the Bluetooth on your phone!" This next-generation robot uses a new NXT Intelligent Brick ("the brain") and features a powerful 32-bit microprocessor, plus support for USB 2.0. If your tween thinks he's outgrown Legos, bring this home! (800) 233-8756.

■ Morphibians

(Kid Galaxy $24.99 ●●●●½) These snappy vehicles run on land and water! With one-button full-function radio control, these are less complex than some of the larger RCs and have the added fun of float-ablilty. 5 & up. (800) 816-1135.

■ Roboreptile and RS Media 2007

(WowWee $350) RS promises to provide all of your media needs in the package of an interactive robot. Comes with a small color LCD screen on his chest, tweeters and woofer, a USB connector, and music playback; you can input data from your PC. Comes loaded with four personalities (each with its own distinct animations and expressions). Comes with 50 MB of internal memory or you can use an external memory card (additional purchase required). Also new, **Roboreptile** ($120 ○○○○), the latest in the robo "creature" line, 2¼' long, is truly creepy in that Jurassic Park/Terminator kind of way, with 28 remote functions. We found him less responsive to commands than his predecessors. 8 & up. Still top rated, the less expensive earlier versions: **Robosapien** ($99) and **Robosapien V2** ($250); and **Roboraptor** ($100 ○○○○), a scary 32"-long white robotic dino that thinks he's in a scene from "Jurassic Park." He hisses and snaps. For our older toy testers this was cool. (Some little siblings may truly be freaked out by his aggressive nature). 10 & up. (800) 310-3033.

Construction Toys

What Kids Learn from Construction Toys

Builders learn to follow directions and develop dexterity, problem-solving skills, and stick-to-itiveness. Success is not always instant. Updated classics such as **Lincoln Logs** are more appropriate for this age even though they are labeled for preschoolers. **Glueless Snap Models** are also a good place to start for beginning model builders. A relatively open-ended bucket of Legos, such as the **Ultimate House Building Set** ($24.99 ○○○○), works for beginners.

EARLY SCHOOL YEARS • Five to Ten Years

What You Should Know Before You Buy:

- As their dexterity develops, kids can handle smaller pieces and more-complex building sets.

- A variety of building sets is better than just one because building with Legos and K'nex, for example, involve different, but equally valuable, skills.

- Open-ended sets that can be built in multiple ways are a great place to start. As your child becomes a more confident builder, move on to small models.

- Age labels on most building sets are not accurate. If the box says 5 & up and your 5-year-old needs a lot of assistance, the problem is with the label, not your child.

- Working on one of these sets together can be rewarding. Be careful not to take over; break the project into doable parts to build confidence.

- Less can be more, which is helpful to keep in mind. Start with smaller doable sets that help your child learn particular building strategies.

- Girls as well as boys need to develop spatial/visual skills that are built into construction toys.

■ **Airport** 2007 PLATINUM AWARDS

(Lego Systems $79.99/700 pieces ●●●●●) You can't go wrong with any of the new airport/plane sets from Lego—they're all Lego at its best in terms of design. Really depends on what size plane you want and how much you like helicopters.
The **Airport** set is wonderful, comes with a passenger plane, control tower, and baggage truck. Our testers loved the see-through ramp to the plane and the revolving door. 5–12. The **City Airport** ($89.99/863 pieces ●●●●●) comes with two helicopters, a smaller plane, control tower, and vehicles. Marked 9 & up. **Passenger Plane** 2007 PLATINUM AWARD ($39.99/401 pieces ●●●●●) is fun to put together down to the beverage cart, swivel chairs, and cockpit controls. The age label 5–12 is misleading on both this set and the Airport. You'd need to be an experience Lego builder to do this on your own—although we agree that 5s would love to play with this plane after putting it together with a parent. For a chunkier plane,

look at **Airport Action** on page TK. The **City Hospital** ($49.99/377 pieces ❍❍❍❍) also has a lot of play value after it's built, with building, helicopter, and ambulance. For race fans, you'll want to bring home the **Lego Competition Racers** set ($64.99/573 pieces) that features a Ferrari, pit stop, and all the props for race day. 8 & up. (800) 223-8756.

■ Prehistoric Planet Dinosaur Fossils T-Rex 2007

(Toysmith $19.99 ❍❍❍❍) Much like their original sets, but now the pieces have a laminated design instead of plain wood. We tested the 40"-long **T-Rex** (watch out!). This is way too hard for 5s & up (as marked), but a good parent/child project. 9 & up. Still one of our favorites (but again needs parental help), **B.C. Bones Empire State Building** ($19.99 & up ❍❍❍❍) one of a series of stunning wooden structures that includes the Eiffel Tower and Golden Gate Bridge. The company has updated their instructions, which we found to be an improvement but still not enough for the starting age on the box. (800) 356-0474.

■ Star Wars 2007

(Lego Systems $34.95 & up) For Star Wars fans there are several new kits worth noting: **Jabba's Sail Barge** ($74.99/781 pieces ❍❍❍❍): Our 11-year old tester thought the age label (8–12) was off—you'd need to be older to do this kit. He liked the toy, but had tough comments for the directions: "pictures were too dark on the instructions and that really threw off some of the building." For the hard-core Star Wars/Lego fan, consider the **Imperial Star Destroyer** ($99.99/1366 pieces), and of course you'll need the **B-wing Fighter** ($34.99/435 pieces) to go along with that! (800) 223-8756.

■ K'nex Vertical Vengeance Coaster 2007

(K'nex $59.99 & up ❍❍❍) Here is the latest twist on a K'nex roller coaster. This one is over 5 feet high, with a motorized chain lift that takes two cars to the top—where they zoom down the loops and spiral turns of 33 feet of track. Our crack K'nex testers gave the directions very poor ratings. Ages 10 & up. For younger K'nex builders, **Light ups! 30 Models Kit** ($29.99) looks challenging with rods that light, but not available for

EARLY SCHOOL YEARS • Five to Ten Years

testing; also **Gear Action Building Sets** ($29.99 ●●●) that have gear-driven motion; these work, but directions are not clear. 7 & up. (800) 543-5639.

■ Gears! Gears! Gears! BLUE CHIP

(Learning Resources $20/$40 ●●●●●) These open-ended sets develop problem-solving skills as kids make their own moving machines with plastic gears. Our testers preferred the big set of gears to many of the newer themed sets. **Wacky Wigglers** ($39.95 ●●●½) got high marks from our 6-year-old tester who loved its big teeth, motorized glowing parts, and glow-in-the-dark eyeballs. He loves how it moves! We found it quite ugly. 5 & up. (800) 222-3909.

COMPARISON SHOPPER
Magnetic Building Sets

We love these open-ended magnetic sets. Put one on the coffee table and everyone will take a turn! Shop around because we found prices do vary. You want to bring home at least a medium-sized set (they range from $25 to $35). You won't go wrong with any of the basic sets of the following brands: **Magz-x** (Progressive Trading ●●●●) Our testers gave high marks to their unique "x" design. (800) 903-6249. **Supermag** (Plastwood ●●●●) has thinner and more tapered rods than most. Our testers, at first excited by their new model sets, gave them a so-so review: "Once you built the Ferrari the wheels really didn't work well enough to drive around and it felt like it was going to fall apart. We like the originals better!" (800) 770-9550. **MagStruction** (Educational Insights ●●●●) These sets come with plastic panels in a variety of sizes and shapes. 6 & up. (800) 995-4436.

■ Mag XL Magformers
2007 PLATINUM AWARD

(Rainbow Products $16.99–$27.99 ●●●●●) Here's the newest fun in magnetic toys! Choose a set of either 14 or 30 geometric squares and triangles that can be set down on a flat surface. Give them a lift and—abracadabra—you have a 3-D ball that clicks together! Kids will have fun exploring the countless ways to invent new connections and constructions. Safe enough to leave out on the coffee table with no small magnets to worry over. This will entice grownups as well as kids. 5 & up. (541) 826-9007.

■ Tall Stacker Pegs Building Set 2007

(Lauri $40 ●●●●½) Our tester was not sure at first about this toy, an unusual combo of big chunky pegs with crepe rubber shape pads with peg holes. Kids can build horizontally as well as vertically. Our tester wrote, "In my kindergarten class, the children . . . didn't seem to tire of it . . . I also loaned it to friends with children who are 5 and 7 . . . they absolutely loved it!!! They kept building hotels, etc." This unusual construction set builds eye-hand coordination along with open-ended creative designing. Set has 100 pegs, large base, and 17 mats in varying colors, sizes and shapes. 4 & up. (800) 451-0520.

■ Quadrilla

(HaPe $49.95 & up ●●●●●) This line of imported marble run toys caught our attention for their design (they are beautiful). An unusual funnel-shaped piece is the center post of both the **Basic Set** ($49.95) and the big **Twist Set** ($159.95). Their **Rail Set** ($139.95) is also a beauty, with releases that add surprise motion. The first batch of these sets had some rough pieces that impeded the marble from rolling, but this issue has been addressed. If you got one of the old sets, exchange it. PLATINUM AWARD '06. (800) 661-4142.

Games

Classic and New Games

Now's the time when kids really begin to enjoy playing games with rules with both friends and family. Of course, winning is still more fun than losing, and playing by the rules isn't always easy. That's the bad news. The good news is that many of the best board games are both entertaining and educational. Many games can improve math, spelling, memory, and reading skills in a more enjoyable way than with the old flash card/extra workbook routine. Game playing also builds important cooperative social skills.

For 5s and 6s, now's the time for classic BLUE CHIP games such as:

EARLY SCHOOL YEARS • Five to Ten Years

Parcheesi	Dominoes	Chutes and Ladders
Checkers	I Spy Bingo Lotto	Pick-up-Sticks
Uno	Trouble	What's My Name?
Connect 4	Lite-Brite	

For 7s, 8s, and up, try classics such as:

Battleship Bingo	Boggle	Chess
Chinese Checkers	Clue	Life
Mancala	Monopoly Jr.	Operation
Othello	Pictionary Jr.	Scattergories Jr.
Scrabble	Sorry	Twister
Upwards Quarto!	Yahtzee	

Active & Group Games

■ Cosmic Catch *2007* PLATINUM AWARD

(Hasbro $24.99 ●●●●●) A great game for the whole family! Everyone wears a different colored band on their hands and the ball then identifies each player by passing it around once. Our favorite game mode is much like Simon Says—the ball calls out the color that it should be passed to next. If you make a mistake, the game is over. There are more challenging games, in which you have to break the "code" the ball has in mind. 7 & up, but will also be enjoyed by older siblings and family members. 2–6 players. (888) 836-7025.

■ Scavenger Hunt for Kids *2007*

(Pazow $6.98 ●●●● ½) Here's a great card game for a play date, birthday party, or sleep-over. Sure, you can write your own cards for a scavenger hunt; in fact, this comes with some blanks for that purpose. But this comes ready-made with a basic game, a race version, and a team variation. There are three items on each card and players must find all of them. Bonus points are also awarded for the first to put the found objects away. Designed for 8 & up. (415) 885-5006.

Zooreka *2007*

(Cranium $16.99 ●●●● ½) Kids build their dream zoos by amassing resources and trading them in for habitat cards such as Elephant Alley, Penguin Peninsula, or Hippo Hideaway. The first one to get four habitats wins! Our testers said, "This is great!" 8 & up. Still top rated, **Family Fun Game** ($19.95 ●●●●½). Designed for teams of adults and kids to play together, using visual memory, creativity, facts, cooperation, and communication skills. 7 & up. Also still top rated for younger players, PLATINUM AWARD-winners **Balloon Lagoon** ($19.99 ●●●●●, 5 & up) and **Cranium Cadoo for Kids** ($19.99 ●●●●●) 7 & up. (877) 272-6486.

Beginner Games

■ Pandabo

(HaPe $9.95 ●●●●●) Beautifully crafted, this is a balancing game with a wooden panda holding up round, half-round, and square rods. Fine motor skills help as players take turns trying not to be the one who upsets the stack. New for *2007*, **Pisa** ($17.99 ●●●●½). Construct a tower with colored rods between disks of wood. Roll the colored die, remove a rod of that color; but watch out, or the whole tower will fall! Harder than Pandabo. They say 4 & up, we'd say more like 6 or 7 for both. (800) 661-4142.

■ Storefront Bingo

(eeBoo $14 ●●●●●) Each playing board is a different store. Dealer draws a picture tile and names the object; player who has the store for that item calls out name of store. Winner is first to match and fill card pictures. PLATINUM AWARD '06. Also new, **Life on Earth Matching Game** ($12.95 ●●●●), a concentration-style matching game with pleasing images of birds, snakes, kangaroos, and other earthly creatures. Also top rated, **Candy Matching** ($12.95 ●●●●) with yummy-looking candies to match. All 5 & up. (212) 222-0823.

■ Zingo! Heroes *2007*

(Thinkfun $16.99 ●●●●) Updated with a superhero theme, this is a fun variation on Vingo. Each player gets a card with Marvel comic heroes such as the Thing and the Hulk. The dealer pushes down on the superhero tile dispenser. Be the first to see a match and the tile is yours. Will appeal to boys—quick to learn and to play. 4 & up. Thinkfun has also added the Marvel license to other past award winners including **Hopper Heroes** ($16.99 ●●●●) and

EARLY SCHOOL YEARS • Five to Ten Years

City Crossing, now with Spiderman ($16.99 ●●●●). Still top rated, last year's **Toot and Otto Game** ($7.99 ●●●●), a fun variation on Connect 4. (800) 468-1864.

Drawing Games
■ Doodle Tales *2007* PLATINUM AWARD

(Cranium $16.95 ●●●●●) Players are shown a picture with a missing image and asked to draw what they think fits best on their secret doodle pad. The judge then redistributes everyone's drawings and spins the "caption wheel." All players have to finish captions such as: "While we were on vacation" or "late last night . . ." The judge chooses her favorite creation (very subjective but everyone gets to be the judge!). 8 & up. (877) 272-6486.

■ Luck of the Draw *2007*

(Gamewright $19.99 ●●●●) Our testers enjoyed playing Luck of the Draw, the newest "drawing" game on the market. As with most of the games in this genre, you have to draw an image as dictated by the cards, but here in a fun twist everyone votes on the different categories when judging all the drawings: "neatest," "strangest," "most detailed." 10 & up. Younger players will prefer **Who? What? Where?** (see review below). (800) 638-7568.

■ Who? What? Where? Jr.

(Pazow $19.95 ●●●●●) Each player takes a *who*, a *what*, and a *where* card, which combine to ask you to draw a certain image—Abraham Lincoln fishing in Paris, for example. Players get points for guessing each other's drawings. A fun family game for 7 & up. A follow-up to the original PLATINUM AWARD-winning version for 12 & up. (415) 885-5006.

Visual Discrimination and Logic
■ Chaturanga

(Front Porch Classics $44.95 ●●●●●) Our older testers loved this Indian game, said to be the earliest form of chess. It's a strategy game with an element of chance, as players roll wooden dice and play one-on-one or in teams. They say 8 & up—we'd say more like 10 & up. PLATINUM AWARD '06. Also noteworthy, a Bookshelf version of **Raceway '57** (PLATINUM AWARD '06). Our players did not love the design or play pattern of the new **Wordspot** (ooo); "there are more exciting word games like this." (206) 826-3202.

■ Da Vinci's Challenge

(Briarpatch $24.99 ooooo) For 2–4 players, this is a truly challenging game where the object is to create ancient patterns on the pre-printed circular game board. Each pattern you create has different point values, but of course there is a twist. Your opponents can block your patterns. "The game became more interesting as more pieces were put on the board and sometimes a bigger pattern emerges when you're not paying attention!" PLATINUM AWARD '06. They say 8 & up, we'd say more like 10 & up. The connection to Da Vinci? He studied the Egyptian symbol called the Flower of Life. (800) 232-7427.

■ Ringgz 2007 PLATINUM AWARD

(Blue Orange Games $19.95 ooooo) A strategy game that becomes more interesting the more you play it. The idea is to capture as many territories on the board as possible by having the "majority of color" on any given territory. You place your colors down by placing either a colored disc (which captures the entire space) or rings of color. The added difficulty: you can only add your color to an adjacent space that already has your color, which means you can quickly be blocked off from adding any pieces. All wood. 8 & up. (415) 252-6372.

■ Wallamoppi 2007 PLATINUM AWARD

(Out of the Box $21 ooooo) Here's a clever variation on the classic game of Jenga. Players must remove their dark or light wooden playing pieces from a pyramid and add them to a tower on top of the pyramid. Wait, there's one more thing! Do all of this before a marble races down a runway into the wooden storage box. Not easy! A quick two-player game that builds dexterity and strategy skills. 8 & up. (616) 844-5263.

EARLY SCHOOL YEARS • Five to Ten Years

Word Games
For 5s & up

■ Curious George A B See Game 2007

(Rose Art $12.99 ○○○○) Curious George is just an icon on the game boards of this "I spy" style game. Players take turns turning two cards, a letter and color card. Then players all race to find the color of that letter on the playing boards. Flip the boards and players must find objects that start with that letter. They say 4 & up, we say just right for kindergarteners and 1st graders working on letter sounds and visual discrimination. (800) 272-9667.

■ 4-Way Spelldown!

(Cadaco $19.99 ○○○○○) Roll the two "letter" dice, then try to make a word with the letters thrown and as many of the 10 letter keys already on the playing board. For example, if you roll a "t" and an "o," and you have a "y" and an "s," you can spell "toys." The first to flip all of their keys wins. Marked 6 & up, but we'd say more like 8 and up. PLATINUM AWARD '05. (800) 621-5426.

■ Pick Two Deluxe & Bananagrams 2007

(Outset Media $19.99 ○○○○½ & Bananagrams $14.95 ○○○○½) Both of these games are a version of "speed scrabble," in which players build their own word grid and try to be the first to use up their letters. When a player uses all letters she shouts, "Pick Two!" or "Peel!" and others must take two or three letters. Either is a fun word game. Pick Two tiles have number values, so there's more math involved in scoring. Otherwise they are pretty much the same. We do like the banana-shaped bag for take-along play. www.outsetmedia.com or www.bananagrams-int.com.

■ You've Been Sentenced! 2007

(McNeil Designs $24.95 ○○○○½) Forget sentence diagrams. This is much more fun! Players take 10 cards and have to use as many as possible in a sentence. Cards have famous names; places; and places plus verbs, adverbs and adjectives. No grammar words are used, but good grammar must be used and other players can judge the sentences. Good family fun for kids 8 & up. www.youvebeensentenced.com

Top-Rated Card Games

Aside from a deck of cards for a fierce game of Rummy, War, or Old Maid, don't overlook deck-specific classics such as **Uno** or **Mille Bourne.** Here are other card games to play that are fun and quick and even have some learning power built in:

■ Fuddy Duddy 2007

(Let's Play Games $6.99 ●●●●½) Quick and easy, players must collect a run of one color, 1 to 4, or a run of "duds" that have no color. 8 & up. (856) 988-1980.

■ Game Night 2007

(Chronicle $24.95 ●●●●) Okay, if you know how to play all the card and dice games in the book, you don't need this set. But if you are like most of us, this deck of cards, dice and cup, score board, stickers, and most important of all, game book, explains and allow you to play 11 games such as Crazy Eights, Hearts, Rummy, Hooligan, Snakes, and others. 6 & up.

■ Thing-a-ma BOTS 2007

(Gamewright $5.99 ●●●●½) Players turn over cards and name the funny looking robots. Others must remember the names others give and say that name when they recognize a matching robot that is turned up. Person who calls out name of match takes the stack and play continues. A quick 12-minute game that calls for listening, looking, and remembering. Kids will have less trouble coming up with silly names than most self-conscious adults. 6 & up. **Match of the Penguins** ($9.99 ●●●●) is also a matching game, but the fine differences are much tougher to spot. (800) 638-7568.

■ Ugly Doll 2007 PLATINUM AWARD

(Gamewright $9.99 ●●●●●) This is like a disorderly game of concentration. Do not place the cards in neat rows. Spread all 70 out on the top of the table and turn three at a time. Do not turn them back down. Next player turns three over. First person to spot three that match calls out, "Ugly" three times and takes them. Silly, but fun and calls for speedy visual discrimination. 6 & up. Game based on **Ugly Dolls** ($20 each ●●●●), Japanese animation-inspired dolls (created in Brooklyn!). Very quirky—not going to be everyone's cup of tea, but fun. (800) 638-7568.

EARLY SCHOOL YEARS • Five to Ten Years

■ Whoonu

(Cranium $16.95 ●●●●●) It's all about knowing the people you are playing with; players take turns at being the "Whoozit" and others get points by guessing what objects named on the playing cards the "Whoozit" likes best. Even testers who do not like board games love this card game for three or more players. PLATINUM AWARD '06. Still top rated, **Zigity** ($12.95 ●●●●). Visual discrimination and word and number play are all part of the fun. 8 & up. (877) 272-6486.

Geography Games

■ Borderline

(Borderline $9.95 ●●●●) Whether you play with the **USA** or new **World Edition,** here's a painless way to make maps fun! The object is to get rid of all your cards, but you can only put cards down on a card that "borders" the state, body of water, or country in your hand. If you don't know, flip your card for a map that shows the borderlines. A no-tears-or-fears geography game! 8 & up. (800) 641-9996.

■ Great States

(International Playthings $20 ●●●●) This U.S.A. map game includes a board and cards that help young readers learn their state capitals, birds, flowers, and landmarks. What we really liked is that you use the map to find the answers—you're not expected to know them all already. Older players will enjoy playing with the timer, but it's not essential. 7 & up. We'd pass on the **Junior** edition, which doesn't work as well as the original. (800) 445-8347.

■ The Scrambled States 2

(Gamewright $6 ●●●●) There are 50 state cards, each with four different attributes for that card (region, population, land mass, and color). Fifteen cards are placed face up, one card from the draw pile is turned over. The first player to "slap" one of the 15 cards that has a shared attribute with the face card, wins that round. A fun way to introduce kids to geography. Some parents may find it light on content, but it's a good way to get the subject introduced in a nonthreatening manner. 6 & up. Still recommended, the board edition. (800) 638-7568.

Math Games and Equipment

■ Buy It Right Shopping Game

(Learning Resources $19.95 ●●●●½) Making change is not always easy for kids who don't get to handle more than their milk money. This game involves a lot of buying and selling and some flexible thinking. Kids roll three numeral dice and decide whether they want to call a 4, 2, 1, $4.21, or $1.24 . . . a choice that depends on whether they are buying or selling. Unlike most shopping games, which are aimed at girls, this is a gender-free game. 6 & up. 7 & up. (800) 222-3909.

■ Combo King *2007* PLATINUM AWARD

(Gamewright $14.99 ●●●●●) Our testing family thought this was a kinder, friendlier form of Yahtzee. The cards you draw determine what kind of roll you need to get in order to win the round (e.g., three 5s, two 3s). Some dice challenges invite everyone to compete (e.g, first person to roll a four wins). Not difficult to learn and fun to play. You win chips for winning the rounds (so there is a poker-like element to the game as well); first player to make all their combos is the Combo King. 8 & up but you'll need an adult. (800) 638-7568.

■ Highrise *2007* PLATINUM AWARD

(Fundex $29.99 ●●●●●) Here is an all-new twist on dominoes—a 3-D game with 36 dominoes stacked on top of each other. Matching is done on two adjoining dominoes below. Easy to learn, quick to play, and fun! Calls for seeing spatial relationships, not just simple matching skills. 8 & up. (800) 486-9787.

■ Math Dash *2007*

(Learning Resources $24.95 ●●●●½) This is like Scrabble with numbers instead of letters. Players use tiles to make math equations on the crossword-style grid. Each time a player completes an equation he calls out, "Take three!" and others must take three more tiles. Object is to be the first to use up all your tiles. Fast-paced fun that can be played by kids at differing skills levels. 6 & up. Also new for *2007*, **Head Full of Numbers** ($14.95 ●●●●½). Like Boggle with numbers, players roll six dice and toss for all to see. Players write as many equations as possible using those numbers. 7 & up. (800) 222-3909.

EARLY SCHOOL YEARS • Five to Ten Years

■ Number Chase 2007

(Playroom $8 ●●●●½) Put the numbers cards out from one to fifty (that alone is a good learning task for 6s and 7s). One person thinks of a secret number. Other player turns one card over at a time and asks question that helps discover the secret number. A good game for learning number value and sequencing. 6 & up. (866) 999-9654. www.playrooment.com.

■ Tangoes Jr. 2007

(Rex Games $25 ●●●●½) A handsome new game based on Tangrams, the classic geometric puzzle game. Seven puzzle pieces with magnets inside fit into a tray that stores under a magnetic playing board. There are two levels of play. Level one cards allow for matching geometric shapes on the card; level 2 shows only a silhouette that child builds on. So this grows more challenging. Excellent for travel or home. They say 4 & up; we'd say save this for 5–8. (800) 542-6375.

■ Uno Spin 2007 PLATINUM AWARD

(Mattel $15.99 ●●●●●) Right off the bat, we loved the sound of the click play board as it spins. The spinning board adds interesting twists to the game (as you play the regular game of trying to discard all of your cards), including trading your hand with another player, showing all your cards to your opponents, or a variation on war. 7 & up. (800) 524-8697.

■ 4-Way Countdown

(Cadaco $19.95 ●●●●●) The object is to be the first player to turn over all ten of your pegs by rolling dice. Players may add, subtract, multiply, or divide the numbers they roll in order to get the number they need. 6 & up. PLATINUM AWARD '05. (800) 621-5426.

■ Mad Math BLUE CHIP

(Patrix $22.95 ●●●●●) If math facts are a source of tension in your house, here are two games for working on those skills. Mad Math has a self-correcting board with addition facts on one side and multiplication on the other. Your goal is to collect three spaces by rolling the dice and finding the corresponding math fact on the playing board. New for 2007, **Delicio** ($18.99 ●●●●), a clever memory game that teaches food families (in French and English). (888) 834-2380.

TOYS

■ Old Century Shut-the-Box

(Front Porch Classics $49.95 ●●●●●) Here's a handsome wooden chest with numbered tiles that players flip after they roll the big wooden dice. Object is to turn over all the tiles or to have the lowest number of points left when you can no longer make a move. There's room for flexible thinking here since a roll of 7 and 2 means you can flip any combination of 9. Fun for reinforcing addition and place value. 8 & up. PLATINUM AWARD '04. (206) 826-3202.

■ Rapido

(HaPe $17.95 ●●●● ½) An elegant sequencing game. Players compete to pick up colored wooden marbles in special cylinders matching the pattern on their playing paddle. Seeing the pattern and responding quickly calls for good eye-hand coordination and memory. Fun quick rounds for 2–4 players. They say 4 & up, but we'd say more like 5–8. (800) 661-4142.

■ Roll 'n Multiply 2007

(Emines $24.99 ●●●●) Our testers agreed this is a good way to work on multiplication facts. Roll the dice and multiply, then take the disk with that number and place it on the board. Your objective is to get four of your color tiles in a row while blocking your opponent. Beginners check answers with multiplication table—more advanced players must multiply without the table. (408) 247-3298.

■ Sudoku 2007 PLATINUM AWARD

(Briarpatch $19.95 ●●●●●) The object of this seemingly simple game is to put all the numbers in order from one to nine in a nine grid board. But this is a real brainteaser that calls for logic, problem solving, and patience. Unlike the book versions with lots of erasing, this elegantly designed board has Scrabble-like playing pieces printed in red on one side and black on the other. Set up the puzzle with red side chips and solve with black side showing. Comes with booklet of 100 puzzles waiting to be solved. Addictive! 7 to 77+. (800) 232-7427.

PREVIOUS WINNERS FOR SOLVING MATH PROBLEMS: Practicing simple addition and subtraction: **Sum Swamp** ($14.95). Help

EARLY SCHOOL YEARS • Five to Ten Years

with fractions: **Pie in the Sky** ($12.95 ●●●●). Telling time: **Tick, Tac, Tock!** ($14.95 ●●●●). (800) 222-3909.

Math Manipulatives

Concrete materials give kids a greater understanding of counting and calculating. Don't rush to take these materials away from kids. They help make the transition to abstract thinking easier. A BLUE CHIP choice is **Unifix Ready for Math Kit** (Didax $12.95 set of 100 ●●●●●). Beginning math students use these cubes, book, and stickers for understanding early math concepts. We'd recommend pairing them with their activity books. (800) 458-0024.

■ Talking Clever Clock

(Learning Resources $34.95 ●●●●½) Hands down, the best electronic clock for teaching kids how to tell time. Our nine-year-old tester had given up on ever learning how to tell time—but within minutes he was having fun using the clock that has self-checking features with both digital and analog clock faces. 5 & up. (800) 222-3909.

Math Electronic Quiz Machines

Most math-quiz machines are like electronic flash cards—good for picking up speed, but if your child doesn't have the basic concepts down, these machines won't help. **What to Avoid:** many machines require that two-digit answers be entered with tens first. This is contrary to the way kids are taught, especially when regrouping is involved, so machines may be confusing. Our best advice: try them before you buy.

■ Talking Math Mat Challenge

(Learning Resources $29.95 ●●●●½) Kids step on this talking mat to answer math quizzes programmed at two levels of difficulty. Level One asks kids to find the numeral named and do simple addition and subtraction. More fun than flash cards, but not that different in content. It's for kids who are ready for drill. Labeled 4–7, most fours will do only the numeral game. Far more appropriate for mid-first and second graders. Forget the newer **Factor Frenzy** (●●●) and **Light 'N Strike Math** (●●●). Both require too many steps to enter an answer—totally frustrating. We passed on the **Alpha-Bug Step 'n Spell** (●●●), which became too difficult too quickly and was not especially responsive. Also, testers gave the new-for-2007 **ABC Chalk Talk!** ($39.95 ●●) thumbs down because it is "buggy." Players correctly identified "c" as the first letter of cup, but were told repeatedly that they were wrong. The tone of the machine isn't mean but isn't very pleasant, either. (800) 222-3909.

Other Electronic Equipment and Learning Tools

■ Word Whammer Fridge Phonics 2007

(LeapFrog $24.99 ●●●●) Kids can create more than 325 three-letter words with magnetic letters that speak and sing. This is step beyond the original **Fridge Phonics Letters Set** (see Preschool), which plays one letter at a time. **Word Whammer** is played with three letters to help kids learn to blend sounds and make words. It includes single letter names and sounds, plus word hunt games with rhyming words. Some 4s may be ready, but this is really a better game for 5–7. (800) 701-5327.

■ FLY Pentop Computer

(LeapFrog $99 ●●●●●) Truly an innovation in electronic learning toys! FLY is a computer in a pen that works with special paper to create a variety of options: a working calculator that you draw, a translator (great for beginner language students), and we loved the musical keyboard you can draw and then play on your paper. There are also games that involve special baseball trading cards. All very George Jetson . . . will appeal most to 'tweens. PLATINUM AWARD '06. New for 2007, **Alegbra** and **Writing** on the educational side and **Sudoku, Harry Potter,** and **Totally Stumped** on the game side. Not ready for testing. (800) 701-5327.

■ Leap Pad Plus Writing Learning System

(LeapFrog $39.99 ●●●●) We were delighted that many Dr. Seuss classics, such as *Fox in Socks* and *One Fish Two Fish*, have been adapted for this platform or the Leap Pad. Unfortunately, this year there were only new licensed titles (**Bratz, Madagasacar,** etc.). We still believe this is a lost opportunity of bringing great literature together with innovative technology. Kids who are learning to write their letters and numbers will like this electronic workbook with stylus

EARLY SCHOOL YEARS • Five to Ten Years

that really writes. Although the toy is marked 3 & up, the skills are more appropriate for 5s & up. (800) 701-5327.

> **COMPARISON SHOPPER**
> **Talking Globes**
> Although less expensive than they used to be, they don't work as well. Why ask questions that can't be answered by looking at the globe? Our testers liked pushing the buttons but quickly felt frustrated. The **LeapFrog Explorer Smart Globe** (LeapFrog $99 ●●) comes with a sensor pen and lots of information (the pace is frenetic). (800) 701-5327. The **GeoSafari World** (Educational Insights $59.95 ●●●) has 5,000 questions, but again you'd need an atlas to answer many of them. (800) 995-4436.

Puzzles

Putting jigsaw puzzles together calls for visual perception, eye-hand coordination, patience, and problem-solving skills. During their early school years, kids should build puzzles from 25 pieces to 50- and 100-plus pieces.

Beginners' Puzzles—Under 50 pieces

■ **Alphabet Puzzle Boards** *2007*
(Lauri $29.99 ●●●●) Like the old A–Z puzzles, this new set goes one step further with a familiar object for each of the letter pairs, adding sound recognition to the mix of 26 puzzles with upper and lower case and object. Handling the 3-D letters gives kids a feel for their shapes. Still top rated, **Kids Perception Puzzle** ($7.99 ●●●●●); figures in slightly different poses that help kids look at small differences, just as they must when reading words that look almost alike, such as *cap* and *cup*. 4–7. (800) 451-0520.

■ **Alphabet & Number Puzzle Pairs**
(eeBoo $14 ●●●●) A handsome set of two-piece puzzles with easy-to-recognize objects to pair with upper- and

lower-case letters or objects and numerals. The letter/number sides are color-coded along the edges to help make the matches. Illustrated by Saxton Freymann, well-known artist of *How are You Peeling?* and *Food for Thought*. These can be used for simple games or solo puzzle play. (212) 222-0823.

COMPARISON SHOPPER
Parquetry Blocks

Making a design with these multicolored blocks takes visual perception as well as patience and problem-solving skills. We suggest a classic BLUE CHIP **Parquetry Blocks Super Set** (Learning Resources $26.95 ●●●●●), thirty-two geometrically shaped tiles kids arrange on top of 20 colorful patterns. Advanced players use tiles with patterns to the side or out of sight. Develops skills in matching and sequencing patterns—skills that are needed in putting letters together to make words. 5–8. (800) 222-3909. New for 2007, **Trapecolo** (HaPe $24.99 ●●●●½). Create colorful patterns with 180 trapezoid shapes that fit into a large six-sided wooden frame. Patterns are shown in the brochure, but not full size, so these are more challenging. Marked 4–99, we'd say more like 6 & up. (800) 661-4142.

■ 1001 Nights 2007

(Haba $35 ●●●●½) This is a handsome set of tiles that can be used in open-ended format to create a skyline of minarets and domes, à la 1001 Arabian Nights. There are multiple patterns that children can follow, and matching the tiles calls for visual perception. A good quiet time activity. (800) 468-6873.

Intermediate & Advanced—
50 &100+ Pieces and Shaped Puzzles

■ Bug Tumble

(The Orb Factory $14.99 ●●●●) The graphics of this box don't do justice to the stunning puzzle inside. Much like a DK book, the collage of bugs, worms, and other creepy things will appeal to bug-fascinated kids. While there  are 48 pieces, it is still a very challenging puzzle with a pleasing oversized 2' x 3' size. Puzzle comes with a big poster chockful of info on the

EARLY SCHOOL YEARS • Five to Ten Years

creepy crawlies in the puzzle. Marked 4 & up, but we'd say most 6s will find it challenging. Really depends on the child. (800) 741-0089.

■ Egyptology Puzzle 2007 PLATINUM AWARD

(Mudpuppy $11 ●●●●●) Based on the book *Egyptology* from Candlewick, this handsome 100-piece puzzle is smartly designed with good clues in the graphics. If you have a child in the midst of all things Egyptian, this will be a prize! Puzzle image is printed on the metal storage tin. 7 & up. (212) 354-8840.

■ Lego City Puzzles 2007 PLATINUM AWARD

(Ravensburger $10 ●●●●●) Choose from two cityscape scenes, one of a fire with Lego trucks and helicopter or a police station with police copter. Both puzzles are 60 pieces and include a bonus Lego vehicle to build and play with after the puzzle is assembled. Also top rated, **City Scenes** ($10 ●●●●). Three 49-piece puzzles with different patterns on the back to sort them. Small pieces for more advanced puzzlers. 5 & up. (800) 886-1236.

COMPARISON SHOPPER
USA & World Map Puzzles

The Scrambled States of America (Ceaco $9.95 ●●●●): Our testers loved the unusual ways the pieces of this 150-piece puzzle were cut. The variation in colors makes the experience "challenging" but "doable." A good parent/child puzzle, but not the puzzle for learning the states, since the states are not done in whole pieces. (800) 638-7568. For more traditional maps, consider: **Puzzibilities USA Puzzles** (Small World Toys $20 ●●●●), a classic wooden version with landmarks, capitals, and a vinyl sheet for arranging pieces out of the frame is a good choice. 6 & up. (800) 421-4153. **Wonderfoam Giant USA Puzzle Map** (Chenille Kraft $44 ●●●●): testers enjoyed putting together this giant-sized (4' w x 2½' h) floor puzzle with 73 thick foam pieces. State names are printed on the map with 16 landmarks (state capitals marked by a star but not named—you might want to add the

capitals with a marker on the back of each state). Also, **Wonderfoam Giant World Puzzle Map** ($44 oooo). (800) 621-1261.

Activity Kits and Art Supplies

For school-age kids, art class is seldom long enough. Besides, such classes are usually teacher directed, with little chance for kids to explore their own ideas. Giving kids the tools and space for art projects at home provides more than pure entertainment. Art helps kids develop their ability to communicate ideas and feelings visually, to refine eye-hand skills, and to learn how to stick with a task.

> **BASIC GEAR CHECKLIST FOR EARLY SCHOOL YEARS ARTISTS**
>
> ✓ Crayons, chalk, colored pencils, and pastels
> ✓ Watercolor and acrylic paints
> ✓ Watercolor markers
> ✓ Paper for origami
> ✓ Sewing supplies
> ✓ Lanyard kits
> ✓ Rug hooking supplies
> ✓ Woodworking supplies
> ✓ Flower press
> ✓ Stamps
> ✓ Loom (weaving, beads)
> ✓ Sand art supplies
> ✓ Colored wax
> ✓ Needlepoint supplies
> ✓ Cutting/pasting supplies
> ✓ Fabric paints
> ✓ Air-hardening clay

Activity and Craft Kits

Again this year there seemed to be more craft kits than ever before. We had our network of testers get to work—with a mixed bag of results. Some kits that looked fantastic were disappointing; others were surprisingly good. Our testers complained that the packaging was deceiving, making products look bigger than they actually were. Both boys and girls love making things they can play with, wear, or give as gifts. Many require adult assistance. Here's a sampling of our testing. For even more reviews, visit our website.

EARLY SCHOOL YEARS • Five to Ten Years

Drawing, Painting, Coloring, and Gluing

■ **Beautiful Beaded Mirror** *2007*

(Creativity for Kids $17.99 ●●●½) This would have been a top winner if it included more materials. A beautiful kit that requires more attention to detail than can be expected from 8s & up. (800) 311-8684. Still top rated, **Beaded Dresser Set** ($14.99 ●●●●) that comes with a small mirror set in wood, a ceramic heart frame and heart-shaped box, pastel colored beads, ribbons, and glue. A straightforward, easier project that requires kids to spread the glue out and then spill beads onto the glue for decoration. The light beads have a "princess/fairy" look to them and will appeal to younger girls. 6 & up. (800) 311-8684.

Let's go to the races! We often complain that there are not a lot of great craft kits for boys. Here are three sets that will be a hit.

■ **Cast & Paint: Krazy Kars** *2007* PLATINUM AWARD
(Skullduggery $14.95 ●●●●●) "Let's do another," and "so neat"—our testers really liked these fun model kits that are easy to do and produce Hot Wheels/Matchbox-scaled cars. Sets come with enough modeling material for four cars (but enough decorations for two). The cars take 30 minutes to set. New kits feature NASCAR winners like Jeff Gordon and Jimmie Johnson. Kits come with NASCAR decals, paint, and blo-pens (not our favorites), but our testers really were less concerned with the decorating and more intent on making a toy they could really use! (800) 336-7745.

■ **Monster Trucks Custom Shop**
2007 PLATINUM AWARD

(Creativity for Kids $24.99 ●●●●●) Customize the four monster trucks with paint and stickers, then let 'em rip! With pull-back mechanisms, these are ready for racing. The stickers go on well. The paint isn't great, but really is beside the point. These four monster trucks are just FUN! For smaller vehicles, check out **Fast Car Race Cars** ($14.99 ●●●●). Set of three wooden cars with pull-back mechanisms to paint (our kids used markers to play with the cars sooner). With either the trucks or the cars, set up a roadway with some empty small boxes for simulated crashes and road races. (800) 311-8684.

■ **Create Your Own Books** *2007*

(Creativity for Kids $15.99 ●●●●½) Two blank books, one with a "window" cut out of the cover and pages that a photograph will show through. This could make a great book that's all about one person or a pet or a special place. A second book is notebook-sized and has lined paper with spaces for illustrations, plus colored pencils and stickers. These are open-ended materials for the budding author/artist. Comes with some suggestions for creating rough drafts and a list of story starter ideas. Says 4 & up, but this is likely to be a better choice for 5–9s. (800) 311-8684.

■ **Decoupage Diva Jewelry Keeper**
2007 PLATINUM AWARD

(Creativity for Kids $21.99 ●●●●●) Kids get a test run on decoupage with this mini-armoire with mirrored lid, doors that hold bracelets, interior for necklaces, and bottom drawer for pins and such. Comes with paper accents, sequins, and sparkle glaze. 8 & up. (800) 311-8684.

■ **Musical Jewelry Box** BLUE CHIP

(Alex $19.99 ●●●●●) This is the quintessential jewelry box with spinning ballerina. Comes with sparkling gems to glue on top and a frou-frou tutu of pink tulle on a hot pink ribbon to attach to the box. A very girlie-girlie gift, but likely to win the oo-oohs and ah-h-h-hs of beginners. The box is finished in pink so there's not a lot to do, but it's showy and quick. 6 & up. (800) 666-2539.

■ **Paint-a-Doggie Diner** *2007*

(Alex $19.99 ●●●●) Wouldn't Snoopy have loved this fancy food stand when supper time rolled around? Two metal food dishes lift in and out of the wooden white platform

EARLY SCHOOL YEARS • Five to Ten Years

for your pet's water and food. Kids can personalize the platform with their pet's name and stamp-on images. Note: Dishes are too small for big eaters and stand is too low for tall dogs. 16" w x 9.5" d; comes with paints, stampers, brushes, and mixing tray. (800) 666-2539.

■ Paint A Paper Lantern 2007

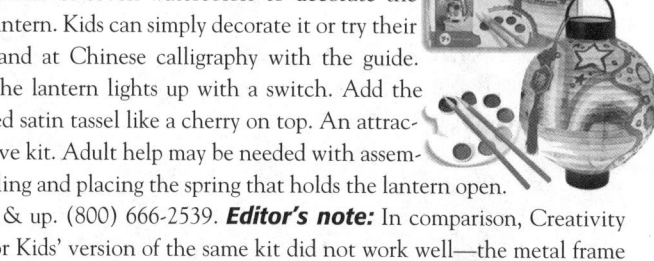

(Alex $9.99 ●●●●½) A charming white paper lantern comes with two bamboo brushes and a palette of seven watercolors to decorate the lantern. Kids can simply decorate it or try their hand at Chinese calligraphy with the guide. The lantern lights up with a switch. Add the red satin tassel like a cherry on top. An attractive kit. Adult help may be needed with assembling and placing the spring that holds the lantern open. 7 & up. (800) 666-2539. **Editor's note:** In comparison, Creativity for Kids' version of the same kit did not work well—the metal frame was too tall and we kept tearing the lantern. (800) 666-2539.

■ Scratch Art Light Catcher Fun Kits 2007

(Scratch Art $2.99 ●●●●½) Kids scratch away the black paint to give the open spaces a stained glass look when the finished product is hung on a window (themes include birds, flowers, and a sailboat). Quick, pleasing projects that are a good party favor/activity. Also new, **Scratch Magic Stickers** ($5.99 ●●●●) comes in 20 animal shapes. For a bigger kit, **Draw & Learn Deluxe Kit** ($16.99 ●●●●) has over 50 stencil shapes of dinosaurs, underwater, jungle, and outer space themes. This just might attract boys in particular who often need to develop the fine motor skills of holding a pencil—without the challenge of writing letters. (508) 583-8085.

■ Works of Ahhh Star Box 2007

(Balitono $18 ●●●●●) Our tester painted and then gave this star-shaped box as a gift for Mother's Day. A real hit! A keepsake for any gift-giving season. PLATINUM AWARD '06. Also fun, **My Pinball Game Kit** ($22 ●●●●½). Finding kits that will appeal to boys as well as girls is not always easy. This one was a hit with our eight-year old tester. Okay, it won't compete with the electronic versions, but it will be unique! Also fun for dramatic play,

Dog House and Dog ($22 ●●●●), with pooch, house, and feeding bowl. Still top rated, **Horse Stable** ($25 ●●●●●) and **Jewelry Box** ($22 ●●●●●). Platinum Award '05. (609) 936-8807.

Comparison Shopper
Scrapbooking 2007

Scrapbook and Memory Box Gift Set (Creativity for Kids $28.99 ●●●●●) Scrapbook fans are going to love this commodious box with picture-frame cover that holds a spiral-bound scrapbook plus 16 sheets of patterned paper, stickers, stencil, scalloped scissors, paper punch, stamper, pens, glue stick, and great ideas. This will appeal to older girls ready to memorialize a school year, trip, or big event. Marked 7 & up, but was coveted by our 10- and 11-year-old testers. Platinum Award '05. 7 & up. (800) 311-8684. **My Scrapbook Case** 2007 (Alex $16.99 ●●●●½): sized for less ambitious or beginner scrap-bookers, this comes with a small 6½" x 6½" spiral scrapbook with multicolored pages. Kit comes in a sturdy decorative box with magnetic closure. Kit includes puncher, sequins, glue stick, scallop edge scissors, and stickers. 5 & up. (800) 666-2539.

Candles, Cooking, and Mixing

■ Beeswax Candles BLUE CHIP

(Creativity for Kids $16 ●●●●●) The best candle making kit—fun to do and makes great presents. Comes with five sheets of colored wax that you can cut to make different-sized candles. 6 & up. (800) 311-8684. We'd skip Alex's **Candle Painting** set, which our testers found disappointing—"my candle doesn't look like the box." 6 & up.

■ Wax Works BLUE CHIP

(Chenille Kraft $5.49 ●●●●●) These waxy sticks can be twisted and shaped into free-form sculptures. Great for developing fine motor skills. 5 & up. (800) 621-1261.

EARLY SCHOOL YEARS • Five to Ten Years

Beads, Jewelry, & Accessory Kits
Using beads is more than engaging in a creative craft; it's helping kids develop fine-motor skills.

■ JellLoopdeLoops Sparkle Jelly Jewelry Kit 2007

(Fashion Angels Enterprises $14.99 ●●●●½) Our testers really enjoyed this kit with 48' of glitter tubing so that crafters can make 36 bracelets and 20 rings. One parent noted: "love the creativity factor and including the pliers was an excellent idea", but thought the seed beads were too tiny to manage. 8 & up. (800) 492-3237.

■ Funky Bead Chest
(Bead Bazaar $19.99 ●●●●●) A dream gift for a beader! A tall, brightly painted wooden chest with three lined drawers comes topped with a juicy collection of wooden beads, charms, and colorful string to match. PLATINUM AWARD '06. If you're having a party, consider **Totally Fun Beads** ($18.99 ●●●●½); comes with 30 charms, 1000+ beads, and 30 strings. Plenty for a group! Our testers also raved about this company's **Hemp** and **Mystic** bead kits ($9.99 ●●●●) that will appeal to tweens, teens, and their mothers! (800) 838-1769.

■ Wrist Pix 2007

(Fashion Angels Enterprises $16 ●●●●½) Set comes with small metal frames that you decorate using either the enclosed designs (ready for coloring with markers) or your own drawings or digital photos. Once you place your design, put a small acrylic cover over it; then you're ready to make your bracelets by stringing the metal frames together using the enclosed elastic and glass beads. Still top rated, **World Colors** ($19.99 ●●●●), a more advanced kit with four colors of hemp to weave with a generous supply of shells, bells, wooden beads, and painted beads for bracelets, necklaces, and rings; **Alphadot Bracelet Kit** ($19.99 ●●●●●), with 85 Alphadot beads that slide onto three thin watch-like bands; **Ribbon Raps** ($14 ●●●●●), has beads to string on gossamer ribbon; and Mystix ($16 ●●●●), which includes semiprecious stones. 8 & up. (800) 492-3237. *Editors' Note:* these new kits are marked 8 & up, but we

TOYS

found that kids often needed help getting started.

Needlecrafts
Knitting, Crocheting & Sewing

Knitting continues to be a big trend for adults and kids. While we believe that nothing replaces a real instructor for knitting, these kits will appeal to kids. Here are our top picks:

■ EZ-Fleec-Y Knitting 2007

(Alex $16.99 ○○○○½) Two big wooden knitting needles are used to knit the thick rolls of colorful fleece strips. Big needles and big "yarn" make for big and fast projects. Make a hat or scarf and wear it, all in the same day! A good choice for experienced knitters. ***Editors' Note:*** we found the directions in the crochet kits in this line harder to follow. 8 & up. A better choice: last year's **Knitting Circle** ($39.99 ○○○○½) comes with chunky yarn and needles. The new **Knot-A-Quilt** ($20 ○○○½) fared less well with our testers: "takes too long," and "boring" were the surprising remarks we got back on this kit, which requires kids to tie 48 fringed squares together to make a big 36" x 48" quilt. It does take a really long time and it's not that much fun to put together. (800) 666-2539.

■ Hug This Shrug Kit 2007 PLATINUM AWARD

(Fashion Angels Enterprises $17.99 ○○○○○) Picking up on a big fashion trend, this kit provides clear directions and materials for making a small black shrug as well as a big fashion beaded safety pin for closure. Marked 8 & up, but we'd say more like 10 & up, and then new knitters will need assistance. Flash Dance, anyone? Check out **Leg Warminators** ($17.99 ○○○○○), which allow another generation to make their own with very bright colors using a large plastic spool knitter. Still top rated, **I Knit this Poncho!** ($16 ○○○○½). (800) 492-3237.

■ Super Embroidery Kit
2007 PLATINUM AWARD

(Alex $19.99 ○○○○○) Packaged in a red felt bag with a pocket, this is a charming sewing set for beginners. There's an embroidery hoop and one practice cloth for trying out stitches as well as a dozen colors of floss, scissors, needles, transfer patterns to iron on, felt letters, shapes, and pieces to decorate with beads

EARLY SCHOOL YEARS • Five to Ten Years

and sequins. A clear stitching guide is included. They have even included some buttons for practical needle-work. Marked 7 & up, we'd say more like 9 to 'tweens. (800) 666-2539.

Weaving

■ Weaving Fashion Weaving Loom

(Alex $18 ●●●●) Cleverly packaged with very current chunky, fluffy yarn, this kit gives weaving an updated look. Our testers gave high ratings to both this kit and the **Giant Weaving Loom** ($29.99 ●●●●). Must be threaded, but easy to use. (800) 666-2539.

■ Potholders & Other Loopy Projects

(Klutz $16.95 ●●●●●) Don't look any further—this is the best potholder set on the market. The supplies are vibrant and inviting and the book really does explain what to do. Weaving not only develops eye-hand coordination, it also involves following patterns and problem solving. Marked 6 & up; we'd say more like 7 & up. PLATINUM AWARD '04. (800) 737-4123.

Musical Instruments

■ Chimalong & Mini Chimalong
BLUE CHIP

(Woodstock Percussion $20 & up ●●●●●) The tone of this metal-chime xylophone is lovely, and it can be played by number/color or musical notation. Reinforces reading from left to right. Mini-version is not as sweet sounding. Marked 3 & up; we'd say 4–8. (800) 422-4463.

■ The Flea Ukulele

(Flea Market Music $159 ●●●● ½) Here's a handsome four-string soprano-size ukulele with a solid musical sound. Perfect for beginners and available in multiple colors. The back is made of plastic and the top is wood. It comes with a storage bag and instructions. (800) 459-5558.

■ Kids' Tom Tom

(Remo $53 ●●●●) If you're lucky, they'll let you play this colorful drum while they dance! Comes with mallets, but testers say that tones are better when played by hand. Also terrific: a **Kids' Konga Drum** ($63 ●●●●) and **Two-Headed Bongo** ($50 ●●●●). Their new line of less expensive instruments does not have the same rich sound. (800) 422-4463.

■ Music Maker Harp BLUE CHIP

(European Expressions $32 ●●●●●) No electronic sounds here. This is a cross between a zither and an autoharp, but much easier to learn to play. Slip one of 12 follow-the-dot song sheets under the strings and pluck. Has a soft and lovely tone. Includes folk, Beatles, and classical music sheets. 6 & up. (800) 779-2205.

■ Zoundz *2007* PLATINUM AWARD

(Zizzle $49.99 ●●●●●) This translucent white board lights up and, depending on the placement of the various shaped play pieces, it plays contemporary sounding music. Can also be used as a speaker for an MP3 player. (866) 494-9963. Also fun, **Ozone Space Rocker** (Funhouse $39.99 ●●●●), a very retro looking blowup vinyl chair with built in speakers for your MP3 player. (800) 929-4666.

Active Play

■ Backyard Flyer

(Kid Galaxy $14.95 ●●●●●) "One of the best toys of the year" was the consensus among our tween testers. They were thrilled with this small blue-and-yellow plane that is launched by using the battery-powered handheld launcher. It kept our testers (parents included) well occupied for part of an afternoon—even when it went flying into the neighbor's backyard! A great toy for the price. PLATINUM AWARD '06. Improved this year with an easier-to-use launcher. (800) 816-1135.

■ Beamo

(Stuff Design $25 ●●●●●) We really wish that we had had one of these when we were young! These fabric discs are about two feet wide and have a foam outer core that doesn't hurt as much as a regular frisbee if you miss! Great for multi-generational play. 6 & up. PLATINUM AWARD '04. (888) 946-7464.

EARLY SCHOOL YEARS • Five to Ten Years

■ Fun Roller

(Small World Toys $33.99 ●●●●) Looks like a prop for a circus clown. After inflating the big circle (four-foot diameter), kids can walk forward on it and make it go. Will require a certain level of coordination and balancing skill. Lots of fun, but is too small for taller 5s and 6s. (800) 421-4153. 4 & up.

■ Mattel Hot Wheels ESS Radar Gun *2007*

(Mattel $24.99 ●●●●½) This really works! We tracked cars (we don't recommend this to kids—but we couldn't help ourselves), baseball pitches, and bicycles going by. Fun for outdoor play. (800) 542-8697. Our testers also tried the **Discovery Speed Detector** ($39.95 ●●●●) and gave it strong reviews as well. In a head-to-head competition, the Mattel gun is more sensitive and responds better than the Discovery version, which takes more finesse to work. That said, both did well with our kid testers. Both 8 & up. (800) 938-0333.

■ Speed Stacks *2007*

(Play Along $39.99 ●●●●½) This is a game that has caught on in gym classes in middle schools and high schools across the country. It's a great way to build eye-hand coordination as well as concentration. The idea is to stack and unstack the cups in the shortest amount of time. Fun and active—and great for the age that usually just wants to plug into their video games. (954) 596-2210.

Wheel Toys
Shopping Checklist

◉ Fives will continue to enjoy many of the wheel toys in the Preschool chapter.

◉ By 6 or 7, most kids are ready and eager for a two-wheeler with training wheels. Steer clear of bikes with gears or hand brakes. Learning to balance is a big enough deal.

◉ Tempting as it may be to surprise your child, your best bet is to take your child to the store.

TOYS

○ Buy a bike that fits, rather than one to grow into. When kids straddle a bike they should be able to put a foot on the ground for balance.

○ Budget and size will dictate the choices. **Schwinn, Huffy,** and **Razor** ($100 & up) offer solidly built 16" bikes with adjustable training wheels and an assortment of accessories.

○ Helmets do help! According to the Consumer Product Safety Commission, one in seven children suffers head injuries in bike-related accidents. While studies show that wearing helmets reduces the risk of injury by 85 percent, the sad fact is that only 5 percent of bike-riding kids actually wear helmets. See Safety Guidelines for helmet standards.

■ Green Machine

(Huffy $100 ●●●●○) You'll want a turn on this truly innovative ride-on. Steer the two chunky rear wheels by moving the two hand levers (one also has a brake). Solidly made even for bigger kids (and small adults!). PLATINUM AWARD '04. (800) 872-2453.

■ Flying Turtle

(Mason Co. $69.95 ●●●●) Low to the ground, this seat on skate wheels zips along on any smooth surface by twisting the handlebars from side to side. No pedals, no batteries, no motor! This is kid powered and fun for kids up to 150 pounds. One test family keeps this indoors and claims that all visiting kids from 4–12 enjoy it! (800) 821-4141.

■ Trikke 5

(Trikke Tech $139 ●●●●●) Our testers wrote: "A HUGE HIT! The kids love this! It works well, and looks super cool, too. It operates much like the flying turtle." Designed for kids 7–11 with a maximum rider weight of 150 lbs., the three-wheeled scooter will go where the rider leans. The company sells bigger models for teens and grown-ups but we did not test them. 8 & up. PLATINUM AWARD '05. (877) 487-4553.

EARLY SCHOOL YEARS • Five to Ten Years

Science Toys and Equipment

■ Big Bad Boomin' Bugs Observation Station 2007
(Little Kids $19.99 ●●●●) Catch your bug with the capture-and-carry bug scooper, drop it into the 12" x 8" dome with powerful 3X magnifying lens on top. Plug in the earphones and you can listen to the bug chew, crawl, chirp, click, or buzz! A multi-sensory bug experience. (800) 545-5437. For a smaller bug chamber, **Backyard Safari Bug Scope** (Summit Toys $12.99 ●●●●) Hunters have to catch the bug under the open end of this temporary trap. Designed with a light to aid viewing. (205) 661-1174.

■ Box of Rocks
(GeoCentral $21.99 ●●●●) If you have a young rock hound in the family, this box with 16 specimens and an informative booklet will be a hit and may inspire further discoveries. **Activity Rocks** ($5.25 ●●●●) has four specimens—including one that floats! (800) 231-6083.

■ Dinosaur Excavation Kit 2007
(Usborne $17.99 ●●●●½) Archeologists in training will have fun digging out the bones of a T-Rex from the clay block. Complete with goggles*, brush, chisel, and hammer. Assemble the bones and read the book, which introduces beginning readers to the many kinds of dinosaurs. No glue included. *These goggles are not actually safety devices.

■ Discovery Kids SL-70 Telescope
(Discovery Kids $149.95 ●●●●●) With many of the same features usually found on expensive adult models, this is a terrific value. Includes precision ground lenses, an erecting prism, and universal 10mm and 25mm Kellner eyepieces. Comes with a tripod that extends to 55" viewing height, and a padded shoulder carry bag—the whole kit (tripod, scope, bag) weighs just 16 lbs. Ultra neat are the illuminated night-vision dials. PLATINUM AWARD '04. 7 & up. (800) 938-0333.

■ Hook Fortune Finder 2007
(Wild Planet $19.95 ●●●●) Movie merchandise is not usually on our list. But this pirate toy à la Captain Hook, inspired by *Pirates of the Caribbean*, is a metal detector that happens to work better than many we've tested. Also fun in the same line, a **Treasure Hunter** ($24.95 ●●●●). Hide the treasure chest and give kids the finder that lights up red when they get close to the chest. We passed on the **Light Scope,** which has a really bright red light. 5 & up. (800) 247-6570.

TOYS

■ Marshall Brodien Magic Wand Set 2007

(Cadaco $19.99 ●●●●) It takes some reading and practice to perfect these showy magic tricks with a light-up magic wand. Don't tell—the magic is all based on the use of magnets. 7 & up. (800) 621-5426.

■ Perfumery

(Scientific Explorer $20 ●●●●) Lots of perfume kits come with such cheap-smelling scents that we usually pass on them. This is the exception. It really is a chemistry kit with directions to read and recipes to stir up—with pleasant payoffs that kids can use or give as gifts. 8 & up. (800) 900-1182.

■ Perryscope 2007

(Kid Galaxy $14.99 ●●●●) Fun for land or water. An adjustable periscope that rises 10" above the water. Has a soft eyecup and adjustable handles. 6 & up. (800) 816-1135.

Nature Houses & Lodges

■ My Birdhouse Kit

(Balitono $20 ●●●●) One of the best outdoor crafts is to prepare a birdhouse for backyard visitors. This wooden house is pre-constructed (7½" x 5½" x 6½") with drainage holes, removable roof, and a ventilation slot for added comfort! Kids can enjoy painting the house. We'd recommend pairing this kit with a bird guidebook, a pair of binoculars, and a log. 7 & up. (609) 936-8807.

■ Hanging Bird Feeder and Bird Houses Kits

(TWC of America $17–$20 ●●●●) If you'd like to build your own birdhouse, these beautifully crafted pine kits come with rounded edges and predrilled holes, making them the best kids' kits on the market. Adult assistance required. Also, **Deluxe Clear-View Nature House** ($17.99 ●●●●½), a sturdy hut-shaped wooden house, half see-through, half screened, with sliding door; a perfect temporary habitat for observing bugs and small critters. 6 & up. Also, **Soil Dweller Nature House Kit** ($20 ●●●●) for making a wooden-framed house for earthworms. 8 & up. (800) 301-7592.

EARLY SCHOOL YEARS • Five to Ten Years

Best Travel Toys and Games

As kids get older they enjoy traditional games such as I Spy, Twenty Questions, Geography, or Facts of Five. They are also ready for word games and travel books. While we don't recommend plugging your kids into electronics for long stretches of time, there are times when everyone needs some down time! **Leapster, Pixter, PSP, Nintendo DS** and **Gameboy DS** are among our testers' favorites. For reviews of top-rated games, see pp. 174, 202. Be sure to bring along some story tapes. Here are some neat take-alongs:

■ Connect Four 2007

(Milton Bradley $19.99 ●●●●) Large enough to handle with ease and compact enough to take along for travel or the beach. A zip fabric case opens and the four-in-a-row checkerboard stands up; there is storage for the playing pieces. Learning this game of strategy gets better as kids become familiar with it. You can even stop in mid-play and continue a round later. 7 & up. (888) 836-7025.

■ Crayola Color Explosion Neon 2007

(Binney & Smith $7.99 ●●●) Okay, before you open the package you should know that the warnings inside are longer than the directions for use. That said, this is a bit like scratch art black pages with colors that are revealed with a marker. You get better results using the side of the marker than the tip, and you need a bit of pressure to make it work. Not a bad product for travel, unless you have wet hands and get the black ink on your hands and clothes! Good luck to you. This is pretty neat (or maybe messy) on a dark plane. 6 & up. (800) 272-9652.

■ Games to Go 2007

(Alex $25.99 ●●●●) Six oversized 36" game boards for classics such as checkers, mancala, tic-tac-toe, snakes and ladders, backgammon, and Chinese checkers are printed with colorful graphics on fabric. Games are bound together like a giant book along with big playing pieces that all store in a zip-up bag. Clever way to take games along to beach or grandmas or a sleep over party. 5 & up. 5 & up. (800) 666-2539.

TOYS

■ Grab & Go Super Jacks and Hoppity Winks

(Cranium $9.95 each ●●●●) Two nonelectronic take-along games are also perfect stocking stuffers. **Super Jacks** are oversized plastic jacks for beginners; **Hoppity Winks** are tiddly-winks in the shape of colorful frogs that leap on lily pads! 6 & up. (877) 272-6486.

■ The Greatest Dot to Dot Books *2007*

(Monkeying Around $5.95 & up ●●●●) These are not your grandpa's dot to dot book! Smallest books use numerals from 40–140; larger books use numerals from 50–460. 7–'tweens. (800) 553-4300.

■ Imaginetics *2007*

(International Playthings $6.99 ●●●●) These are similar to the Colorforms we grew up with, but they are magnetic. 5s and 6s will enjoy playing with these in the car and airport on their own or with you. New sets include **Angelina Ballerina Friends Forever** and **Bob the Builder Sunflower Valley.** (800) 445-8347.

■ It's All About Me *2007*

(Klutz $14.95 ●●●●) Our testers loved filling in the answers to this personality quiz. This book allows kids to share their thoughts and write down feelings about themselves, their parents and friends. 8 & up. If you have a detail-oriented child, **Paper Stained Glass** ($19.95 ●●●●) will make the time fly. It is really an advanced form of color-by-number. Working on sheer vellum with felt markers, this craft takes up a lot of "are we there yet?" restlessness. For fun once you arrive, bring along **The Foam Airplane Book** ($14.95 ●●●●). 8 & up. (800) 737-4123.

■ Lonpos 101 Pyramid and Rectangle Game *2007*

(Mic O Mic Americas $16.99 ●●●●½) Imagine a puzzle with 566 combinations that fits in a box that is only 3" x 5.5"! A brain teaser game with multicolored balls, connected in various forms, that are a challenge to connect into many patterns. 10 & up. (877) 642-6642.

■ Play Scenes *2007*

(Mudpuppy $11 ●●●●½) These are sturdy play boards that open up like a portfolio and come with cling play pieces. We highly recom-

EARLY SCHOOL YEARS • Five to Ten Years

mend the charming **Fairytale Theater,** which has lots of storytelling play power with characters, props, and a wonderful stage for acting out original stories! There is also an attractive **Map of the U.S.A.** (○○○), with all the states noted (except poor New England, where the states are delineated on the map but collectively labeled "New England"). 5 & up. (800) 670-7441.

■ Magnetic Checkers & Slides & Ladders

(eeBoo $10 each ○○○○) Packed in their own carrying bag, each of these traditional games is done with magnetic playing pieces and a playing board that opens like a book. Charming illustrations give these classic games a new and lively look. Still top rated, **Travel Bingo** ($10 ○○○○), with four bingo pads and four pencils. Objects to look for include stop signs, bikes, flags, cows, railroad crossing signs, etc. 4 & up. (212) 222-0823.

■ Super Story Recorder 2007

(Cranium $19.99 ○○○○) Much like a Mad Lib, Super Story Recorder prompts players to answer certain questions that are then incorporated into a themed story (which you pick with a spin of the dial). Once we got the hang of waiting for beeps to record our answers, it was fun to play. 6 & up. (877) 272-6486.

■ Top Speed 2007

(Gamewright $5.99 ○○○○) Racing car fans will like this game. Players race to put down vehicle parts without matching colors or parts in any row . . . sort of like a simpler form of Sudoku with pictures instead of numbers. Great for developing speedy visual memory and discrimination. Still top rated, **There's a Moose in the House** (Gamewright $9.99 ○○○○○), one of the most innovative card games we've played in years. The object is to place as many moose as possible in your opponents' house of cards. Easy to learn and a lot of fun to play! 2–5 players. 15 mins. 8 & up. PLATINUM AWARD '05. (800) 638-7568.

TOYS

Electronics

■ 20Q 2007

(Radica $9.99 ●●●●●) How does it know? Play twenty questions with this handheld machine and it really seems like magic! The programmed answers also have a sense of humor. Updated this year with a larger screen and buttons. PLATINUM AWARD '05. New for 2007, themed versions ($14.99 ●●● sports, music or movies) were too hard for our testers. (800) 803-9611.

■ Kid Tough Digital Camera 2007
PLATINUM AWARD

(Fisher-Price $69.95 ●●●●●) Designed for beginners, this digital camera works surprisingly easily. There is a two-eye view finder as well as a small but adequate screen. It's easy to use with chunky handgrips and big button. Comes with built-in flash, runs on four AA batteries, and you can add a card for extra memory. Compatible with Mac or PC. They say 3 & up, we'd say more like 6 & up. Available in pink or blue. (800) 432-5437.

■ Leapster L-MAX 2007

(LeapFrog $99 ●●●●●) We have told you about the Leapster before. It's still a great travel toy, but now there's a simple cable connection that will put Leapster games on your TV screen, so it can be used either way. Now it's a good take-along that can also be plugged in at Grandma's. Without the usual frenetic pace, this responds to your child and has more than just zap-and-blast games. If you have been looking for a handheld game machine that's more age-appropriate than Gameboy, look no further. Billed as a learning machine, it's a lot more playful than most. The games and skills are well targeted to older preschoolers and early school-age kids. It has a larger screen and games that can be played at three levels of difficulty. There are math, phonics, reading, and spelling games, as well as an art program that takes some help to learn how to use. Best of the new-for- 2007 games, **Letterpillar,** and **Cosmic Math** with addition, subtraction, multiplication, and division. 4–8. PLATINUM AWARD '06. (800) 701-5327.

■ Pixter Multi-Media

(Fisher-Price $84.99 ●●●●●) A handheld, no-mess art platform that allows kids to create countless combinations of designs with the easy-

EARLY SCHOOL YEARS • Five to Ten Years

to-use stylus on the touch-sensitive back-lit screen. An interesting cartridge, **Symphony Painter** ($19.99), allows kids to draw and experiment with composing music. Will work with both the new and old models. (800) 432-5437.

■ **Talking Picture Book**

(Cranium $19.99 ❍❍❍❍½) Kids create their own story book pages combining reusable stickers, wipe-off colorful pens, and their own voices. A story starter wheel suggests things to include in your story, and there are sound effects to record along with your own words. Crayola's **Story Creator** looks like this, but Talking Picture Book is more versatile and records better. 5 & up. (877) 272-6486.

Best Birthday Gifts for Every Budget

Big Ticket $100 plus
: **Mindstorm NXT** (Lego Systems) or **Castle** (Playmobil) or **Trikke5** (Trikke Tech)

Under $100
: **The American Girls Collection Doll** (American Girl) or **Leapster L-MAX** or **FLY Pentop Compuer** (LeapFrog) or **Pixter Multi-Media** (Fisher-Price)

Under $80
: **Kid Tough Digital Camera** (Fisher-Price)

Under $40
: **City Airport** (Lego Systems) or **YOUniverse ATM Machine** (Summit)

Under $30
: **Cosmic Catch** (Hasbro) or **Mag XL Magformers** (Rainbow Products) **Scrapbook and Memory Box Gift Set** (Creativity for Kids)

Under $25
: **Morphibians** (Kid Galaxy) or **Combo King** (Gamewright)

Under $20
: **Sudoku** (Briarpatch) or **Uno Spin** (Mattel) or **Leg Warminators** (Fashion Angels Enterprises) or **Doodle Tales** (Cranium)

Under $10   **Ugly Doll** (Gamewright) or **Fuddy Duddy** (Let's Play Games) or **Scratch Art Light Catcher Fun Kit** (Scratch Art)

Books for Early and Later School Years

As children learn to read independently, they continue to enjoy hearing stories read aloud to them. Often they can comprehend more complex books than they can read on their own. You'll want to find books of many genres, as children are hungry for information as well as all kinds of fiction. Before long they graduate from the easy-to-read books to chapter books that they can read to themselves. Our book **Read It! Play It!** suggests 50+ books and activities for the early school-age group. For both early and later school years, look for past winners and current Gold and Platinum winners on our website at Toyportfolio.com. For our PLATINUM AWARD 2007 books, see page 177.

OPPENHEIM TOY PORTFOLIO
PLATINUM BOOK AWARDS 2007

Reading to children is more than a great way to entertain them. Studies show that young children who are read to every day learn to read earlier and with greater ease. But quite aside from the academic benefits, sharing books with children is one of the most pleasurable ways of being together. With books, we can share the thrill of adventure, the excitement of suspense, and the warm satisfaction of happily-ever-afters. Through books, we can help children find answers to their questions about real things and how they work. Books give grown-ups and children a ticket that transports them from everyday events to a world of faraway, long ago, and once upon a time.

There are wonderful new choices this year for all ages. Below you'll find our PLATINUM AWARD winners. Be sure to visit our website, www.toyportfolio.com for current GOLD AWARD winners as well as our archive of reviews.

Babies and Toddlers

■ Amazing Baby Soft Book 2007

(Kids Preferred $12 ●●●●●) An adorable fabric book for beginners with bold black-and-white grab handle. Each page has an interesting texture and shape for little hands to explore—a shimmery star, a lift-up baby face with mirror underneath, a squeaky duck with shiny yellow body, a knit fabric bear, and a pink satin heart. (866) 763-8869.

■ Baby Animals 2007

(by Anne N. Nguyen, Chronicle $19.95 ●●●●●) There are 18 little board books in this library. Each fits perfectly in little hands and opens to reveal a tiny story about a featured animal. Illustrations are in color photos and text is short but clear and about familiar animals. 6 mos & up.

■ Baby Love & My Blanket 2007

(by Sandra Magsaman, Little Brown $14.99 each ooooo) Two charming fabric "books" with lots of color, texture, and peek-a-boo surprises. **Baby Love** opens into a long fold-out with lots of animal faces that lift to reveal a loving sentiment; **My Blanket** keeps opening into a blanket with interesting patterns and textures and many flaps to turn.

■ Maisy's Book Tower 2007

(by Lucy Cousins, Candlewick $9.99 ooooo) We've written about these chunky "knowing and naming" books before. Now they come boxed together, a set of four little books that fit into tiny hands. You'll find lots to talk about as you name the familiar items in **Maisy's Favorite Animals, Toys, Things,** or **Clothes.** These are sturdy enough for babies and toddlers to handle as they discover the mechanics of turning pages and pointing to objects.

■ Nursery Rhyme Books 2007

(Sassy $12 each ooooo) These vinyl books—**Twinkle, Twinkle, Little Star; Rock-a-Bye Baby;** and **I'm a Little Teapot**—can be enjoyed with sound on or off. They can be "played" with music alone or with music with singing. Pleasant music, not overly loud, makes these an entertaining novelty for sing-along fun. Another book, **Baby's Book of Small Talk,** is a knowing-and-naming book showing single objects on each page, with accompanying text written in English, Spanish, or French—take your choice. (800) 323-6336.

■ Yes 2007

(by Jez Alborough, Candlewick $15.99 ooooo) Bobo, the young chimp of few words, is happy to say "Yes!" to a bath, but not to bedtime. Like earlier adventures in *Hug* and *Tall*, Bobo's story is almost wordless, but children will have no trouble telling the story as they enjoy the pictures. There are plenty of opportunities for them to say both "yes" and "no" in this

dandy little tale for 2 & up.

■ You and Me, Baby 2007

(by Lynn Reiser/photographs by Penny Gentieu, Knopf $15.95 ●●●●●) A celebration of the you and me-ness of parent and child as they connect in everyday simple ways . . . smiling, waving, splashing, hugging, and just plain loving each other! Marvelous photos of diverse parents and children add much to this happy book for babies and toddlers.

■ "I'm not cute!" 2007

(by Jonathan Allen, Hyperion $14.99 ●●●●●) Older toddlers and preschoolers will identify with Baby Owl. It seems everyone just has to say how cute he is, but Baby Owl prefers to think of himself as a big, strong hunting machine. That is true until Mama Owl tries to please him by going along with his powerful self-image. Then poor Baby Owl struggles with his ambivalent feelings of wanting to be both big, and small and cute. A true slice of life tale! 2½ & up.

Preschool

■ Art 2007

(by Patrick McDonnell, Little, Brown $14.99 ●●●●●) A breezy child-like conception of art without the usual museum solemnity. The book captures all the exuberance that children bring to their early explorations of color and form . . . free-form, especially. Here is a child who loves art and his mother, who loves both the child and his art. 3 & up.

■ Boo and Baa Have Company 2007

(by Lena and Loof Landstrom, Farrar Straus $15 ●●●●●) In a delightful comedy of errors, Boo and Baa, two resourceful sheep, try rescuing a cat up a tree. Boo finds himself out on a limb and unable to get down. A clever little story that builds on the concept of friendship. 3–6.

■ Dooby Dooby Moo 2007

(by Doreen Cronin & Betsy Lewin, Atheneum $16.95 ●●●●●) Once again, Farmer Brown's barnyard critters are trying to pull a fast one.

This time they are rehearsing for a talent show at the county fair and the sounds emanating from the barn have Farmer Brown puzzled. With all the singing, this is sure to be a noisy and funny read-aloud opportunity. 4–8.

■ **Elusive Moose** 2007

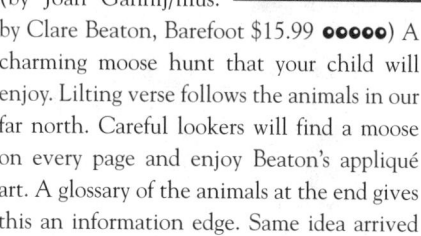

(by Joan Gannij/illus. by Clare Beaton, Barefoot $15.99 ●●●●●) A charming moose hunt that your child will enjoy. Lilting verse follows the animals in our far north. Careful lookers will find a moose on every page and enjoy Beaton's appliqué art. A glossary of the animals at the end gives this an information edge. Same idea arrived late with lots of playful language and a moose to find in **Looking for a Moose** (by Phyllis Root/illus. by Randy Cecil, Candlewick $15.99 ●●●●●). Both are winning choices! 3 & up.

■ **Fast Food** 2007

(by Saxton Freymann & Joost Elffers, Scholastic $12.99 ●●●●●) Get ready to roll! This "transportation" book takes mushroom and radish creatures riding, gliding, and rolling along. Zany creations are coupled with zippy rhymes that are fun to read aloud. There's a ginger reindeer and a red pear sleigh on green bean runners. Delightful! 4 & up.

■ **The Gingerbread Girl** 2007

(by Lisa Campbell Ernst, Dutton $16.99 ●●●●●) A year has passed since the fox outsmarted the Gingerbread Boy. When the lonely old couple decide to try again, they create a spunky Gingerbread Girl who leads them on a merry chase, proving that history need not repeat itself! 4–8.

■ **Move Over Rover** 2007

(by Karen Beaumont/illus. by Jane Dyer, Harcourt $16 ●●●●●) It's raining! It's pouring! Rover's in the dog house and one by one so are cat, squirrel, raccoon, blue jay, and

snake. Almost like *The Napping House* until . . . a certain black-and-white creature tries to join them. A lively read-aloud that will tickle preschoolers. 3–7.

■ Library Lion 2007

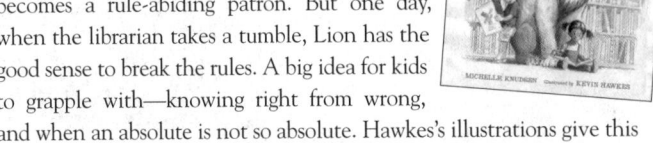

(by Michelle Knudsen/illus. by Kevin Hawkes, Candlewick $15.99 ●●●●○) A very satisfying story of a lion who comes inside the library and becomes a rule-abiding patron. But one day, when the librarian takes a tumble, Lion has the good sense to break the rules. A big idea for kids to grapple with—knowing right from wrong, and when an absolute is not so absolute. Hawkes's illustrations give this an old-fashioned "Robert McCloskey" look that fits the story. 4–7.

■ Oscar: The Big Adventure of a Little Sock Monkey 2007

(by Amy Schwartz and Leonard S. Marcus, HarperCollins $16.99 ●●●●○) Move over, Curious George, Oscar may be little but he needs no Man with a Yellow Hat to save him from his journey out into the big world. When Susie goes off to school without a key she will need, Oscar, an independent little monkey, takes responsibility and no easy trip to reach Susie just in the nick of time. A fast-paced fantasy. 3–7.

■ A Particular Cow 2007

(by Mem Fox/illus. by Terry Denton, Harcourt $16 ●●●●○) What happens on one particular day to one particular cow is enough to turn a not-too-particular day into a very eventful one. This is one of those yarns that just keeps growing sillier and sillier. 4–7.

■ Silly Billy 2007

(by Anthony Browne, Candlewick $15.99 ●●●●○) Poor Billy has a lot of trouble sleeping with all the things on his mind. Although others tell him not to worry, his grandmother assures him that she had the same problem. She shares her small "worry dolls" with Billy and they save the nights! Based on a Central American custom, this just might catch on in your house, too.

Pop-Up Books

■ My Little Yellow Taxi 2007

(by Stephen T. Johnson, Harcourt $19.95 ●●●●○) This is one of those books that is more of a toy than a story. Surprisingly heavy in the hand, maybe it will build muscles, too, as kids play with the lift-out parts of the taxi and the moving parts on the sturdy pages.

This is an action-packed book for city kids with a typical fascination with taxis. 3 & up.

■ Ruff! Ruff! Where's Scruff? 2007

(by David A. Carter, Harcourt $13.95 ●●●●○) Scruff is one muddy dog who is due for a bath. Turn the lift-the-flap pages and try to find Scruff hidden behind the cows, the pigs, and other barnyard animals. Children as young as two will like this, but it is easy to tear—so make it a parent-and-child book to share. 2–5.

■ Sharks and Other Sea Monsters 2007

(by Robert Sabuda & Matthew Reinhart, Candlewick $27.99 ●●●●○) In typical fashion, Sabuda has created yet another incredible pop-up book. This is darker and the information denser than most. If your young reader is taken with the world of sharks, whales, scorpions, and prehistoric sea monsters that still live, this is a book to dive into. There will be lots of *ooohs* and *aahhhhs* as the pages, large and small, pop open. They say 5 & up; we think

this will be a waste for kids under 7 or 8 but enjoyed by those well beyond—say 40 & up.

■ MOMMY? 2007

(by Maurice Sendak, Arthur Yorinks, Matthew Reinhart, Scholastic $25 ●●●●○) Sendak has taken a classic theme—the search for a missing mother—and transformed it into a zany one-word pop-up

Pop-Up Books / Early School

joke. Not for the timid, this pops from one page to the next with a boy who looks a lot like Max asking for "Mommy?" From one page to the next, classic monsters such as Frankenstein and Dracula pop off the pages. When Mommy finally pops out of the closet, we think the joke will be lost on anyone under the age of 7 & up.

■ Sabuda and Reinhart Present: Castle 2007

(by Kyle Olman/illus. by Tracy Sabin, Scholastic $19.99 ●●●●●) Fot the child who is taken with medieval times and castles, this is a must-have treasure. Awesome pop-ups of buildings, knights, and serfs all come to life with paper engineered to leap off the pages. An informative text may eventually be read—after all the wows! 7 & up.

Early School

■ Alphabet Explosion! Search and Count from Alien to Zebra 2007

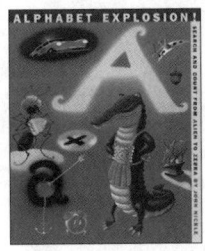

(by John Nickle, Random House $16.95 ●●●●●) Search each of the pages for an amazing number of objects and actions that start with the featured letter. Take the letter G, for example—there are 25 Gs, as in *glass, golfing, golf club, grinning, green*, etc. This is not an alphabet book for beginners. But it is fun for 5–8.

■ Adèle & Simon 2007

(by Barbara MClintock, Farrar, Straus $16 ●●●●●) In turn-of-the-20th-century Paris, young Adèle picks up her little brother Simon after school, warning him not to lose his things on the way home. What follows is a series of lost objects that must be found in the Breugelesque crowd scenes. McClintock's romp through old Paree includes a sighting of Miss Clavell and Madeline, ah *oui*! 5–8.

BOOKS

■ Happy Birthday, Jamela! 2007

(by Niki Daly, Farrar, Straus $16 ooooo) Jamela is about to have a birthday. When she goes shopping for a special dress, she finds "princess shoes" that would be perfect. But Mama says she needs sturdy school shoes. Jamela, inspired by the sparkly shoes, decorates her new school shoes. Although Mama is annoyed, an artist neighbor is impressed. Jamela manages to get her wish—even before she blows out the candles on her cake. 6 & up.

■ Olivia Forms a Band 2007

(by Ian Falconer, Atheneum $17.95 ooooo) It's the Fourth of July, and how can you have fireworks without a band? That is what Olivia wants to know. Fear not, the ever-resourceful Olivia has enough imagination to become a one-pig band! 4–8.

■ Owen & Mzee 2007

(by Isabella Hatkoff et al., Scholastic $16.99 ooooo) A true story that came out of the Tsunami, about when a baby hippo was left stranded after a storm and taken away to a park where an ancient, giant tortoise (and a lot of caring people) take over nurturing the young hippo. Done with photos, this is a good book for talking about feelings and the big concept that even when one feels alone, there are others who are there, if you allow them into your life.

■ Pancakes for Supper! 2007

(by Anne Isaacs/illus. by Mark Teague, Scholastic $16.99 ooooo) Broadly based on the *Little Black Sambo* story, this has none of the usual baggage. Unlike recent retellings, it is not a conscious PC rendering. Here, the heroine falls out of her parents' wagon and cleverly avoids being eaten alive by giving each of five wild animals a piece of her clothing that they believe makes them most

Early School

attractive. When the five disagree on who is the best, they end up in a chase that turns them into maple syrup. You guessed it—young Toby and her parents use that sweet ending on their pancakes. A keeper. 4 & up.

■ Edwina, The Dinosaur Who Didn't Know She Was Extinct 2007

(by Mo Willems, Hyperion $16.99 ❍❍❍❍❍) Remember *Danny's Dinosaur*? Edwina steps from a similar mold and is equally delightful. One doubting Thomas by the name of Reginald Von Hoobie-Doobie tries his best to prove that dinosaurs are extinct, but Edwina manages to prove that facts are not all we need in this world! 4 & up.

■ Flotsam 2007

(by David Wiesner, Clarion $16 ❍❍❍❍❍) What a splendid, imaginative work! Told without words, this seaside fantasy takes off when a camera washes up on the shore. It is found by a boy who has the film developed and discovers in the images a magnificent underwater world—as well as children from all over the world who have seen its wonders. Wiesner spins his own brand of magic! 5–8.

■ Mama, I'll Give you the World 2007

(by Roni Schotter/illus. by S. Saelig Gallagher, Random House $16.95 ❍❍❍❍❍) Luisa goes to Walter's World of Beauty every day after school. That's where her Mama works and Luisa does her homework. Mama works to give Luisa the world—someday. But Luisa decides that she needs to give Mama the world—for her birthday. A warm and charming story of friendship, community, and love between a mother and daughter. A beauty. 4 & up.

■ Museum Trip 2007

(by Barbara Lehman, Houghton Mifflin $15 ❍❍❍❍❍) A wordless gem of an adventure. On a class trip to the museum, a boy gets separated from his group. While looking for them, he finds his way into a small room. There he finds a collection of mazes on display and is transformed to fit into the mazes. As the young reader finds the path through the mazes he and the boy save themselves and leave the museum triumphant. In fact, the young hero of the story and the museum guard both wear the same golden medal. Another winner from the author of **The Red Book.** 5 & up.

■ **Pandora's Box** 2007

(retold and illustrated by Jean Marzollo, Little, Brown $12.99 ●●●●●) Get ready to laugh out loud—a rare event when reading a Greek myth. If you take your myths solemnly, you may be troubled when Prometheus steals fire from Zeus and cooks oatmeal for his brother. On the other hand, there's something wonderfully childlike about the troubles that come flying out of Pandora's box, as well as comforting in knowing that hope and curiosity are not lost. Marzollo's unique telling of this and **Let's Go, Pegasus!** have humor and a good page-turning pace for beginning myth readers. 7 & up.

■ **Snow Globe Family** 2007

(by Jane O'Connor/illus. by S.D. Schindler, Putnam $16.99 ●●●●●) Side by side two families live, one in a house, another in a snow globe, waiting for the first big snowstorm of the season. In this charming fantasy world, the family in the snow globe is noticed only by the baby of the big family. An imaginative story that matches the mesmerizing magic that children often find with a shake of a snow globe. 5 & up.

■ **Take Care, Good Knight** 2007

(by Shelley Moore Thomas/illus. by Paul Meisel, Dutton $15.99 ●●●●●) When the wizard goes off for a day, he leaves his precious cats in the care of three little dragons, not knowing that they do not know how to read his directions. An amusing story that proves how important it is to know how to read! 4–8.

■ **Yoon and the Christmas Mitten** 2007

(by Helen Recorvits/illus. by Gabi Swiatkowska, Farrar, Straus $16

Early School – Historical Fiction

○○○○) A tender story about a Korean girl who believes in Mr. Santa Claus, no matter how many times her parents tell her this is not their custom. When Christmas eve comes, Yoon hangs up a mitten, since she has no stocking. A gem. 5 & up.

Historical Fiction

■ Brothers 2007

(by Yin/illus. by Chris Soentpiet, Philomel $16.99 ○○○○○) Set in San Francisco's Chinatown, this is an immigrant story of Ming, a boy from China, who is befriended by Patrick, the son of Irish immigrants. Though Ming's older brother warns him not to venture out of Chinatown, the boy not only finds friendship, he saves the family business. Soentpiet's memorable illustrations are infused with light, color, and character. 6 & up.

■ Night Boat to Freedom 2007

(by Margot Theis Raven/illus. by E.B. Lewis, Farrar Straus $16 ○○○○○) Granny Judith urges 12-year-old Christmas John to take others across the river from Kentucky to Ohio and freedom under the dark moon. Each time he returns, he tells Franny the color his passengers wore, the colors of freedom. Granny uses her dye pots to make a quilt of freedom that will take them across one day. A moving story inspired by reading hundreds of slave narratives collected in the 1930s. Masterful storytelling and art are perfectly blended! 7 & up.

■ Satchel Paige, Don't Look Back 2007

(by David A. Adler/illus. by Terry Widener, Harcourt $16 ○○○○○) One of the greatest pitchers of all time, Satchel Paige began his career in the Negro Baseball League and stayed with the game well beyond the time when most retire. His goal—playing in the major leagues and in the World Series—took longer than most to accomplish, but speaks to the idea of not looking back. 5–9.

BOOKS

Non-Fiction

■ First Picture Spanish *2007*

(Felicity Brooks & Mairi Mackinnon et al., Usborne $14.99 ●●●●●) Cleverly designed with illustrations and lift up flaps with Spanish phrases that reveal the translations. To hear the phrases spoken, go to the publisher's website. This is an interaction that really can be helpful. 7–70.

■ Rainforest *2007*

(by Thomas Marent, DK $40 ●●●●●) Every coffee table should have this stunning book that is chock full of stunning photographs of the plants, animals, birds, and insects that inhabit this precious habitat. Includes a CD with sounds of the rainforest. Magnificent!

■ John, Paul, George & Ben *2007*

(by Lane Smith, Hyperion $16.99 ●●●●●) A preamble to the Founding Fathers, Lane Smith does a witty send up, playing on the celebrated stories of each. He takes us back to their boyhoods, showing how they were each destined to their greatness. This is a funny book for those who know the legends about these American icons. That said, one has to wonder how many kids today will see the joke. This just might be a book for grownups of a certain age. History in schools these days often skips these old chestnuts about honest George and Clever Ben. 8 & up.

■ The Usborne Book of Art *2007*

(by Rosie Dickins, Usborne $22.95 ●●●●●) Well chosen—from Ancient Egypt to avantgarde art of today. Handsomely illustrated with discussions of techniques as well as artists' materials. This is a comprehensive book that presents clearly written and interesting entry points into the world of art history. With internet links, this is an excellent survey for junior high and beyond. Also by the same author, a simpler version, **Usborne Children's Book**

Early School / Later School Years

of Art ($14.99) for 7 & up.

- **Why Are the Ice Caps Melting?** 2007
- **Who Lives in an Alligator Hole?**

(by Anne Rockwell, HarperCollins $4.99 each ●●●●●) Here are two timely subjects from today's news that may be on your child's worry list. **Global Warming** and **Alligators** give young readers a look to the North and the South. Clearly written in child-accessible prose with illustrations that add to their understanding, these are two fine additions to the *Let's Read and Find Out* series for early school-age readers. 7 & up.

Chapter Books

- **The Looking Glass Wars** 2007

(by Frank Beddor, Dial $16.99 ●●●●●) In the tradition of *Wicked* and *Peter and the Starcatchers*, here's the exciting, compelling (and can you say, "soon to be a screenplay"?) back story of *Alice in Wonderland*. What we soon discover is that Mr. Carroll took great liberties in twisting the true story of Princess Alyss Heart of Wonderland. Her story will appeal to both boys and girls. You'll want the next installment at once! 8 & up.

- **Peter and the Shadow Thieves** 2007

(by Dave Barry and Ridley Pearson, Hyperion $18.99 ●●●●●) Sometimes sequels can be disappointing, but Barry and Pearson deliver another fast-paced adventure that continues to tell the prequel adventures of Peter Pan. Here, Peter leaves Mollusk Island with Tinker Bell to help his friend Molly rescue her mother from the evil hands of Lord Ombra.

- **Toys Go Out: Being the Adventures of a Knowledgeable Stingray, a Tough Little Buffalo, and Someone Called Plastic** 2007

(by Emily Jenkins/illus. by Paul O. Zelinsky, Random House $16.95 ●●●●●) A charming book just right for sharing at bedtime. Readers come to know three favorite toys of a little girl. Someone Called Plastic discovers he's really a rubber bouncing ball. Stingray discovers he's not a real Stingray and the Little Buffalo discovers that he is truly treasured by the little girl and his friends. A calmer, less action-packed version of *Toy Story*.

■ Water Street 2007

(by Patricia Reilly Giff, Random House $15.95 ●●●●●) With the construction of the Brooklyn Bridge as the backdrop, Giff makes the struggles of working-class families in Brooklyn in 1875 come to life for young readers. Here the focus is on Nory's (of Nory Ryan's Song fame) daughter Byrd and her upstairs neighbor Thomas Neary.

■ Weedflower 2007

(by Cynthia Kadohata, Simon & Schuster $16.95 ●●●●●) While Sumiko experiences discrimination in her home town before the war, the attack on Pearl Harbor changes her life forever. Her family is sent to an internment camp where she befriends a Native American. A compelling view of this dark period in American history (for a non-fiction account, see **Dear Miss Breed,** review below).

■ The Miraculous Journey of Edward Tulane 2007

(by Kate DiCamillo/illus. by Bagram Ibatoulline, Candlewick $18.99 ●●●●●) This story will remind you of Rachel Field's classic **Hitty,** but the tale of Edward Tulane is far more accessible. As always, Kate DiCamillo whisks you away into a special place, where she spins a tale, this time, of a china rabbit who must survive many losses before understanding what it is to love and be loved in return. 7 & up.

■ Sherlock Holmes and the Baker Street Irregulars, The Fall of the Amazing Zalindas 2007

(by Tracy Mack and Michael Citrin, Orchard Books $16.99 ●●●●●) The famous detective is aided in his work by a gang of homeless boys, the Baker Street Irregulars. Engaging mystery told from the perspective of these young sleuths. 8 & up.

While we don't give ourselves awards, here are two books that are highly recommended.

■ The Prince's Bedtime 2007

(by Joanne Oppenheim/illus. by Miriam Latimer, Barefoot Books $16.99 ●●●●●) Truly one of our family's favorite bedtime stories. There's a little prince who can't fall asleep no matter what his parents try . . . wiz-

ards, musicians . . . but with no success. A much simpler approach does the trick. A must-read for reluctant young sleepers! 3–7.

■ **Dear Miss Breed: True Stories of the Japanese American Incarceration During World War II and a Librarian Who Made a Difference** 2007

(by Joanne Oppenheim, Scholastic $22.99 ●●●●○) Kids often struggle with how they can make a difference. Here's the story of a remarkable young children's librarian who did just that. Clara Breed was horrified when her young Japanese American patrons and their families were sent to incarceration camps. She corresponded with many throughout the war, sending them books, supplies, and most importantly, her hope and friendship. Joanne was captivated by this story. She located and took oral histories from many of Miss Breed's "children," now in their 70s and 80s. Given the current climate we live in, with the ever-present threat of terrorism, this book provides a chilling lesson about what can happen to a nation when fear overcomes reason. 12 & up.

OPPENHEIM TOY PORTFOLIO PLATINUM DVD AWARDS 2007

Why No Baby DVDs? Developmentally, babies learn from active, real-life experiences rather than from being "plugged in" to passively watching others at such an early age. We believe that a mirror would be more interactive and age-appropriate than a video screen. Reading books and talking about the pictures, or interacting as you sing songs and recite rhymes, will do more to build language than plugging babies into the TV to look at pretty pictures with music. For kids under 2 (and beyond), less is more! We are delighted that the American Pediatric Association has agreed with our position.

The golden age of children's videos has passed. Most of what fills the shelves at the store are canned cartoons (unfortunate) or rereleases on DVD. Be forewarned: don't judge a DVD by its title. The lead story may be the same, but other stories on the same disk are often totally different form the original. By mixing them up this way they appear to be "new"—but once again, "new" is not always better.

Never-ending. With the new format it's more likely that you will slide the disk in and let it play from one end to another. If you are traveling cross-country these long DVDs might make the miles fly by. But at home, they can be seductive and hard to turn off—another example of too much of a good thing. We've also found that they are harder to navigate, so it's sometimes hard to skip ahead, and kids are unlikely to push the pause button. Parents will need to monitor the length of time spent. Nor are all the stories equally worthwhile. Some of the choices are better than others and often there are too many "properties" that are downright forgettable. Ideally, you would be able to select a trio of films and then the DVD would shut down. But that is not possible. So, the new bigger and better DVDs are a mixed blessing that once again require parental management.

More Scare for Your Dollar. Entertainment that looks like children's fare sometimes comes laced with a heavy dose of adult-sized violence. While many of us remember watching the Wicked Witch of the West from behind a blanket, most of us were school-age, not three. Some filmmakers seem to forget that young children are still working on the distinction between real and make-believe. DVDs, like toys, are not "one size fits all."

Screen Your DVDs. Whenever possible, take the time to preview videos, or at least watch with your children the first time around. You may be surprised at the number of videos you choose not to watch to the end. Series still need to be viewed one title at a time, otherwise you are apt to come home with a video for toddlers with story lines about aliens, witches, and ghosts (*Kipper*); or how about a "legend" for 2- and 3-year-olds told by a fairy who comes from a blue moon (*Blue's Clues*)? We even received a preschool video about a boy who has good parents, nice toys . . . everything . . . except a body. Teaching kids to turn off a film because it's just not worth watching is also not a bad lesson to pass on.

Here are the top choices of the year:

■ Bear Snores On *2007*

(Scholastic Video Collection $14.95 ◉◉◉◉◉) One of our all-time favorite storybooks is brought to life with the same charm as the book. Bear sleeps all winter long and awakes to find a lair full of his woodland friends. Charming. DVD also includes **Waiting for Wings,** featuring the stunning artwork of Lois Ehlert and **Come On, Rain!** by Karen Hess. 3 &up.

■ Caillou, The Everyday Hero *2007*

(PBS $14.98 ◉◉◉◉◉) As always, Caillou delivers slice-of-life stories that are right on target for preschoolers. Caillou helps his little sister Rosie, he faces his fears about a waterslide, and plays with his friends as they construct a road and a bridge. No big surprises or scares here. Just right!

DVDs

■ Cars 2007

(Pixar $TBA ●●●●●) From the team that brought us The Incredibles and Toy Story, Cars delivers both stunning animation and an engaging story. A very ambitious race car, Lightning McQueen (Owen Wilson) finds himself in the the forgotten Route 66 town of Radiator Springs with such notable car characters as Doc Hudson (Paul Newman), a VW van (George Carlin), and Sally (Bonnie Hunt). A little long in places, but it delivers a solid message that family and friends are more important than celebrity or fortune. Humor, amazing graphics, and heart challenge the Hollywood myth of the go-it-alone macho-man, giving us a new kinder, gentler hero.

■ Growing Up with Winnie the Pooh: Love & Friendship 2007

(Disney $14.99 ●●●●●) From the kinder and gentler collection of Disney's Winnie the Pooh, these stories focus on honesty, helping friends, and respect. Calm and fuzzy, just as Pooh should be. (Be careful—there are a couple of Poohs that include scenes that are over-the-top suspenseful for younger viewers).

■ Popular Mechanics for Kids: Lightning and Other Forces of Nature 2007

(Koch Vision $14.98 ●●●●●) For kids who are weather fanatics this is a must see. Includes info on generators, a visit to Niagara Falls, an actual lightning storm, and a visit to the Boston Museum of Science. Hosted by two 'tween kids, this is really informative and engaging.

■ Wallace & Gromit: The Curse of the Were-Rabbit 2007

(Dreamworks $29.98 ●●●●●) We are big fans of Wallace (the inventor) & Gromit (his canine sidekick) and their latest film is wonderful. Together they run the Anti-Pesto pest control company and when prized veggies start disappearing prior to the big local veggie competition they are called into action. They're inventive and always fun to watch. Not intended for very young children.

■ The Greatest Game Ever Played 2007

(Disney $29.99 ●●●●●) Much like *The Legend of Bagger Vance*, but without the sexual tension (or scenes), **The Greatest Game Ever**

Played is the story of the local boy who against all odds gets an opportunity to play in the U.S. Open and of course, wins. Even better because it's based on a true story. Long in parts, but engaging, and continues in the tradition of great sports movies from this studio.

Blue Chip and Notable Past Winners: Feature-Length Films

These are widely available films that you'll find in the video store or library. They also are shown frequently on TV, but the video versions lack interrupting commercials—a real plus! Most of these are for early school years and beyond.

- Anne of Green Gables
- Apollo 13
- Babe
- Beauty and the Beast
- Beethoven Lives Upstairs
- The Borrowers
- Cinderella and Cinderella II
- Charlotte's Web
- Chicken Run
- Chitty Chitty Bang Bang
- E.T.
- Finding Nemo
- Fly Away Home
- Freaky Friday
- Gulliver's Travels
- Harriet the Spy
- Harry Potter series
- Holes
- Homeward Bound and Homeward Bound II
- Honey, We Shrunk Ourselves
- The Indian in the Cupboard
- The Lion King and The Lion King II
- The Little Mermaid
- Madeline
- Mary Poppins
- The Miracle
- Mulan
- My Dog Skip
- The Nutcracker (with Baryshnikov)
- October Sky
- Peter Pan (Mary Martin version)
- The Red Balloon
- Remember the Titans
- The Rookie
- The Santa Clause
- Sarah, Plain and Tall
- The Secret Garden
- Shrek and Shrek 2
- The Sound of Music
- Snow White
- Sounder
- Stuart Little and Stuart Little 2
- Tarzan
- To Kill a Mockingbird
- Willy Wonka and the Chocolate Factory
- The Wizard of Oz

DVD Plug-ins and Game Platforms

This is a big year for electronic gaming. In addition to three new next-gen game home platforms (Microsoft's Xbox 360, Nintendo's Wii, and the Sony Playstation 3), there are now multiple choices for gaming on the go (Game Boy and the DS from Nintendo, and Sony's PSP). Additionally, there are a huge number of plug & play games for the TV, games for computers, and even software for everyday DVD players.

High Tech For Preschool and Early School Years

■ Cranium Hullabaloo DVD Game
2007 PLATINUM AWARD

(Cranium $24.95 ●●●●●) Fun for a party or play date, this is an active game that involves kids in wiggling like an octopus, crawling like a lizard, and hopping like a kangaroo. As they move to  different colored and shaped playmates, kids may find themselves on the same square as a friend. No problem. It's not a competitive game. Winning is completely by chance as the caller announces the "Lucky Pad" that three kids may be standing on. With live-action video of animals and how they move, this game offers lots of opportunities for active play as well as quick rounds for multiple winners. A delightful adaptation of the original Hullabaloo game. 4–8. (877) 272-6486.

DVD Plug Ins

■ GeoTrax Rail & Road System *2007* PLATINUM AWARD

(Fisher-Price $24.99 ●●●●●) This expandable train set with a motorized diesel engine named Geo, will take kids on adventures on their own tracks, and in the accompanying DVD, which combines animated and real footage of all types of trains. (800) 432-5437.

■ Books by You *PREVIEW 2007*

(Knowledge Adventure $19.99) Kids help write a 70-page book by answering interactive questions asked by John Lithgow. The collaborative book can be read on the computer, printed at home, or even (for an additional fee) professionally bound. 8 & up.

■ Jump Start World *PREVIEW 2007*

(Knowledge Adventure $19.99 plus content updates) Knowledge Adventure, long known for its educational software, moves to the internet this year with a virtual world of learning. Kids earn badges to play arcade-style games by practicing school skills. 4–8.

■ ION *2007*

(Hasbro $119.99/additional cartridges $19.99 ●●●) The goal of **ION** is to bring high tech, age appropriate play to the preschool crowd. A built-in camera puts kids literally *into* the game. They see themselves onscreen along with the bubbles they must "break," operating the game by moving their whole bodies. The game is similar to (but less extensive and expensive than) Sony's **EyeToy Play** for the PS2. Our impression from the prototype was extremely positive, but the early production product we tested did not live up to our expectations in terms of graphics (poor) and the game was not responsive enough—creating a lot of frustration for our players. Great idea, needs more tweaking. We will post a final review on our website. (888) 836-7025.

■ Time-to-Learn Preschool *2007* PLATINUM AWARD

(Fisher-Price $89.95 ●●●●●) The stand-alone preschool playset is wonderfully complemented by a claymation DVD featuring the Little People kids that come with the preschool. Colors, numbers, and shapes are the focus of this school, and there are multiple features to help reinforce these concepts. (800) 432-5437.

DVD Plug Ins

■ Candy Land DVD Game

(Milton Bradley $29.99 ●●●●●) Put the playmats on the floor, plug this into your DVD player, and kids are ready for an active, but not too fast, moving game that gets them up off the couch. Players move from one of 24 color playmats to another collecting tokens as they go. An ideal game for developing listening skills and color concepts in a playful manner. Grown-up supervision is a must. 2–4 players. PLATINUM AWARD '06. (888) 836-7025.

■ Black Belts Karate Studio

(Spinmaster $24.99 ●●●●) Billed as a way to introduce preschoolers to karate, this comes with a DVD and mat. Our 5- to 7-year-old testers enjoyed following along. **Bella Dancerella** ($29.99 ●●●) did not impress our testers or their moms. One word: "Boring," said our 8-year-old testers who felt the intro took way too long. The references to using your left and right foot are going to be well beyond most 4s, 5s, and 6s. Our testers felt that the new **Cheerleading DVD** (●●●) went too quickly for them to follow. (800) 622-8339.

Educational Plug-Ins

For reviews of educational plug-ins, see pp. 102 and 174.

High Tech for Older School Years and Teens

Gaming Platforms

With the price of next-generation game platforms approaching the price of a personal computer, making the right choice is more important than ever. The selection criteria are different for kids from those for adult gamers, and the good news is that for kids, less is probably more.

Here are the questions we are most often asked about these machines.

Which next-gen platform would be most appropriate for younger children?

We don't recommend the purchase of a game platform for kids under 10.

What about for 'tweens?

Of the three choices—Wii, PS3, and Xbox360—the only clear choice for 'tweens and family gaming is Nintendo's Wii. Cheaper than the others, it also has the widest selection of age-appropriate games. While Sony and Microsoft have focused on hard-core, violent gaming, Nintendo has created a revolutionary game platform that gets kids using more than their thumbs. Once you've tried the motion-sensitive Wii controller you'll be hooked: it can swing like a tennis racket, spin like bicycle pedals, or beat like a baton. Brain and body power are engaged in many of the Nintendo Wii titles; the emphasis is on fun rather than bloodshed.

Are there family friendly titles for the other home game platforms?

Yes! Sports titles are a good bet, and we also like dancing games like the Konami's **Dance, Dance, Revolution** series, and **Pump It Up** (Mastiff). **Play2** and **Kenetic** (Sony) for the PS2 are also favorites: game play is activated and controlled by the EyeToy camera that senses a player's movement. We can't say for certain whether the EyeToy games will be forward-compatible with the PS3.

With the exception of sports titles, family friendly titles for the Xbox 360 are few and far between. Microsoft is dedicating a lot of resources to **Viva Piñata!** for Xbox 360 (and also for PCs) based on the TV show of the same name. Borrowing elements from Zoo Tycoon, kids build a fantasy habitat for fanciful living piñatas like the "Horsetachio." The low-key game has kids cultivating and landscaping gardens, and taming and training animals. Sadly, at a time when Microsoft has drastically cut back on its educational software offerings, the emphasis here is on "entertainment" and not skills. However, it is a good sign that children haven't been completely forgotten by Microsoft as it moves to its next-gen platform. We're also excited by Lucasarts **Thrillville,** an amusement park sim that in previews looks every bit as much fun as the PC's **Rollercoaster Tycoon** (see page 204).

Another good source of games for Xbox360 is the Xbox Live Arcade. Here you can download puzzle and arcade games such as **Zuma** and **Hexen** that have no violence, and some strategizing.

As of this writing we haven't seen any title designed exclusively for the PS3 that is kids-oriented. Upcoming titles we've heard of set the crimson palette for the new platform: **Tom Clancy's Splinter Cell Double Agent, Brothers In Arms Hell's Highway, Full Auto 2: Battlelines.** This may change as time goes by, and many of the family friendly titles that work on the PS2 may be able to run on a PS3, but it is too soon to tell.

If you already have a PS2, Xbox, or Game Cube, and don't want to be an early adopter of the Nintendo Wii, you might want to consider holding out until more family friendly titles come to market.

Notable PS2 Games and/or Xbox games

■ Karaoke Revolution Series

(Konami $50 ●●●●●) Konami knows how to throw a good party—witness the popularity of the **Dance Dance Revolution Series.** Now they've taken the karaoke craze to the next level with a series of games for the PS2, Xbox, and Xbox360 that monitor how well you sing. (For some of us that's more painful than fun!) The closer to pitch and rhythm, the more the crowd cheers. Depending on your platform, there are rock, country, and even American Idol versions. 8 & up.

■ EyeToy, Play, Play2, and Kenetics *2007*

(Sony $49.99 ●●●●●) The EyeToy is a camera that acts as a game controller, and is available only for the PS2. Kids see themselves on the TV screen, in the video games, where they use their whole body to play. Originally bundled with **Play,** a series of arcade mini-games, the technology found its way into many games, including **Harry Potter** for PS2. **Play** and **Play 2** (●●●●½) are active games for all ages, while **Kenetics** (●●●●½) is designed as a workout program for 'tweens, teens, and adults.

■ Dance Dance Revolution Series

(Konami $50 ●●●●●) This series continues to pump out delightfully difficult dance challenges featuring hot, current songs. The new version has EyeToy and DancePad support. The difficulty factor makes this game better for kids 10 & up.

Portable Game Platforms
What is the difference between Nintendo's Gameboy Mini, GameboyDS, and the Sony PSP? Which one is better?

The Gameboy DS (and its sleeker upgrade, the DS Lite) offer the most innovative, fun, and mentally challenging games for 'tweens on the go. Games designed for the DS use two screens (one of which is touch sensitive). It is rumored that there will be some cross-functionality between the DS and Wii home platform.

For most kids under 10, the Gameboy Mini, a micro-refit of the GameBoy, will be more than enough, though the games on the DS—particularly NintenDogs—will be reason enough to upgrade to the more powerful (and expensive) dual-screen platform.

It is clear from the cutting edge, Darth Vader gloss-black style of the Sony PSP that it was designed for teens and adults looking to take the gaming experience, together with music and movies, wherever they go. The PSP has an enormous 4.3"-wide screen, wireless connectivity, optical drive, and memory card support—and a price that is nearly two times that of the DS. Like the DS, a number of puzzle games are available, but there are even more titles that center on shooting and violence.

Among our favorite DS games:

■ Electroplankton

(Nintendo $34.99 ●●●○) Electroplankton is like no other program you're likely to have tried: Not really a game, but more of a creative playground that mixes music and art. The electronic creatures within your DS can be poked, prodded, and twirled into fantastic patterns to create mesmerizing soundscapes. 10 & up. Rated E.

■ New Super Mario Bros. *2007*

(Nintendo $34.99 ●●●○) This is a portable update to the side-scrolling action-game style that made Nintendo what it is today; it makes no pretense to educational merit. 10 & up. Rated E.

■ Animal Crossing Wild World *2007*

(Nintendo $34.99 ●●●○) Another reenvisioning by Nintendo of what electronic play can be. Not so much a game, but a living world to explore. You'll be exploring, decorating, and otherwise interacting with cyber creatures in this electronic world. 10 & up. Rated E.

■ WarioWare: Touched! *2007*

(Nintendo $39.99 ●●●●) This collection of fast-paced games pushes the DS's touch pad to the limit. It's not just about how fast you can solve the puzzles, it's about figuring out how to solve them that makes the game so much fun. Testers told us they liked it for short, quick game breaks when they didn't have time to get deep into more complicated fare. 10 & up.

■ Brain Age *2007*

(Nintendo $19.95 ●●●●) The strangest game of the year, Brain Age is a series of mini-games designed to "exercise" your brain. Soduko and other brain teasers break the expectations we have of mobile gaming. Controlled entirely by voice or touchpad, featuring no violence, and with a focus on developing minds rather than on shooting bullets, Brain Age may herald the dawn of a new age in gaming. 10 & up.

Favorite PSP games:

■ Bust-A-Move

(Majesco $19.99 ●●●) Single and multiplayer on-the-go fun, this is a puzzler game that mixes dexterity and strategic thinking as you "bust" bubbles that look like multicolored grape clusters by making similarly colored groups. The game style has been around on many platforms, but this is the best looking version you can take with you. 10 & up.

■ Lumines

(Ubisoft $19.99 ●●●●) This game reminds us of Tetris, but with a difference: it is faster and more fluid. It is up to you to build the biggest area possible using multi-colored cubes. Sounds easy, until the pulsating beat and frenetic graphics begin to get under your skin. It requires concentration, an ability to think ahead, and visual conceptualization. 10 & up.

What about Computers as gaming, learning, and creativity platforms?

Sadly, the supply of new educational software for home consumption has dwindled. Good deals, though, can still be had on classic drill-and-review titles from Knowledge Adventure and The Learning Company, often in bundles at greatly reduced prices.

But the computer is still an excellent platform for exploring, creativity, and gaming. Be sure to check that your computer is powerful enough to handle the requirements of new games, as older machines won't cut it. Also, as with all software, check the ESRB rating on the package. While we think the ESRB sometimes lets games go with too soft a rating, if they say it is violent, it certainly is.

Some of our favorite computer titles are:

■ Roller Coaster Tycoon 3

(Atari $29.99 ●●●●●) Roller Coaster Tycoon 3 puts you in charge of every aspect of an amusement park, from roller coaster design to how much to charge for the cotton candy. Though the subject matter seems "light," the game is a learn-by-doing school on subjects as diverse as physics and economics. Best of all, you can even "ride" the coasters.

■ Zoo Tycoon 2 series

(Microsoft $29.99 ●●●●) Though not as full of thrills as Roller Coaster Tycoon, the gentler pace, easier learning curve, and more in-depth information about animals made this a better fit for many of our testers. New expansion packs feature aerial trams and jeep rides that let you explore the 3-D parks that you create. 10 & up.

■ Digital Blue Microscope *2007*

(Digital Blue $74.99 ●●●●●) Updated and improved, this gadget has a still and motion picture camera that lets kids view and record the microscopic world on their computer. 10 & up.

■ Piano Wizard

(Piano Wizard $199.95 ●●●●) This bundled piano keyboard/software combo teaches kids the fundamentals of reading music by turning the process into a video game! 8 & up.

Plug-Ins

Jakks, Tiger Games, Radica, and others manufacture game gadgets that plug directly into the TV. Unlike the PS2 or Xbox, they usually are not very expandable and have limited quality graphics. However, we like these two plug-ins because they get kids up and moving.

■ Play TV Baseball 3

(Radica $39.99 ●●●●) At first our 'tween and teen testers thought this simulation baseball game was too hard, but 30 minutes later they were having a great time taking turns at bat. They also liked the opportunity to work on pitching. The set comes with a tethered ball

DVD Plug Ins

(that you don't actually throw—we had trouble with that concept, our testers did not) and a plastic bat that keeps track of how you're doing! Marked 8 & up, we'd say more like 10 to 45. (800) 803-9611.

■ Star Wars Game Saga Edition
(Tiger Games $49.99 ●●●●) Plug the training droid into your TV and players with wireless light saber are ready to become Jedi warriors. Testers had an aerobic workout swinging the light saber and ridding the galaxy of droids and other evildoers! We don't usually review zap-it games, but this is more fantasy than war, and multi-generational—it may even get parents up and on their feet! May the Force be with you. 8 & up. (888) 836-7025.

DVD Games

■ Harry Potter Deluxe Edition Scene It?
(Screenlife $49.95 ●●●●) Chances are you've seen and even played Scene It? before. Players race to identify and answer questions from old films or TV shows. This one is especially for Harry Potter film aficionados, with images and questions from all the Harry Potter films including "Harry Potter and the Goblet of Fire." (866) 383-4263.

■ American Idol All Star Challenge *2007*
(Screen Life $34.95 ●●) Unlike the American Idol show, where contestants are judged on the quality of their performances, players of this game are rewarded (or not) arbitrarily by the DVD. There is no skill, performance, or strategy necessary to keep this game moving. Even worse than false praise, you could give the performance of a lifetime, and then get roasted by a video clip of Simon, just because the game randomly chose it. (866) 384-4263.

■ Digi Makeover *2007*
(Radica $59.99 ●●●) The concept here is kind of fun. You take your picture with the built-in camera, load your picture to the TV screen and then you can use the interactive console to change your hair, makeup, eye color, etc. Not the most introspective toy, but fun in theory. Unfortunately, our testers did not think the added graphics were very good. **Jibbi** ($29.99 ●●●) is a voice-activated interactive pet that lives on your child's television. Our testers found that he was not very responsive and was often confused by regular background noise. Testers preferred Neopets on line to Jibbi. (800) 803-9611.

■Family Tetris *2007* Platinum Award

(Radica $29.99 ●●●●○) Everyone wanted a turn playing this head-to-head Tetris game that you connect to your television. Comes loaded with five different versions of the classic game. This version got high marks for being able to set different skill levels on each of the two controllers. Marked 3 & up, but will be best enjoyed by 7s & up. (800) 803-9611.

OPPENHEIM TOY PORTFOLIO
SNAP AWARDS 2007

This is a sampling of the new **Special Needs Adaptable Product (SNAP) Awards** for 2007. Many toys throughout this book will be of interest to kids with special needs. You will also find SNAP awards and activities from previous years on our website, www.toyportfolio.com.

■ ActiviTot Developmental Gym 2007
(Tiny Love $83 ❍❍❍❍❍) This oversized pear-shaped mat will be welcome, especially for older babies who may be delayed, as it's bigger than typical playmats that are quickly outgrown. This has built-in toys, mirror, and music box that can be moved about for tummy-time activities. (800) 843-6292.

■ Lamaze Clap With Me Monkey 2007
(RC2/Learning Curve $19.99 ❍❍❍❍❍) Clap monkey's hands and sing the familiar tune, "If you're happy and you know it, clap your hands!" Beginners will love the ability to activate the music and will soon learn to make the monkey clap with a squeeze at the right moment. **Activity:** Sing the song without the monkey and clap your child's hands on cue. Add other motions such as stamping your feet, wiggling your nose, throwing a kiss. (800) 704-8697.

■ Toss the Taggie 2007
(Taggies $19.95 ❍❍❍❍❍) Perfect for encouraging crawling and chasing games, this soft fabric ball is slightly under-stuffed; it has ribbon Taggies for easy grabbing and a jolly jingle sound inside.

Activity: Use the jingle ball for your own back-and-forth roly-poly games, or set up some soft animals in a stack and roll the ball to make them go "Boom!" (877) 482-4443.

■ Peek-a-Blocks Bucket of Builders 2007

(Fisher-Price $19.95 ooooo) A large bucket with a "bristle" lid comes loaded with fifteen interesting blocks. Each has see-through sides and colorful items inside to talk about. For youngest players, this is a good toy for filling-and-dumping games. **Activity:** Count how many you can stack on the lid before they fall down. Use these for talking about colors, too. (800) 432-5437.

■ My First Quatro Set 2007

(Lego Systems $9.99 ooooo) Twenty bricks are twice the size of Duplo blocks and a favorite for stacking. Or bring home the Large Quatro Bucket ($19.95/75 pieces). **Activity:** Play a color sorting game. Do you have more of one color? What color has the smallest number of pieces? Which color makes the tallest stack? The shortest? (800) 233-8756.

■ iPlay Zoom Around Garage 2007

(International Playthings $59.99 ooooo) A multilevel garage with an elevator and four chunky magnetic cars that can ride up and roll down the chutes. It has sound effects and flashing lights for dramatic play. **Activity:** Use the cars for talking about colors and using the position words *up, down, inside, outside, first, last*. Using these abstract position words in context gives them hands-on meaning. (800) 445-8347.

■ Little People Lil' School Bus 2007

(Fisher-Price $16.99 ooooo) Push down on the bus driver and the lights flash, horn beeps, and music plays on this yellow bus that plays "Wheels on the Bus." Bus includes a wheelchair but unlike earlier versions, no ramp for getting on and off. (800) 432-5437.

■ Lucky the Incredible Wonder Pup 2007

(Zizzle $49.99 ooooo) Looking for a toy that encourages language? This is it! Lucky is a plush dog that responds to 15 commands including "lie down," "come here," and "shake hands." But you must remember to say "Lucky" first, and wait for him to bark, indicating that he's ready. A lovable, well trained pooch that needs no housebreaking! (866) 494-9953.

■ Jumbo Jungle Animals 2007

(Learning Resources $25.99 ●●●●●) These are perfect props for blocks and pretend play. A 13" giraffe, an elephant, a lion, a tiger, and a gorilla. **Activity:** Put the animals in a row. Have your child turn around. Now, rearrange two of the animals. When your child turns back, can she tell which ones were moved? A good visual memory game. (800) 222-3909.

■ Funky Artist 2007

(Alex $19.99 ●●●●●) One step above finger paints, this set of three brushes is like nothing you have seen before. One is like a string mop, one like the soft brush in a car wash, and one like a flower. Each produces a different texture. Comes with three bottles of paint and big flat dishes for the paint. **Activity:** Make the most of mixed paint by discovering how colors blend to make a new color. (800) 699-2539.

■ Thomas & Friends Echo Tunnel 2007

(RC2/Learning Curve $49.99 ●●●●●) Here's another toy to encourage talking. A prop for the wooden train set. Push the button and talk into the tunnel, and it echoes what you say. (800) 704-8697.

■ Magneatos Intermediate 2007

(Guidecraft $15–$100 ●●●●●) Smaller in scale than the Jumbo Magneatos, they are still the right size rods and magnetic balls designed for easy handling. However, the short rods do fit into a choke tube, so they are not for kids who are still mouthing their toys. For them we suggest staying with the Jumbo Magneatos. (800) 465-6342.

■ Caterpillar Race 2007

(Edushape/PlaySound $12.95 ●●●●●) Two caterpillars race to the finish line. Players roll the dice and move forward the matching color piece of the caterpillar's body. A fun color concept game with easy rules to learn and good fun to play. (800) 404-4744.

Using Ordinary Toys for Kids with Special Needs

■ Tea Party Game 2007

(eeBoo $15 ●●●●○) Players use a spinner to collect the pieces of the tea set needed for their party. There are no skills involved in this luck-of-the-draw game. Graphics are beautiful. **Activity:** Have a pretend tea party with your child and some of his favorite dolls/bears. (212) 222-0823.

■ Word Whammer Fridge Phonics 2007

(LeapFrog $24.99 ●●●●●) Use this for letter name and sound recognition games. An electronic toy that sticks to the fridge and not only says letters, but blends sounds. Like last year's **Fridge Phonics Magnetic Letters,** this "speaks" and goes one step further with spelling games for older kids. We still love the original **Fridge Phonics** and love that they have added lowercase letters this year! Buy both sets and have kids play upper- and lowercase matching games free-form on the fridge door! (800) 701-5327.

■ Alphabet Puzzle Boards 2007

(Lauri $29.99 ●●●●●) Like the old A–Z puzzle board, these go a step further with an object for each letter in the alphabet. Each board has both upper- and lowercase letters. Handling the letters gives children a feel for their shapes. **Activity:** Use these for tracing or pressing into to play dough, or place a piece of paper on top of the letter(s) in the child's name and use a crayon to make a rubbing. It is like magic when the letter or name appears! (800) 451-0520.

Contact Companies

Company	Consumer Number	Website
Aeromax Toys	877-776-2291	aeromaxtoys.com
Alex	800-666-2539	alextoys.com
American Girl	800-845-0005	americangirl.com
Automoblox	973-364-8090	automoblox.com
Baby Einstein	800-793-1454	babyeinstein.com
Back to Basics	800-356-5360	backtobasicstoys.com
Balitono	609-936-8807	balitono.com
Bead Bazaar	800-838-1769	beadkit.com
Binney & Smith	800-272-9652	binney-smith.com
Blue Orange Games	415-252-0372	blueorangegames.com
Borderline	800-641-9996	borderlinegames.com
Briarpatch	800-232-7427	briarpatch.com
Brio	888-274-6869	knex.com
Cadaco	800-621-5426	cadaco.com
Ceaco	800-638-7568	ceaco.com
Chenille Craft	800-621-1261	chenillecraft.com
Community Playthings	800-777-4244	communityplaythings.com
Constructive Playthings	800-832-0572	constplay.com
Coop Kids	760-931-5733	coopsport.com
Corolle	800-668-4846	corolledolls.com
Cranium	877-272-6486	cranium.com
Creativity for Kids	800-311-8684	creativityforkids.com
Didax	800-458-0024	didax.com
Discovery Kids	800-938-0333	kids.discovery.com
Educational Insights	800-995-4436	edin.com
Edushape	800-404-4744	edushape.com
eeBoo	212-222-0823	eeboo.com
Emines	408-247-3298	emines.com
Enchantmints	888-440-6468	enchantmints.com
European Expressions	800-779-2205	europeanexpressions.com
Fashion Angels Ent.	800-492-3237	thebeadshoponline.com
Fisher Price	800-432-5437	fisher-price.com
Flea Market Music	800-459-5559	fleamarketmusic.com
Folkmanis	800-654-8922	folkmanis.com
Franklin	800-225-8647	franklinsports.com
Front Porch Classics	206-826-3202	frontporchclassics.com
Fundex	800-486-9787	fundexgames.com

Contact Companies

Funhouse	800-929-4666	beteshgroup.com
Galt	899-899-4258	galttoys.com
Gamewright	800-638-7568	gamewright.com
GeoCentral	800-231-6083	geocentral.com
Guidecraft	800-524-3555	guidecraft.com
Gund	800-448-4863	gund.com
Haba	800-468-6873	constructiontoys.com
HaPe	800-661-4142	hapetoys.com
Hasbro	888-836-7025	hasbro.com
Huffy	800-872-2453	huffy.com
Infantino	800-840-4916	infantino.com
Insect Lore	800-548-3284	insectlore.com
International Playthings	800-445-8347	intplay.com
Jakks Pacific	877-875-2557	jakkspacific.com
Kettler	757-427-2400	kettlerusa.com
Kid Galaxy	800-816-1135	kidgalaxy.com
Kids II	800-230-8190	kidsii.com
Kids Preferred	866-763-8869	kidspreferred.com
Klutz	800-737-4123	klutz.com
K'Nex	800-543-5639	knex.com
Language Littles	212-535-8122	languagelittles.com
Latitude Enfant	800-544-9183	latitudeenfant.com
Lauri	800-451-0520	lauritoys.com
Let's Play Games	856-988-1980	made2Bplayed.com
Leap Frog	800-701-5327	leapfrog.com
Learning Resources	800-222-3909	learningresources.com
Lego Systems	800-233-8756	lego.com
Little Kids	800-545-5437	littlekidsinc.com
Little Tikes	800-321-0183	littletikes.com
Manhattan Toy	800-541-1345	manhattantoy.com
Mary Meyer	800-451-4387	marymeyer.com
Mason Co.	800-821-4141	masoncorporation.com
Mattel	800-524-8697	mattel.com
Maxim Enterprises	888-266-2946	maximenterprise.com
McNeil Designs	302-478-2757	youvebeensentenced.com
Mega Bloks	800-465-6342	megabloks.com
Melissa and Doug	800-284-3948	melissaanddoug.com
Mic O Mic Americas	877-642-6642	micamericas.com
Milton Bradley	888-836-7025	hasbro.com
Monkeying Around	800-553-4300	monkeyingaround.com
Mudpuppy	800-670-7441	galison.com
North American Bear Co.	800-682-3427	nabear.com
Ohio Art	800-641-6226	world-of-toys.com
Outset Media	877-592-7374	outsetmedia.com

Contact Companies

Company	Phone	Website
Overbreak	888-537-6501	overbreak.com
Pamela Drake	800-966-3762	woodkins.com
Patrix	888-834-2380	patrix.tv
Pazow	415-885-5006	pazow.com
Pint Size Productions	800-544-9183	pintsizeproductions.com
Plasmart	877-289-0730	plasmacar.com
Plastwood	800-770-9550	plastwood.com
Play Along	954-596-2210	playalongtoys.com
Playhut	808-752-9488	playhut.com
Playmobil	800-752-9662	playmobil.com
Playskool	800-327-8267	hasbro.com
Progressive Trading	800-903-6249	magz.com
Radica	800-809-9611	radicagames.com
Radio Flyer	800-621-7613	radioflyer.com
Rainbow Products	541-826-9007	rainbowproducts.com
Ravensburger	800-886-1236	ravensburger.com
RC2/Learning Curve	800-704-8697	learningcurve.com
Remo	800-525-5134	remo.com
Rex Games	800-542-6375	rexgames.com
Rich Frog	802-865-9225	richfrog.com
Rockabye	310-631-2222	rockabye.com
Rose Art	800-272-9667	megabloks.com
Sassy	800-323-6336	sassybaby.com
Schylling	800-541-2929	schylling.com
Scientific Explorer	800-900-1182	scientificexplorer.com
Scratch Art	508-583-8085	scratchart.com
Skullduggery	800-336-7745	skullduggery.com
Small Miracles	888-281-1798	smallmiracles.com
Small World Toys	800-421-4153	neurosmith.com
Spinmaster	800-622-8339	spinmaster.com
Step 2	800-347-8372	step2.com
Stuff Design	888-946-7464	beamo.com
Taggies	877-482-4443	taggies.com
The Orb Factory	800-741-0089	orbfactory.com
Thinkfun	800-468-1864	thinkfun.com
Tiny Love	800-843-6292	tinylove.com
Toysmith	800-356-0474	toysmith.com
Trikke Tech	805-693-0800	trikke.com
TWC of America	800-301-7592	tweber.com
VTech	800-521-2010	vtech.com
Waba Fun	303-926-0848	superstructs.com
Wikki Stix	800-869-4554	wikkistix.com
Woodstock Percussion	800-422-4463	chimes.com
WowWee	800-310-3033	wowwee.com

Contact Companies

Zapf Creation	877-629-9273	zapf-creation.com
Zizzle	866-494-9953	zizzle.com

Safety Guidelines

Many people assume that before toys reach the marketplace they are subjected to the same kind of governmental scrutiny as food and drugs. The fact is that although the government sets specific safety standards, there is no agency like the FDA that pretests and approves or disapproves products.

The toy industry is charged with the responsibility to comply with federal safety standards, but they are self-regulating, which means it's not until there are complaints or reports of accidents that the Consumer Product Safety Commission (CPSC) enters into the picture. The CPSC is the federal government agency charged with policing the toy industry—but not until the products are already on the shelf!

What does all this mean to you as a consumer? Basically it means "Let the buyer beware!" Both small and large manufacturers have run into problems with small parts, lead paint, strangulation hazards and projectile parts.

The CPSC releases useful recall warnings that are posted in most major toy stores, and manufacturers are required to release recalls to the wire services. The CPSC has a hotline if you want further information about a recalled product or want to report one that perhaps should be recalled; you can call (800) 638-CPSC. The CPSC also publishes a safety handbook that you can request.

To protect your child, here is a safety checklist to keep in mind when you're shopping for playthings:

For infants and toddlers:

- **Dolls and stuffed animals.** Select velour, terry or non-fuzzy fabrics. Remove any and all bows, bells and doo-dads that can be swallowed. Stick to dolls with stitched-on features rather than buttons and plastic parts that may be bitten or pulled off.
- **Crib toys.** Toys should never be attached to an infant's crib with any kind of ribbon, string, or elastic. Babies

and their clothing have been known to get entangled and strangled by such toys.

- **Soft but safe.** Be sure that soft toys such as rattles, squeakers and small dolls are not small enough to be compressed and possibly jammed into a baby's mouth.
- **Heirlooms.** Antique rattles and other treasures often do not meet today's safety standards and can be a choking hazard.
- **Wall hangings and mobiles.** Decorative hangings near or on the crib are interesting for newborns to gaze at but pose a safety hazard once a child can reach out and touch. They need to be removed when an infant is able to touch them.
- **Foam toys.** Avoid foam toys that can be chewed on and swallowed and present a choking hazard.
- **Push-and-straddle toys.** If you're looking for your child's first push toy, make sure it's stable and your child can touch the ground when sitting on the toy.
- **Toy chests.** Old toy chests with lids that can fall do not meet today's safety standards. They can severely injure and even entrap small children. New chests have removable lids or safety latches. We recommend open shelves and containers for safe and easy access instead of the jumble of a deep toy chest.
- **Age labels and small parts.** When you see a toy labeled "Not for children under 3," that's a warning signal! It usually means there are small parts. Such products are unsafe for toddlers—no matter how smart they may be! They are also unsafe for some threes and fours who frequently put things in their mouths.
- **Batteries.** Toys that run on batteries should be designed so that kids cannot get to the batteries.
- **Quality control.** Run your fingers around edges of toys to be sure there are no rough, sharp or splintery, hidden thorns. Check for products that can entrap or pinch little fingers.

For older children:

- **Eye and ear injuries.** Avoid toys with flying projectiles. Many action figures come with a number of small projectile parts that can pose a safety hazard if pointed in the wrong direction and that certainly pose a danger if there are younger children in the house.

- **High-power water guns.** Doctors report many emergency room visits from children with eye and ear abrasions caused by the trendy high-powered water guns.

- **Burns.** Avoid toys that heat up when used. Many of the toy ovens and baking toys become hot enough to cause burns.

- **Safety limits.** Establish clear rules with kids for sports equipment, wheel toys, and chemistry sets.

- **Adult supervision.** Avoid toys labeled "Adult supervision required" if you don't have the time or patience to be there.

For mixed ages:

Families with children of mixed ages need to establish and maintain safety rules about toys with small parts.

- Older children need a place where they can work on projects that younger sibs can't get hurt by or destroy.

- Establishing a work space for the older sib gives your big child the privilege of privacy along with a sense of responsibility.

- Old toys need to be checked from time to time for broken parts, sharp edges, or open seams. Occasionally clearing out the clutter can foster heightened interest in playtime. It also brings old gems to the surface that may have been forgotten.

Safety Standard for Bike Helmets

Do little kids really need helmets? Look at the data and you decide:

About 900 people, including more than 200 children, are

killed annually in bicycle-related incidents; about 60% of these deaths involve a head injury. Data shows that very young bike riders incur a higher proportion of head injuries! More than 500,000 people are treated annually in U.S. emergency rooms for bicycle-related injuries. Research indicates that a helmet can reduce the risk of head injury by up to 85%!

New helmets must adequately protect the head, and have chin straps strong enough to prevent the helmet from coming off in a crash, collision, or fall. Helmets for children up to age five will cover more of the head to provide added protection to the more fragile areas of a young child's skull. New helmets will carry a label stating that they meet CPSC's new standards, to eliminate confusion about which certification mark to look for on helmets.

CPSC offers the following tips on how to wear a helmet correctly:

- Wear the helmet flat atop your head, not tilted back at an angle.
- Make sure the helmet fits snugly and does not obstruct your field of vision.
- Make sure the chin strap fits securely and that the buckle stays fastened.

Noisy Toys

In addition to all the above criteria, we have always considered the noise level of products. Loud toys are more than just annoying—they can actually pose a risk to your child's hearing. Recently, with the generous assistance of Nancy Nadler of the League for the Hard of Hearing, we tested the sound level of many new toys. In doing so, we discovered that many ordinary rattles and squeakers produce sounds measured at 110 to 130 decibels. Yet experts say that sustained exposure, over time, to noise above 85 decibels will cause hearing damage. Because current regulations allow manufacturers to make toys which produce sounds up to 138 decibels at a distance of 25cm, parents must be informed consumers. We suggest that you:

Safety Guidelines

- consider noise levels of toys before purchasing them.
- remember that musical toys, such as electric guitars, drums, and horns, emit sounds as loud as 120 decibels.
- stop and listen before purchasing a toy that makes a noise. If it sounds too loud for your ears, it probably is! Don't buy it.
- be very careful with toys designed to go next to the ear (such as toy phones and toys with headsets).
- remember that noisy floor toys are best listened to at a distance... teach your child not to place his ears on the speaker of the toy.

These guidelines have been prepared in conjunction with the League for the Hard of Hearing.

Brand Name and Title Index

NOTE: Toys and equipment are listed under manufacturer or distributor. The following codes are used for titles of works: (A) = Audio tape; (B) = Book; (DVD) = DVD and DVD Plug Ins.

Acting Out
  Hokey Pokey Musical Skirt, 119
Adèle & Simon (B), 183
Aeromax Toys
  Get Real Gear, 79
Alex
  Candle Painting set, 162
  Car Wash, 108
  Dough Party, 119
  EZ-Fleec-Y Knitting, 164
  Finger Painting Party, 116
  Funky Artist, 65–66, 209
  Games to Go, 171–172
  Giant Art Jar, 116
  Giant Weaving Loom, 165
  Jungle Toss Bean Bag Game, 110, 124
  Kitch 'n Carry Sets, 78
  Knitting Circle, 164
  Knot-A-Quilt, 164
  lacing games, 105–106
  Mini Golf, 110–111
  Musical Jewelry Box, 160
  My Creativity Center, 121
  My Dollhouse, 88
  My First Sink, 78
  My First Stove, 78
  My First Table, 121
  My Giant Floor Puzzle, 46
  My Picnic Basket, 131
  My Playhouse/Theatre, 114
  My Scrapbook Case, 162
  No-Mess Finger Paint Tray, 116
  Paint-a-Doggie Diner, 160–161
  Paint a Paper Lantern, 161
  Piggy Ballerina Bank, 132
  Puppet Theater, 86–87
  Rub a Dub Jungle Waterfall Bathtub Set, 69
  Super Art Table, 118
  Super Embroidery Kit, 164–165
  Super Rolling Art Center, 118
  Tabletop Easel, 118
  Weaving Fashion Weaving Loom, 165
  Whistling Hippos, 69
Alphabet Explosion! Search and Count from Alien to Zebra (B), 183
Amazing Baby
  Developmental Blanket Teether, 28
  Developmental Butterfly, 28
  Developmental Duck, 28
  Developmental Light Up Musical, 3
  Sound Balls, 25
  Teether Mirror Rattles, 14
Amazing Baby Soft Book (B), 177
American Girl, 175
  Elizabeth, 133
  Emily, 133
  Nellie O'Malley, 133
  Stroller, 123
American Idol All Star Challenge (DVD), 205
Anne of Green Gables (DVD), 196
Apollo 13 (DVD), 196
Art (B), 179
Atari
  Roller Coaster Tycoon 3, 204
Atheneum
  Dooby Dooby Moo, 179–180
  Olivia Forms a Band, 184

Babe (DVD), 196
Baby Animals (B), 177–178
Baby Einstein
  Bath Puppets, 69
  Discover & Play Color Blocks, 18
Baby Love (B), 178
Baby's Book of Small Talk (B), 178
Back to Basics blocks, 94
Balitono
  Dog House and Dog, 162
  Horse Stable, 162
  Jewelry Box, 162
  My Birdhouse Kit, 170
  My Pinball Game Kit, 161–162
  Works of Ahhh Star Box, 161–162
Barefoot Books
  Elusive Moose, 180
  Looking for a Moose, 180
  Prince's Bedtime, The, 190–191
Bead Bazaar
  Funky Bead Chest, 163
  Hemp kit, 163
  Mystic bead kit, 163
  Nature Barrel of Beads, 117
  Totally Fun Beads, 163
Bear Snores On (DVD), 194
Beauty and the Beast (DVD), 196
Beethoven Lives Upstairs (DVD), 196
Binney & Smith
  Crayola
    Color Wonder Finger Paints, 65
    Color Cyclone, 118
    Color Explosion Neon, 171
    Color Wonder Paper & Markers, 65, 73, 116, 124
    Grand Canvas, 117–118
    Kid's Large Washable Crayons, 65
    Model Magic Bucket, 119, 124
    Super Brush, 118
Black Belts Karate Studio (DVD), 199
Blue Orange Games
  CooCoo the Rocking Clown!, 99
  Ringgz, 146
  Zimbbos!, 99
Boo and Baa Have Company (B), 179
Books by You (DVD), 198
Borrowers, The (DVD), 196
Briarpatch
  Da Vinci's Challenge, 146
  Sudoku, 152, 175
Brio
  Double Suspension Bridge, 93
Brothers (B), 187

Cadaco
  4–Way Countdown, 151
  4–Way Spelldown!, 147
  Marshall Brodien Magic Wand Set, 170
Caillou, The Everyday Hero (DVD), 194
Candlewick
  Library Lion, 181
  Maisy's Book Tower, 178
  Maisy's Favorite Animals, 178
  Maisy's Favorite Clothes, 178
  Maisy's Favorite Things, 178
  Maisy's Favorite Toys, 178
  Miraculous Journey of Edward Toulane, The, 190
  Sharks and Other Sea Monsters, 182
  Silly Billy, 181–182
  Yes, 178–179
Cars (DVD), 195
Castle (B), 183
Ceaco
  Scrambled States of America, The, 157
Charlotte's Web (DVD), 196
Chenille Kraft
  Colossal Barrel of Crafts, 116, 124
  Little Pretenders, 80
  Wax Works, 162
  WonderFoam Dominoes, 101, 124
  WonderFoam Giant USA

220

Brand Name and Title Index

Puzzle Map, 157–158
WonderFoam Giant World Puzzle Map, 158
Chicken Run (DVD), 196
Chitty Chitty Bang Bang (DVD), 196
Chronicle
  Baby Animals, 177–178
  Game Night, 148
Cinderella (DVD), 196
Cinderella II (DVD), 196
Clarion
  Flotsam, 185
Community Playthings
  Wooden Doll Cradle, 58, 86
Constructive Playthings blocks, 94
Giant Constructive Blocks, 51, 73
  Windows and Doors Blocks, 95
Coop Kids
  2 in 1 Hitting Trainer Hit-a-Way Jr., 109
Corolle
  African American Bebe Do, 81
  Babicorolle, 55
  Babipouce, 27, 31
  Baby Chou Twins, 81, 124
  Bebe Do, 82
  Bebe Do Emma, 84
  Bebe Do with Moses Basket, 81
  Bitty Twins Double Stroller, 86
  Chouquettes, 82
  Collapsible Stroller, 86
  Jules, 81
  Les Cheries, 134
  Les Minis Calins, 82
  Miss Corolle Collection: Doucette, 82
  Miss Grenadine, 27, 55
  Paul Fait Pipi, 84
  Play Crib, 86
  Puppet Blue, Puppet Raspberry, 27
  Tidoo, 55
Cranium
  Balloon Lagoon, 144
  Cadoo for Kids, 144
  Clippity Clop Horse, 79
  Doodle Tales, 145, 175
  Family Fun Game, 144
  Get-up Fairy, 79
  Giggle Gear Magical Unicorn, 79
  Grade & Go Super Jacks and Hoppity Winks, 172
  Hullabaloo (DVD), 197
  Roaring Dinosaur, 79
  Super Story Recorder, 173
  Talking Picture Book, 175
  Whoonu, 149
  Zigity, 149
  Zooreka, 143–144
Crayola
  Color Cyclone, 118
  Color Explosion Neon, 171
  Color Wonder Paper & Markers, 65, 73, 116, 124
  Grand Canvas, 117–118
  Kid's Large Washable Crayons, 65
  Model Magic Bucket, 119, 124
  Story Creator, 175
Creativity for Kids
  Beaded Dresser Set, 159
  Beautiful Beaded Mirror, 159
  Beeswax Candles, 162
  Ceramic Allowance Bank, 132
  Create Your Own Books, 160
  Decoupage Diva Jewelry Keeper, 160
  Fast Race Cars, 160
  Monster Trucks Custom Shop, 159–160
  Scrapbook and Memory Box Gift Set, 162, 175
  Wake Up! Alarm Clock, 132
Curious George Activity Books, 122

Dear Miss Breed (B), 190, 191
Dial
  The Looking Glass Wars, 189
Didax
  Unifix Ready for Math Kit, 153
Digital Blue Microscope (C), 204
Discovery Kids
  SL-70 Telescope, 169
Discovery Speed Detector, 167
Disney
  Greatest Game Ever Played, The, 195–196
  Growing Up with Winnie the Pooh: Love & Friendship, 195
DK Adult
  Rainforest, 188
Dooby Dooby Moo (B), 179–180
Dreamworks
  Wallace & Gromit: The Curse of the Were-Rabbit, 195
Duplo. See Lego Systems
Dutton
  Gingerbread Girl, The, 180
  Take Care, Good Knight, 186

Earlyears
  See International Playthings
Educational Insights
  GeoSafari World, 155
  MagStruction, 141
Edushape
  Caterpillar Race, 99, 209
  EduBlocks, 51
  Educolor Blocks, 51
  Kiddy Connects, 49, 73
  Rollipop Toddler Starter and Advanced Sets, 48, 73
  Smart Mat, 10
  Soft Wood-Like Blocks, 51
  Taf Toys 2 in 1 Smart Gym, 10
Edwina, The Dinosaur Who Didn't Know She Was Extinct (B), 185
eeBoo
  Alphabet & Number Puzzle Pairs, 155–156
  Animal Bingo, 99–100
  Baby Animals puzzles, 104
  Candy Matching, 144
  Color Dominoes, 101
  Fairies of the Field lacing game, 105
  I Never Forget a Face Memory Game, 100
  Life on Earth Matching Game, 144
  Magnetic Checkers, 173
  Musical Friends lacing game, 105
  Pin the Tail on the Donkey, 98
  Read to Me Tot Tower, 31, 53
  Rhyming Words puzzle sets, 104
  Slides & Ladders, 173
  Storefront Bingo, 144
  Tea Party Game, 100–101, 124, 210
  Travel Bingo, 173
Elusive Moose (B), 180
Emines
  Roll 'n Multiply, 152
Enchantmints
  Puppet Palace, 135
E.T. (DVD), 196
European Expressions
  Music Maker Harp, 166

Farrar Straus
  Adèle & Simon, 183
  Boo and Baa Have Company, 179
  Happy Birthday Jamela!, 184
  Night Boat to Freedom, 187
  Yoon and the Christmas Mitten, 186–187
Fashion Angels Enterprises
  Alphadot Bracelet Kit, 163–164
  Hug This Shrug, 164
  I Knit This Poncho!, 164
  JellLoopdeLoops Sparkle Jelly Jewelry Kit, 163
  Leg Warminators, 164, 175
  Ribbon Raps, 163–164
  World Colors, 163–164
  Wrist Pix, 163–164
Fast Food (B), 180
Finding Nemo (DVD), 196
First Picture Spanish (B), 188
Fisher-Price
  Activity Tunnel, 24
  Baby Gymnastic Playwall, 23–24
  Baby's First Blocks, 19
  Bird's the Word Elmo, 83

Brand Name and Title Index

Bounce & Spin Zebra, 40
Bubble Mower, 46
Check Up Center, 56
Classical Stacker, 20, 52
Color Pixter, 123
Corn Popper, 41
ESPN Grow to Pro Baseball, 109
ESPN Grow to Pro Basketball, 109
GeoTrax Coast Winds Airport, 92
GeoTrax Rail & Road System (DVD), 198
GeoTrax Workin' Town Railway, 92
Jungle Friends Treehouse, 22, 23
Kid Tough Digital Camera, 174, 175
Laugh and Learn Learning Home, 24, 31, 64
Little Mommy Newborn Twin Dolls, 55–56
Little People Animal Sound Farm, 61
Little People Cement Mixer Truck, 60
Little People Dinosaurs, 61
Little People Lil' Kingdom Palace, 60–61
Little People Lil' Movers Airplane, 60, 73
Little People Lil' School Bus, 60, 208
Little People Pirate Ship, 60–61
Little People Time-to-Learn, 61
Medical Kit, 80
Mega T-Rex, 95
Melody Push Chime, 41
Mower, 46
On-the-Go Microphone, 121
Peek-a-Blocks Bucket o'Builders, 50, 208
Pixter Multi-Media, 123, 171, 174–175
Pixter Symphony Painter, 175
Pop 'n Musical Big Top, 48
Pop-Onz Pop 'n' Twirl Building Table, 48
Potty Elmo, 84
Roll-a-Rounds Drop & Roar Dinosaur, 23, 31
Roll-a-Rounds Swirlin' Surprise Gumballs, 23, 31
Shake 'n Go Speedway, 92
Sing & Go Choo Choo, 25
Snap-Lock Beads, 19, 31
Song & Story Content Store, 120
SparkArt Creativity System, 118
Star Station On-the-Go Player, 121
Stride-to-Ride Learning Walker, 37
Tickle-Me Elmo, 84
Time-to-Learn Preschool (DVD), 198
TMX Elmo, 84
Twin Time Dollhouse, 87
Fisher-Price/Scholastic
 Read With Me DVD, 102–102
Flea Market Music
 Flea Ukulele 165
Flotsam (B), 185
Fly Away Home (DVD), 196
Foam Airplane Book, The (B), 172
Folkmanis
 hand puppets, 135
Frances England
 Fascinating Creatures, 123
Franklin
 Hopping Sport Balls, 110
Freaky Friday (DVD), 196
Front Porch Classics
 Chaturanga, 145–146
 Old Century Shut-the-Box, 152
 Raceway '57, 146
 Wordspot, 146
Fundex
 Highrise, 150
Funhouse
 Ozone Space Rocker, 166
Funrise
 Tonka Trucks, 89

Galt
 Baby Walker, 38
 Push Cart, 31
Gameboy, 171, 174
Gamewright
 Combo King, 150, 175
 Feed the Kitty, 100
 Hiss, 100
 Luck of the Draw, 145
 Match of the Penguins, 148
 Scrambled States 2, The, 149
 There's a Moose in the House, 173
 Thing-a-ma BOTS, 148
 Top Speeds, 173
 Ugly Doll, 148, 176
GeoCentral
 Activity Rocks, 169
 Box of Rocks, 169
GeoTrax
 Workin' Town Railway, 92
 GeoTrax Rail & Road System (DVD), 198
Gingerbread Girl, The (B), 180
Greatest Game Ever Played, The (DVD), 195–196
Greatest Dot to Dot Books, The (B), 172
Groovy Girl
 Beachy Keen Sand Buggy, 83
 Minis, 88
 PetRageous, 83
Growing Up with Winnie the Pooh: Love & Friendship (DVD), 195
Guidecraft
 Magneatos, 97, 209
 Magneatos Intermediate, 97
Gulliver's Travels (DVD), 196
Gund
 Animal Puppets, 86
 Big Spunky, 56
 Colorfun Ball, 25, 31
 Cuddly Pals Pokey & Spunky, 3, 30
 Goober, 84
 Let's Play Puppets, 6
 Little Lovelies Bunny Ring Rattle, 12
 Mini Pro Grabbies, 12
 My Dolly, 27
 Peter Rabbit Musical, 3
 Snuffles, 56
 Sweet Dolly, 27
 Tutti Fruitti, 56
 Woodles Pull-String Musicals, 3

Haba
 1001 Nights, 156
 Doll Pram, 38, 72
 Pushing Car, 38
HaPe
 Pandabo, 144
 Pisa, 144
 Quadrilla, 142
 Rapido, 152
 Smart Living Holiday Home, 88
 Trapecolo, 156
 Woody Click, 95
Happy Birthday Jamela! (B), 184
Harcourt
 Move Over Rover, 180–181
 My Little Yellow Taxi, 182
 Particular Cow, A, 181
 Ruff! Ruff! Where's Scruff?, 182
 Satchel Paige, Don't Look Back, 187
HarperCollins
 Oscar: The Big Adventure of a Little Sock Monkey, 181
 Who Lives in an Alligator Hole?, 189
 Why Are the Ice Caps Melting?, 189
Harriet the Spy (DVD), 196
Harry Potter Deluxe Edition Scene It? (DVD), 205
Harry Potter for PS2, 201
Harry Potter series (DVD), 196
Hasbro
 Air-powered Action Stadium, 98
 Butterscotch My FurReal Pony, 81
 Cosmic Catch, 143, 175
 ION (DVD), 198
 Peek 'n' Play Discovery Dome, 9–10
 Play-Doh, 119
 Play-Doh Case of Colors, 66, 73
 Tonka Toughest Mighty Crane, 90
 Tummy-Time Together Gym, 10

Brand Name and Title Index

Hexen (DVD), 200
Holes (DVD), 196
Homeward Bound (DVD), 196
Homeward Bound II (DVD), 196
Honey, We Shrunk Ourselves (DVD), 196
Hot Wheels, 24, 59, 89, 124
   ESS Radar Gun, 167
   Flashfire car, 137
   Terrordactyle Track Set, 136
   Turbo Glo, 136–137
Houghton Mifflin
   Museum Trip, 185–186
   The Red Book, 186
Huffy bicycles, 168
   Green Machine, 168
Hullabaloo (DVD), 197
Hyperion
   Edwina, The Dinosaur Who Didn't Know She Was Extinct, 185
   "I'm not cute!", 179
   John, Paul, George & Ben, 188
   Peter and the Shadow Thieves, 189

I'm a Little Teapot (B), 178
"I'm not cute!" (B), 179
Indian in the Cupboard, The (DVD), 196
Infantino
   Alphabet Boat Puzzle, 105
   Baby Mail, 17
   Bee & Me, 29–30
   Bucket Buddies, 17
   Changing Table Flutter Bug Musical Mobile, 4, 30
   Cuddly Teether Blanket, 15
   Hula Hut, 17
   I Spy My House Puzzle, 105
   Jittery Jungle Pal Zebra, 29–30
   Peek Rattle and Teethe, 18
   Penguin Bowling, 42
   Wall Mounted Mobile & Mirror, 4
   Where's My Tail? puzzle, 105
Insect Lore
   Ladybug Land, 106
   Live Butterfly Pavilion, 106
International Playthings
   Angelina Ballerina Friends Forever, 172
   Angelina Ballerina Party Time Picnic Set, 131
   Animal Pairs Game, 100
   Ball Party Bounce, 49
   Busy Bead Rattle, 15
   Calico Critters Townhome, 87
   Castle and Bucket Set, 108
   Earlyears
      Baby Dino Rocker, 40
      Click & Play Triangles, 15
      Click N Spin Highchair Flower, 22
      Crib Mirror, 5
      Soft Busy Blocks, 18
      Sweet Baby Blocks, 18
   Egg and Spoon Race, 98
   Götz Precious Day Mini Muffin Boy & Girl, 55
   Götz Precious Day Muffin Collection, 82
   Great States, 149
   Imaginetics, 172
   iPlay Farm Racers, 59
   iPlay Zoom Around Garage, 59, 72, 208
   Press N Go Inchworm, 24–25
   Smoby
      Star Party Disco Bubble and Light, 132
      Star Party Duo Mix Set, 131–132
   Spinnerific Bye-Bye Balloons, 100
   Super Spiral Play Tower, 48–49, 72
   Tea Set, 131
   Tomy
      Ball Party Bounce, 49
      Ball Party Roll Around Tower, 49
ION (DVD), 198
IQ Preschool
   Block Party, 94
   Follow-Along Frog, 41
   Get-a-Grip Sorter, 54
   Pound-A-Ball, 48
   Pound Around, 48
   Push-Along Block Cart, 51, 72

Jakks Pacific
   TeleStory, 102
John, Paul, George & Ben (B), 188
Jump Start World (DVD), 198

Karaoke Revolution Series (DVD), 201
Kenetics (DVD), 200, 201
Kettler
   Kiddo Supertrike, 112
Kid Galaxy
   Backyard Flyer, 166
   Bendos My First RC Buggies, 89–90, 124
   Morphibians, 137–138, 175
   Old Tyme RC Bumper Cars, 90
   Perryscope, 170
Kids II
   Baby Einstein Bath Puppets, 69
Kids Preferred
   Amazing Baby
      Developmental Blanket Teether, 28
      Developmental Butterfly, 28
      Developmental Duck, 28
      Developmental Light Up Musical, 3
      Soft Book, 177
      Sound Balls, 25
      Teether Mirror Rattles, 14
   Asthma Friendly Puppy Dog, 56, 73
   Asthma Friendly Rattle Teether Security Blanket, 14, 14–15
   Comfort Cuddly Hippo and Cow, 56
   Flower Rattle Baby Doll, 15
   Funny Bunny, 15
   Lucky Ducky, 15
   Pastel Rattle Teether Toy, 15
Klutz
   It's All About Me, 172
   Paper Stained Glass, 172
   Potholders & Other Loopy Projects, 165
K'nex
   Brio Double Suspension Bridge, 93
   Gear Action Building Sets, 141
   Kid K'nex Wild Ones, 96
   Lights up! 30 Models Kit, 140–141
   Vertical Vengeance Coaster, 140
Knopf
   You and Me, Baby, 179
Knowledge Adventure, 203
   Books by You (DVD), 198
   Jump Start World (DVD), 198
Koch Vision
   Popular Mechanics for Kids: Lightning and Other Forces of Nature, 195
Konami
   Dance, Dance, Revolution (DVD), 200, 201
   Karaoke Revolution Series (DVD), 201

Lamaze
   2-in-1 Gym, 10
   Clap with Me Monkey, 21
   Eli Elephant, 29
   First Mirror, 11
   Henry the Hippo, 29
   Lights & Sounds Barnyard Crawl Toy, 24
   Shine On Me Musical Mobile, 4
   Spin n Stack Rings, 52
   Press 'n Spin Safari Friends, 22
   Stack 'n Nest Birds, 17–18
   Traveling Mobile, 29
   Whirl & Twirl Jungle, 22, 31
Latitude Enfant
   Garannimals Collection, 57, 73
   My Sound Cube, 18
Lauri
   Airplane puzzle, 104
   Alphabet Puzzle Boards, 155, 210
   Big Shapes Puzzle Tote, 47
   Birthday Cake puzzle, 104, 124

Brand Name and Title Index

Construction Activity Pack, 122
Farm Lacing and Tracing Set, 105
Farm Puppets Lacing Craft Kit, 136
Farm Scene puzzle, 104
Fire & Rescue Pack, 122
Kids Perception Puzzle, 155
Race Car puzzle, 104
Space Odyssey Pack, 122
Tall Stacker Pegs Building Set, 142
T-Rex puzzle, 104
LeapFrog
100 Hoops, 110
Cosmic Math, 174
Explorer Smart Globe, 155
FLY Pentop Computer, 154, 175
Fridge Farm Magnetic Animal Set, 102
Fridge Phonics Magnetic Letter Set, 102, 124
Leap Pad Plus Writing Learning System, 154–155
Leapster L-Max, 123, 171, 174, 175
Learn-Around Playground, 47
Learning Hoops Basketball, 42
Letterpillar, 174
Lowercase Letters, 102
Word Whammer Fridge Phonics, 102, 154, 210
Learning Company, The, 203
Learning Curve. See RC2/Learning Curve
Learning Resources
ABC Chalk Talk!, 154
Alpha-Bug Step 'n Spell, 153–154
Buy It Right Shopping Game, 150
Emergency Rescue Squad Puppets, 136
Factor Frenzy, 153
Gears! Gears! Gears!, 141
Head Full of Numbers, 150
Jumbo Farm Animals, 95
Jumbo Jungle Animals, 73, 95, 209
Light 'n Strike Math, 153
Math Dash, 150
Mighty Magnet, 106
Parquetry Blocks Super Set, 156
Pretend & Play Dishes, 78
Pretend & Play Doctor Set, 80, 124
Pretend & Play Office, 80
Pretend & Play Teaching Telephone, 79, 124
Talking Clever Clock, 153
Talking Math Mat Challenge, 153–154
Teaching Cash Register, 132
Wacky Wigglers, 141
Lego Systems

Airport, 139–140
Airport Action, 96, 140
Big Bucket, 96–97
Big Farm Set, The, 96
Bob the Builder, 96
City Airport, 139, 175
City Hospital, 140
Competition Racers, 140
Dora the Explorer, 96
Duplo Thomas Load and Carry Train, 50
Duplo Zoo, 50, 73
Fire Station, 96
Grand Soccer Stadium, 131
Mindstorm NXT, 137, 175
My First Quatro Set, 50, 73, 208
Passenger Plane, 139
Pirate Ship, 130
Star Wars kits, 140
Ultimate House Building Set, 138
Vladek's Dark Fortress, 130
Let's Play Games
Fuddy Duddy, 148, 176
Library Lion (B), 181
Lincoln Logs, 138
Lion King, The (DVD), 196
Lion King II, The (DVD), 196
Little Brown
Art, 179
Baby Love, 178
My Blanket, 178
Pandora's Box, 186
Little Kids
Big Bad Boomin' Bugs Observation Station, 169
No-Spill Bubble Tumbler, 45
Super Scoop Bubble Wand, 108
Super Size Bubble Wand, 108, 124
Little Mermaid, The (DVD), 196
Little People
Animal Sound Farm, 61
Cement Mixer Truck, 60
Dinosaurs, 61
Lil' Kingdom Palace, 60–61
Lil' Movers Airplane, 60, 73
Lil' School Bus, 60
Pirate Ship, 60–61
Time-to-Learn, 61
Little Tikes
8-in-1 Adjustable Playground, 43
Bathketball, 70
Bathtime Band, 70
Bathtime Toy Waterfall, 70
Bug Tunes Music Set, 67
Chimes the Caterpillar, 67
Climb and Slide Castle, 43
Construction Trucks, 89
Cozy Coupe, 51, 72
Cozy Coupe II, 39
Discover Sounds Kitchen, 21, 31
Discover Sounds Workshop, 21
Dive, Dodge 'n Slide Bouncer, 114
Double Easel, 117
Easy Score Basketball Set, 109
Endless Adventures Tikes Town House, 113–114
Garden Tools, 107
Hook Line & Sprinkler, 45
Inside Outside Cook n Grill Kitchen, 77
Jump 'n Slide, 114
Jungle Music Set, 67
Light & Go Thomas, 59
Little Champs Sports Center, 41
MagiCook Kitchen, 63
Melody Beads Piano, 22–23
Mulching Mower, 46
Playcenter Playhouse, 114
Playful Paws Sprinkler, 45
Playground, 113
Ride & Rescue Coupe, 112, 123
Rugged Riggz, 90, 124
Shopping Cart, 58
Side-by-Side Kitchen, 63
Super Spiral, 108
Super Star Sing-Along Vanity, 80
Surfin' Elmo Rocker, 40–41
Tikes Patrol Police Car, 112
TotSport Bowling Set, 42
TotSports Golf Set, 110–111
Turtle Sandbox, 45, 72
Wide Tracker Activity Walker, 37–38
Lonpos 101 Pyramid and Rectangle Game, 172
Looking for a Moose (B), 180
Looking Glass Wars, The (B), 189
Lucasarts
Thrillville (DVD), 200
Lumines (DVD), 203

McNeil Designs
You've Been Sentenced!, 147
Madeline (DVD), 196
Maisy's Book Tower (B), 178
Maisy's Favorite Animals (B), 178
Maisy's Favorite Clothes (B), 178
Maisy's Favorite Things (B), 178
Maisy's Favorite Toys (B), 178
Mama, I'll Give You the World! (B), 185
Manhattan Toy
Avena, 82
Baby Stella, 81
Baby Whoozit, 30
Birthday Belles puppets, 135
Car Seat Gallery, 28–29, 31
Chimpanzee Jamboree, 20
Cuddle Pups Puppets, 6
Elonia, 2
Finger Puppets Under the Sea, 135

Brand Name and Title Index

Fluffies, 85
Groovy Girl Beachy Keen Sand Buggy, 83
Groovy Girls and Groovy Boys, 83
Groovy Girls Minis, 88
Groovy Girls' PetRageous, 83
Knightingtales Puppets, 136
Leafy Lounger, 82
Magical Mystique Puppets, 136
Melina, 83
Metropolicity Community puppets, 135
NooBoo Symphonic Stacker, 20
Paws at Play, 135
Puppettos Theatre Stage, 135
Put and Peek Birdhouse, 19–20
Royal Rumpus Finger Puppets, 135
Royal Treatment Theatre Set, 135
Supersized Groovy Girl, 123
Supersize Gwen, 83
Supersize Yvette, 83
Tiptoes Touche Mediterranean Madge, 134
Trixieville, 82
Whoozit, 30
Whoozit Grabbitz Ball, 16
Whoozit Starz Lights & Sound, 30
Whoozit Touch & Teethe, 16
Wimmer-Ferguson Infant Stim-Mobile, 4–5, 30
Zayla, 82
Mary Meyer
 Baby Toodles, 15
 Center Stage Puppets, 86
 Cosmo Club, 56
 Doogie Dog Flip Flops, 85
 Great Big Creamy Bear, 84–85
 Yakety Squeeze Me Critters, 85
Mary Poppins (DVD), 196
Mason Co.
 Flying Turtle, 168
Mastiff
 Pump It Up, 200
Matchbox
 Auto Center, 122
 cars, 24, 59, 89
 Construction Zone Pop Up Adventure Set, 122
 Harbor Patrol, 122
Mattel
 Auto Center, 122
 Barbie, 133–134
 Harbor Patrol, 122
 Hot Wheels
  cars, 24, 59, 89, 124
  ESS Radar Gun, 167
  Flashfire car, 137
  Terrordactyl Track Set, 136
  Turbo Glo car, 136–137
 Kid-Tough FP3 Player, 120
Matchbox
 Auto Center, 122
 cars, 24, 59, 89
 Construction Zone Pop Up Adventure Set, 122
 Harbor Patrol, 122
 Uno Spin, 151, 175
Maximum Enterprises
 Deluxe Tumble Treehouse & Skycoaster, 89
 Sky Coaster, 89
Mega Bloks, 96
 Build Off Lap Desk, 50
 Fill & Dump WEagon, 49–50
 Lil' Cement Truck, 60
 Lil' Copter, 60
 Lil' Dump Truck, 60
 Magtastik, 97
Melissa & Doug
 Beginner Pattern Blocks, 104
 Flocked Animal Sets, 94–95
Microsoft
 Zoo Tycoon 2 series, 204
Milton Bradley
 Candy Land DVD Game, 199
 Connect Four, 171
 Dora the Explorer Cand Land, 99, 124
 Duck Duck Goose, 99
Miracle, The (DVD), 196
Miraculous Journey of Edward Tulane, The, 190
Mommy? (B), 182–183
Move Over Rover (B), 180–181
Mudpuppy
 1, 2, 3 to the Zoo Great Big Puzzle, 103
 Counting Bugs Dominoes, 101
 Egyptology Puzzle, 157
 Fairytale Theater, 173
 Map of the U.S.A., 173
 Our World puzzle, 103–104, 124
 Play Scenes, 172–173
 Very Books Block Puzzle, The, 103, 124
Mulan (DVD), 196
Museum Trip (B), 185–186
My Blanket (B), 178
My Dog Skip (DVD), 196
My Little Yellow Taxi (B), 182

Naturally Playful
 Clubhouse Climber, 43
 Up & Away Sand Table, 107
 Welcome Home Playhouse, 113
 Woodland Climber, 43
Night Boat to Freedom (B), 187
Nintendo
 Animal Crossing Wild World, 202–203
 Brain Age, 203
 Bust-A-Move, 203
 DS, 171
 Electroplankton, 202
  New Super Mario Bros., 202
  WarioWare: Touched!, 203
  Wii, 200
North American Bear
 Baby Cozies & Flatso Baby Cozies, 15
 Creeper Sleeper Cat, 57
 Creeper Sleeper Dog, 57
 Flatobearius, 57
 Flatofrog, 57
 Flatoplant, 57
 Flatopotamus, 57
 Puppies for Sale, 85
 Sleepyhead Bunny, 3, 30
 Smushy Elephant, 57–58, 72
Nutcracker, The (with Baryshnikov) (DVD), 196

October Sky (DVD), 196
OHC Group
 Ballet Studio Theater, 134
 Fantasy Pet collection, 134
 Only Hearts Club Collection, 134
 Sleeper Sofa, 134
 Sleeping Bags, 134
 Stable, 134
Ohio Art
 Magna Doodle, 117
 Magna Doodle Color Plus, 116–117
Olivia Forms a Band (B), 184
Only Hearts Club. See OHC Group
Orb Factory, The
 Bug Tumble, 156–157
 Magnetic Dinosaur Puzzle, 104–105
Orchard Books
 Sherlock Holmes and the Baker Street Irregulars, The Fall of the Amazing Walendas, 191
Oscar: The Big Adventure of a Little Sock Monkey (B), 181
Out of the Box
 Wallamoppi, 146
Outset Media
 Pick Two Deluxe, 147
Owen & Mzee (B), 184

Pamela Drake
 Woodkins, 123
Pancakes for Supper! (B), 184–185
Pandora's Box (B), 186
Particular Cow, A (B), 181
Patrix
 Delicio, 151
 Mad Math, 151
Pazow
 Scavenger Hunt for Kids, 143
 Who? What? Where?, 145
PBS

Brand Name and Title Index

Caillou, The Everyday Hero, 194
Penelope Peapod, 123
Peter and the Shadow Thieves (B), 189
Peter Pan (Mary Martin version) (DVD), 196
Philomel
  Brothers, 187
Pint Size Productions
  Latitude Enfant Grannimals Collection, 57, 73
Pixar
  Cars, 195
Pixter, 123, 171
  Multi-Media, 174–175
  Symphony Painter, 175
PlaSmart
  Plasma Car, 112
Plastwood
  Supermag, 141
Play2 (DVD), 200
Play Along
  Speed Stacks, 167
Playhut
  Crawl N Fun, 109
  Megahouse, 114
  Red Fire Engine, 109
  Yellow School Bus, 109
Playmobil
  Airport, 131
  Crane, 131
  Family Vacation House, 129
  Fire Station, 131
  Grande Mansion, 129
  Knight's Empire Castle, 129–130, 175
  Modern House, 129
  Red Dragon, 130
  Rock Castle, 130
  Sea Lion Pool, 131
  Skull Pirate Ship, 130
  Soccer Match, 130–131
  Zoo, 131
Playroom
  Number Chase, 151
Playskool
  Crank 'n Glow Flashlight, 77
  Dance Along MP3, 120
  Fill 'n Spill Fish, 19
  Sing Along Spider, 29
  Triple Track Tower, 49, 73
Play TV Baseball 3 (Plug-in), 204–205
Popular Mechanics for Kids: Lightning and Other Forces of Nature (DVD), 195
Prince's Bedtime, The (B), 190–191
Progressive Trading
  Magz-x, 141
PS2, 200–201
Pump It Up (DVD), 200
Putnam
  Snow Globe Family, 186

Radica
  20Q, 174
  Play TV Baseball 3, 204–205
Radio Flyer
  Classic Walker Wagon, 38
  Liberty spring rocker, 111
  Red Roadster, 39
  Retro Rocket, 39, 72
Rainbow Products
  Mag XL Magformers, 141–142, 175
Rainforest (B), 188
Random House
  Alphabet Explosion! Search and Count from Alien to Zebra, 183
  Mama, I'll Give You the World!, 185
  Toys Go Out, 189–190
  Water Street, 190
Ravensburger
  City Scenes puzzles, 157
  Lego City Puzzles, 157
RC2/Learning Curve
  Bob the Builder Follow Me Scoop, 90, 124
  Deluxe Aquarium, 91
  Edward the Great Set, 91
  Giggle Bug, 21
Lamaze
  2-in-1 Gym, 10
  Clap with Me Monkey, 21, 207
  Eli Elephant, 29
  First Mirror, 11
  Henry the Hippo, 29
  Lights & Sounds Barnyard Crawl Toy, 24
  Press n' Spin Safari Friends, 22
  Shine On Me Musical Mobile, 4
  Spin n Stack Rings, 52
  Stack 'n Nest Birds, 17–18
  Traveling Mobile, 29
  Whirl & Twirl Jungle, 22, 31
  Rheneas & the Roller Coaster Set, 91
  Sodor Fire Station, 92
  Stacking Shapes Pegboard, 53
  Storm on Sodor Set, 91
  Thomas & Friends Echo Tunnel, 92, 124, 209
  Load & Sort Recycling Center, 92
  Sights & Sounds Deluxe Fire Station, 93
  Water Tower Figure 8 Set, 91
Read It! Play It! With Babies and Toddlers, 32, 73–74, 125, 176
Read With Me DVD, 102–102
Red Balloon, The (DVD), 196
Red Book, The (B), 186
Remember the Titans (DVD), 196
Remo
  Kid's Konga Drum, 165–166
  Kid's Tom Tom, 165–166
  Lollipop Drum, 120
  Lynn Kleiner Babies Make Music Set, 67
  Maracas Shakers, 120
  Two-Headed Bongo, 165–166
Rex Games
  Tangoes Jr., 151
Rich Frog
  Rick the Frog and Friends, 57, 73
Rockabye
  Danny Dinosaur, 40
  Elijah Elephant, 40
Rock-a-Bye Baby (B), 178
Roller Coaster Tycoon 3 (DVD), 204
Rollercoaster Tycoon (DVD), 200
Rose Art
  Curious George A B See Game, 147
RS Media, 138
Ruff! Ruff! Where's Scruff? (B), 182
Ryan's Room
  Adventures Ahoy, 88–89
  Home Is Where the Heart Is Dollhouse, 88
  Majestic Castle & Mighty Knights, 89

Santa Clause, The (DVD), 196
Sarah, Plain and Tall (DVD), 196
Sassy
  Baby's Book of Small Talk, 178
  Bathtime Kitchen Sink, 69–70
  Bendy Beeper, 12
  Broggies in the Tub, 70
  Car Wash, 69–70
  Circle Rattle, 12
  Fascination Station, 21–22, 31
  Fishy Fascination Station, 22
  Gumpy Guppy, 16
  Me in the Mirror, 6, 11, 31
  Nursery Rhyme Books, 178
  Poppin' Push Car, 24, 31
  Pull & Go Elephant Pal, 23
  Sassy's Car Wash, 69–70
  Take 'n' Talk Phone, 61–62
  Talk-to-Me Telephone, 62
Satchel Paige, Don't Look Back (B), 187
Scholastic
  Castle, 183
  Dear Miss Breed, 190, 191
  Fast Food, 180
  Mommy? 182–183
  Owen & Mzee, 184
  Pancakes for Supper!, 184–185
Scholastic Video Collection
  Bear Snores On, 194
Schwinn bicycles, 168
Schylling
  Broom Set, 61
Scientific Explorer

Brand Name and Title Index

Perfumery, 170
Scratch Art
   Draw & Learn Deluxe Kit, 161
   Light Catcher Fun Kits, 161, 176
   Magic Stickers, 161
Screenlife
   American Idol All Star Challenge, 205
   Harry Potter Deluxe Edition Scene It?, 205
Secret Garden, The (DVD), 196
Sharks and Other Sea Monsters (B), 182
Sherlock Holmes and the Baker Street Irregulars, The Fall of the Amazing Zalindas (B), 190
Shrek (DVD), 196
Shrek 2 (DVD), 196
Silly Billy (B), 181–182
Simon & Schuster
   Weedflower, 190
Skullduggery
   Cast & Paint: Krazy Kars, 159
Small Miracles
   Let's Pretend Careers, 79–80
Small World Toys
   Backyard Clubhouse, 88
   Fun Roller, 167
   Gertie Balls, 110, 124
   Home Again, Home Again A-Frame, 88
   Hoppity Ball, 110
   IQ Preschool
   120 Unit Blocks of Fun, 94
   Block Party, 94
   Follow-Along Frog, 41
   Get-a-Grip Sorter, 54
   Pound-A-Ball, 48
   Pound Around, 48
   Push-Along Block Cart, 51, 72
   Mixed-Up Chameleon Maze Board, 106
   Multimedia Mania, 88
   Neurosmith Music Blocks, 67, 72
   Neurosmith Together Tunes Block, 68
   Numbers, 47
   Polar Bear Touch & Stack Blocks, 53
   Puzzibilities Sound Puzzles, 105
   Puzzibilities Sounds on the Go, 47, 73
   Puzzibilities USA Puzzles, 157
   Ryan's Room Adventures Ahoy, 88–89
   Ryan's Room Home Is Where the Heart Is Dollhouse, 88
   Ryan's Room Majestic Castle & Mighty Knights, 89
   Shapes, 47

Small World Living Wooden BBQ Grill, 64, 72
Small World Living Wooden Kitchen Appliances, 64, 72
Sounds on the Farm, 47
Supersized Gertie Balls, 110
Tolo
   Abacus Rattle, 16
   Animal Water Slide, 70
   Baby Concerto, 68
   Bug, 30
   Ibis, 30
   Mobile Phone, 62, 73
   Roller Ball, 16
   Stacking Activity Cubes, 53
   Wiggly Jigglies Collection, 30
   Vehicles, 47
   Wagon Set with Bucket, 44
   Wild Animals, 47
Smoby
   Star Party Disco Bubble and Light, 132
   Star Party Duo Mix Set, 131–132
Snow Globe Family (B), 186
Snow White (DVD), 196
Sony
   EyeToy, 200, 201
   Harry Potter for PS2, 201
   Kenetics, 200, 201
   Play 2, 200
   Play and Play 2, 201
Sounder (DVD), 196
Sound of Music (DVD), 196
Spinmaster
   Air Hogs Helix Helicopter, 137
   Air Hogs Hydro Launcher, 137
   Aquadoodle, 115
   Black Belts Karate Studio (DVD), 199
   Sing 'n' Doodle Mat, 115
Step 2
   Angel Fish Rocker, 40
   Bistro Grille, 77–78
   Cooking Essentials, 78–79
   Crabbie Sandbox, 45, 72
   Easel for Two, 117
   Frog Sandbox, 45, 72
   Lifestyle Deluxe Kitchen, 63, 72
   Lifestyle Designer Kitchen, 63, 72
   Lifestyle Dream Kitchen, 63, 72
   Little Helper's Dining Room & Pots and Pans, 62–63
   Naturally Playful Clubhouse Climber, 43
   Up & Away Sand Table, 107
   Welcome Home Playhouse, 113
   Woodland Climber, 43
   Push Around Buggy, 39
   Safari Wagon, 39

Soft & Sturdy Deluxe Blocks, 94
Turtle Sandbox, 45
WaterWheel Table, 44
Stuart Little (DVD), 196
Stuart Little 2 (DVD), 196
Stuff Design
   Beamo, 166
Summit Inc.
   Amazing Money Jar, 133
   YOUniverse ATM Machine, 132–133, 175
Summit Toys
   Backyard Safari Bug Scope, 169

Taggies
   Toss the Taggie, 25, 207–208
Take Care, Good Knight (B), 186
Tarzan (DVD), 196
Thinkfun
   City Crossing, 144–145
   Hopper Heroes, 144–145
   Toot and Otto Game, 145
   Zingo! Heroes, 144
Thomas & Friends
   Echo Tunnel, 92, 124, 209
   Load & Sort Recycling Center, 92
   Sights & Sounds Deluxe Fire Station, 93
   Water Tower Figure 8 Set, 91
Thrillville (DVD), 200
Tiger Games
   Star Wars Game Saga Edition, 205
Time-to-Learn Preschool (DVD), 198
Tiny Love
   ActiviTot Developmental Gym, 9, 10, 30, 207
   Developlay Activity Center, 21
   Gymini Duet, 9
   Gymini Melody Maker, 9
   Gymini Total Playground Kick & Play, 9
   Musical Stack & Play, 31, 47–48
   Symphony in Motion Deluxe, 4, 30
   Symphony-in-Motion Shapes, 4
To Kill a Mockingbird (DVD), 196
Tolo
   See Small World Toys
Tonka
   Toughest Mighty Crane, 90
   Trucks, 89
Toys Go Out: Being the Adventures of a Knowledgeable Stingray, a Tough Little Buffalo, and Someone Called Plastic (B), 189–190
Toysmith
   B.C. Bones Empire State Building, 140

Brand Name and Title Index

Prehistoric Planet Dinosaur Fossils T-Rex, 140
Trikke Tech
 Trikke 5, 168, 175
TWC of America
 Deluxe Clear-View Nature House, 170
 Hanging Bird Feeder, 170
Soil Dweller Nature House Kit, 170
Twinkle, Twinkle, Little Star (B), 178

Ubisoft
 Lumines (DVD), 203
Usborne
 Dinosaur Excavation Kit, 169
 First Picture Spanish, 188
 The Usborne Book of Art, 188–189
 Usborne Children's Book of Art, 188–189

Viva Piñata! (DVD for Xbox), 200
Vtech
 Art Studio, 103
 V.Smile, 103

Waba Fun
 Superstructs Big Builder, 97–98
Wallace & Gromit: The Curse of the Were-Rabbit (DVD), 195
Water Street (B), 190
Weedflower (B), 190
Who Lives in an Alligator Hole? (B), 189
Why Are the Ice Caps Melting? (B), 189
Wikki Stix
 Curious George Activity Books, 122
Wild Planet
 Hook Fortune Finder, 169
 Light Scope, 169
 Treasure Hunter, 169
Willy Wonka and the Chocolate Factory (DVD), 196
Wizard of Oz, The (DVD), 196
Woodstock Percussion
 Chimalong & Mini Chimalong, 165
 Lollipop Drum, 120, 124
 Woodstock Band, 120
WowWee
 Roboraptor, 138
 Roboreptile, 138
 Robosapian, 138
 Robosapien V2, 138
 RS Media, 138
Wrist Pix, 163–164

Xbox 360, 200–201

Yes (B), 178–179
Yoon and the Christmas Mitten (B), 186–187
You and Me, Baby (B), 179

Zapf Creations
 Baby Born, 84
 Love Me Chou Chou, 83
 My Little Baby Born, 83
 Talking Chou Chou, 83
Zizzle
 Lucky the Incredible Wonder Pup, 85, 123–124, 208–209
Zoundz, 166
Zoon Tycoon 2 series (DVD), 204
Zuma (DVD), 200

Visit our website.

www.toyportfolio.com Updates, reviews of award winners, media listings, and parenting articles.

Don't miss our other great resources!

Read It! Play It! reviews 50 classic storybooks every child from 3–8 should know and provides related activities to develop language, writing, math, and science skills. (ISBN 097210018)

Read It! Play It! With Babies and Toddlers reviews 50 books every baby and toddler should know and introduces new parents to the power of books, songs, stories and play at this crucial time in a child's development. (ISBN 0972105042)

Each book is $10 and available in bookstores, on-line, or by mail from the address below (add $3 for shipping and handling).

Are you in a parenting group or play group?

Contact us about special rates available for fundraisers and bulk orders.

**Oppenheim Toy Portfolio, Inc.
40 East 9th St., Suite 14M
New York, New York 10003
(212) 598-0502
www.toyportfolio.com**